Checkpoint 17	162
pluperfect	163
future perfect	164
conditional perfect	165
Checkpoint 18	166

Present participle, imperative, subjunctive | **167**
present participle	168
imperative	170
Checkpoint 19	173
subjunctive	174
Checkpoint 20	182

Key verbs | **183**
modal verbs	184
devoir	185
pouvoir	186
vouloir	187
impersonal verbs	188
être	190
avoir	191
faire	192
Checkpoint 21	194

Verbs followed by prepositions | **195**
verbs followed by à	196
verbs followed by de	198
verb + à + person + de + infinitive	200
verb + dans, par, pour, en	201
verbs with no preposition in French	201
Checkpoint 22	202

Verb tables	203
Verb tables index	254
Grammar terms	255
Checkpoint answers	260
Index	265

introduction

Talk French Grammar is the essential handbook for anyone setting out to learn French, at home or in a class. With its straightforward approach and clear layout, it promotes a real understanding of how French works and how it relates to English.

It's much more than an ordinary grammar book. Using the tried-and-tested principles of the bestselling **Talk French** and **Talk French 2**, it de-mystifies grammar and guides you through the key structures of French in a way that's really easy to follow even if you have no experience at all of grammar and its terminology.

Its parallel focus is on building a large vocabulary – fast – for you to combine with an understanding of grammar to say whatever you want in French, without having to rely on phrasebooks.

Among its special features you'll find:
- a summary of **the most significant differences** in the way French and English work
- clear, **jargon-free explanations** of French grammar, set out in units and illustrated by hundreds of **practical examples**
- **Word power** pages, tailored to individual units. Some of these focus on the fact that large numbers of French and English words are very similar. **False friends** are highlighted too: words which look as though they might mean one thing but in fact mean something different.
- **learning tips and strategies**, positioned just where you need them
- **dictionary guidance**, with abbreviations and sample entries
- regular **Checkpoints** with practice activities to reinforce the language patterns and help you remember them. These are also useful as revision or to jog your memory.
- **verb tables**: the patterns for widely used regular and irregular verbs
- a **glossary of grammar terms** with examples in English to make them crystal-clear
- a **comprehensive, easy-to-use index**

Talk French Grammar can be used successfully alongside any learning materials, and is also the perfect companion for both levels of **Talk French**. The **Talk** series has online activities at www.bbc.co.uk/languages/french, and if you'd like to practise your grammar online, try out the grammar section of the **Steps** course at the same address.

| TALK |

French

Grammar

SUE PURCELL

Series Editor: Alwena Lamping

Published by BBC Active, an imprint of Educational Publishers LLP, part of the Pearson Education Group, Edinburgh Gate, Harlow, Essex CM20 2JE, England.

© Educational Publishers LLP 2009

First published 2009.
5

ISBN 978-1-4066-7911-3

Cover design: Johanna Gale
Cover photograph: © iStock.com/oksix
Insides design and layout: BBC Active design team
Illustrations © Mark Duffin
Publisher: Debbie Marshall
Development editor: Thierry Semo
Project editor: Emma Brown
Marketing: Fiona Griffiths
Senior production controller: Franco Forgione

Printed and bound in China (CTPSC/05).

The Publisher's policy is to use paper manufactured from sustainable forests.

Contents

Introduction | 6
Getting started | 8
focus on vocabulary | 11

Sounds and spelling | 15
pronunciation | 16
stress and intonation | 18
the French alphabet:
spelling things out | 20
capital letters | 21
Word power | 23
Checkpoint 1 | 24

Numbers, time and date | 25
cardinal numbers | 26
ordinal numbers | 28
time | 29
date: days, months, years | 30
Word power | 31
Checkpoint 2 | 32

Nouns | 33
people | 34
other masculine nouns | 36
other feminine nouns | 37
nouns that can be masculine
or feminine | 38
making nouns plural | 39
Word power | 40
Checkpoint 3 | 42

Articles: the, a, some | 43
a: un, une | 44
the: le, la, l', les | 46
the + a, de | 48
some/any | 49
Checkpoint 4 | 50

Adjectives | 51
Word power | 52
adjective endings
and agreement | 54
spelling changes | 55
irregular adjectives | 57
position of adjectives | 58
Checkpoint 5 | 60

Adverbs and comparisons | 61
Word power | 62
adverbs of quantity | 64
plus and moins | 65
comparisons: plus, moins | 66
superlatives: le plus, le moins | 66
irregular comparatives and
superlatives | 67
Checkpoint 6 | 68

Demonstratives and
possessives | 69
demonstrative adjectives | 70
demonstrative pronouns | 71
cela, ça, ceci, ci, ce | 72
c'est or il est | 73

Checkpoint 7	73	Verbs: overview	109
possessive adjectives	74	moods and tenses	110
possessive pronouns	75	person	112
Checkpoint 8	76	verb groups and	
		irregular verbs	113
Pronouns	77	the infinitive	114
subject pronouns	78	reflexive verbs	116
object pronouns	79	Word power	118
direct or indirect object?	80	Checkpoint 13	120
y	81		
en	82	**Questions and negatives**	121
Checkpoint 9	83	asking questions	122
position of object pronouns	84	qui?, que?, quoi?	124
reflexive pronouns	86	quel?, lequel?	125
emphatic pronouns	87	exclamations	126
Checkpoint 10	88	negatives: **ne … pas**	127
		other negatives	129
Sentence structure	89	negative questions,	
word order	90	imperatives and infinitives	131
joining parts of a sentence	91	Checkpoint 14	132
who, whom, which, that	92		
lequel, laquelle	93	**Verbs: simple tenses**	133
dont, où	94	present tense	134
making conversation flow	95	Checkpoint 15	139
opinions	95	future tense	140
Checkpoint 11	96	conditional	144
		Word power	145
Prepositions	97	imperfect	148
à	98	past historic	150
de	100	Checkpoint 16	152
en	102		
dans	104	**Verbs: compound tenses**	153
sur	104	past participle	154
pour	105	the passive	157
par	105	perfect tense with **avoir**	158
sans	106	perfect tense with **être**	159
depuis	106	object pronouns and the	
compound prepositions	107	perfect tense	161
Checkpoint 12	108		

How to use Talk French Grammar

This book works on several levels – make it work for you!

New to language learning or forgotten everything you've learnt? Or perhaps you already know some French words but have no structure to use them in?
Go to **Getting started** on page 8, which gives you an overview of what grammar is about, introduces you to the keystones of grammar and offers a few short activities to help you recognise and remember them.

New to French but understand the meaning of basic terms such as noun, adjective, verb?
Go to page 10, which prepares you for learning French by highlighting the principal differences between French and English.

Learning French on your own or in a class and need extra support?
Choose the unit you want, work through it then complete the **Checkpoint** at the end to see how much you've understood and remembered. You can select the units in the order that suits you because they're free-standing and they cross-reference to each other so that you can easily check things out if you need to.

Need a clear and comprehensive French grammar reference book?
The index will show you where everything is. It uses key words in English and French as well as grammar terms, making it easy for you to find what you're looking for quickly.

Want to brush up on your French or do some revision?
The first page of each unit summarises the key points. Reading these and trying your hand at the **Checkpoint** activities will pinpoint any gaps in your knowledge so that you know what might be useful to spend some time on.

Just want to generally improve your French, deepen your understanding and boost your vocabulary?
Dip into the book at random, reminding yourself of the structures, reading the examples, checking out the **Word power** pages and using the **Checkpoints**.

getting started

What is grammar?

When we talk we do more than just say words randomly; we use them in a specific order and they relate to one another. Grammar is the explanation of how that works: it provides definitions of the structures of a language and how they're used.

Can't I communicate without learning grammar?

Yes – if you're happy restricting yourself to phrases from a book or pidgin-type communication. You'll just about be able to make yourself understood but conversation will be a strain and communication hit-and-miss.
With relatively little knowledge of grammar, you can produce correct and unambiguous French instead. You'll sound more articulate and it will be a much more constructive and satisfying experience.

How do babies cope without knowing about grammar?

It's true that children learn to talk without ever having heard of a verb or a noun. But if you listen to a toddler you'll often hear words like *hided*, *eated*, *sheeps* or *mans*, showing that the child has in fact absorbed the regular patterns of English and is applying them quite unconsciously – albeit not always correctly. As time goes on, irregularities get ironed out and the child, with no apparent effort, starts saying *hid* and *ate*, *sheep* and *men*.

It takes many months of constant exposure to a language to learn in this way. By the time the average child is starting to form sentences, they will have been hearing their mother tongue for around 4,500 hours over a period of 18 months or so.

Most adults want results more quickly than that. By consciously learning how French is structured and how new words fit within sentences, you shortcut the process considerably. But you'll still experiment and make mistakes, just as children do, because that's part of the learning curve too.

How much grammar will I need?

At the start, you can get by comfortably with the basics. As you carry on with your French, you'll gradually accumulate knowledge, and more pieces of the jigsaw will slot into place. There are some aspects of grammar that you might never need or want to know about – as with most things, there's a level that's largely of interest only to the professional or the enthusiast.

Where do I start?

It pays to become familiar with some of the terms used to describe how a language works because it allows you to make sense of statements that you might come across in course books, such as:

The adjective usually goes after the noun or *The definite article is not used when …*

Focus first on the six main building blocks of a sentence. Read these descriptions, then see if you can pick them out in sentences.

- **Nouns** are the words for living beings, things, places and abstract concepts: *woman, son, doctor, Oliver, dog, table, house, Scotland, time, joy, freedom.*
- **Pronouns** are words used to avoid repeating a noun: *I, me, we, us, you, he/she, him/her, it, they, them.*
- **Articles** are *the, a/an* and *some.*
- **Adjectives** are words that describe nouns and pronouns: ***good** wine; **strong red** wine; **my** wine; I am **tired**; it was **superb**.*
- **Adverbs** add information to adjectives, verbs and other adverbs: ***very** good wine; you speak **clearly**; you speak **really** clearly.*
- **Verbs** are words like *go, sleep, eat, like, have, be, live, die,* that relate to doing and being.

---

1 Have a look at the underlined words and write N by the nouns, V by the verbs and ADJ by the adjectives.
   a) <u>Sofia</u> <u>works</u> for a <u>glossy</u> <u>magazine</u>. She <u>organises</u> <u>interviews</u>, <u>hires</u> <u>professional</u> <u>models</u> and <u>photographers</u> and <u>travels</u> all over the <u>world</u>. Her <u>boyfriend</u> is a <u>well-known</u> <u>actor</u>.
   b) <u>My</u> <u>father</u> <u>comes</u> from <u>Toulouse</u> although he <u>lives</u> in <u>Paris</u> because he <u>works</u> at the <u>central</u> <u>office</u> of a <u>large</u> <u>company</u>.
   c) They <u>prepared</u> a <u>fantastic</u> <u>meal</u> for us. We <u>ate</u> <u>grilled</u> <u>fish</u>, <u>fresh</u> <u>asparagus</u> and <u>new</u> <u>potatoes</u>, <u>drank</u> a <u>superb</u> <u>French</u> red <u>wine</u> – and the <u>dessert</u> was absolutely <u>incredible</u>.

2 Now pick out the adverbs ADV and the adjectives ADJ.
   a) The house was <u>very</u> <u>reasonable</u> but it was <u>rather</u> <u>dilapidated</u> … and the garden was <u>really</u> <u>small</u> and <u>overgrown</u>.
   b) We played <u>superbly</u>. It wasn't our fault that the pitch was <u>terribly</u> <u>uneven</u> and the ref <u>deliberately</u> <u>unfair</u>.

How different are French and English?

On the whole, French grammar is very similar to English, but there are a few aspects which are rather different. If you're prepared for these, you'll find that you get used to them very quickly.

Gender: masculine and feminine

Every single French noun – not just the words for people and animals – is either masculine (m) or feminine (f). There's no sense of *it*, not even for things like cars, furniture, sport or days of the week – everything is *he* or *she*. Words linked to a noun, such as articles and adjectives, also have to be masculine or feminine.

Articles

There are four versions of *the* in French. The one you use depends on whether the following noun is masculine or feminine, singular or plural, and whether it begins with a vowel or a consonant. And there are two words for *a/an*.

Different versions of *you*

In English there's only one word for *you*; in French there are two, depending on who you're talking to. **Tu** conveys familiarity and friendliness when you're talking to one person. When there's more than one person or when you're talking to one person you don't know very well or who is older than you, you use **vous**.

Verb endings; I, we, you, he/she, they

In English a verb generally stays pretty much the same no matter who's carrying it out: *I eat, we eat, you eat, the cats eat, Joe eats.*

In French, as well as using *I, you, she,* etc. you change the ending of the verb to show who's doing what.

Verbs: tenses

English has more tenses than French, which means that one French tense may correspond to two or more English tenses. For instance, **je vais** can mean both *I go* and *I am going*; **j'ai fait** *I did* or *I have done*.

Negatives

There are two words that make up the negative in French: **ne … pas** *not*, **ne … rien** *nothing*, **ne … jamais** *never*, and so on. These words go round the verb.

Word order

On the whole, word order is similar to English. The most noticeable differences are with adjectives, which usually come after nouns, not before them as in English: **la musique classique** *classical music*.

Also, words like *it* and *them* usually come before a verb not after it.

What about vocabulary?

Learning a new language is a several-pronged process. Knowledge of grammar has a key place, with even a few simple structures going a long way towards making sure you're understood. Knowing how to use verbs and when to include words like **mais** *but*, **parce que** *because* or **autrement** *otherwise* take you a big step further, letting you express more complex thoughts.

But all these are of limited use without a good stock of words to slot into the structures – and the most obvious source of these is a dictionary.

What sort of dictionary is best?

When choosing your first English/French dictionary, go for a medium-sized one. Too small and it won't give you enough information; too big and it will confuse you with too much. There are also dictionaries online, many of them free.

Why are dictionaries so full of abbreviations?

Some words are straightforward, with just one meaning: **préférer** *prefer* can only be a verb, **possible** *possible* an adjective.

Others are more complex, with the same word belonging in more than one grammatical category. *Mind* can mean what you think with (noun) and to look after (verb). *Book* can mean something you read (noun) and it can mean to reserve a place (verb). *Calm* can mean peaceful (adjective), peace (noun) and to soothe (verb).

To make sure you find the right category of word, each has an abbreviation next to it. The most common are:

art article	*adj* adjective	*adv* adverb
f feminine	*m* masculine	*n* noun
pl plural	*prep* preposition	*pron* pronoun
sing singular	*v* verb	

You may find slight variations in some dictionaries so it's worth checking with the introduction.

How do I make sure I choose the right translation?
Some words have more than one meaning even within the same grammatical category: the adjective *hard* can mean *solid* and it can mean *difficult*. The noun *habit* can be something a nun wears or it can be something you do on a regular basis. The verb *to press* can mean to iron clothes or to push down on something.

There's often an explanation or a phrase to guide you, but if you've looked up an English word and are still not sure which of the French translations to use, look them all up and see what English translations are given.

hard *adj* **1.** dur: ~ *surface* surface *f* dure **2.** difficile: ~ *work* travail *m* difficile **3.** sévère, dur: ~ *master* maître *m* sévère **4.** rude, rigoureux: ~ *winter* hiver *m* rude **5.** ~ *shoulder* bande *f* d'arrêt d'urgence; *the* ~ *stuff* alcool *m; to learn the* ~ *way* apprendre à ses dépens

habit *n* **1.** habitude *f*, coutume *f*: *out of* ~ par habitude; *to get into bad* ~*s* prendre de mauvaises habitudes **2.** accoutumance *f*: ~*-forming* qui crée une accoutumance **3.** [*relig*] habit *m*

press *v* **1.** appuyer (sur): *to* ~ *the key/button* appuyer sur la touche/le bouton **2.** presser: *to* ~ *oranges* presser des oranges **3.** serrer: *to* ~ *s.o's hand* serrer la main de qn **4.** repasser: *to* ~ *a shirt* repasser une chemise **5.** *to* ~ *on* continuer **6.** insister, faire pression sur (une personne), presser: *to* ~ *s.o. to do sthg* presser qn de faire qch

What if I can't find the word I'm looking for?
This is where your knowledge of grammar comes in. The two main points to remember are that:
- adjectives in a dictionary are in the masculine singular
- verbs are in the infinitive, so you have to replace any other endings with **-er**, **-ir**, or **-re** before you look up a verb. If you still have a problem, it probably means that you've come across part of an irregular verb, the most common of which are written out in full on pages 204-253.

How else can I build up a wide vocabulary?

The most obvious source of French outside France is the internet, where you can find information in French on practically anything. Use a dictionary to find the key words relating to your interests then just browse. You'll be surprised at how much French you absorb when words are in a familiar context that interests you.

Don't forget that you already have a huge latent vocabulary simply because, for historical reasons, French and English have a lot of words in common. Some word groups are all but identical, others have moved apart slightly. These are the main focus of the **Word power** pages, which show you how to 'convert' from one language to the other. Not only will you find your vocabulary increasing dramatically, but you'll also have the knowledge and the confidence to make an educated guess at the meaning of new words.

Is it true that many English words are used in French?

Over the years French and English have borrowed and absorbed many words from each other. Most of them have stayed unchanged but a few have adapted to their adopted language. For example, **boulingrin**, which is a manicured garden or lawn, is from the English *bowling green*, **bifteck** *steak* is from *beef steak* and **footing** means *jogging*.

Similarly, the rules of English grammar are often applied to French imported words: we add an English past participle ending *-ed* to the French **cliché** and **sauté**, for instance, to get *clichéd* and *sautéed*.

Do these shared words sound the same?

Many of them are recognisable for speakers of the other language – but many more are pronounced with a 'local' accent, whether French or English. Some French words routinely used in the UK are not said as a French person would say them – **cul-de-sac**, **lieu** and **bureau de change**, for instance.

The key to good pronunciation is to assume that even words you recognise might sound different in French, and to approach **Sounds and spelling** on page 15 with a completely open mind.

Here are just a few of the French words and expressions used in English:

aide-de-camp   *arabesque*
attaché   *artiste*
au pair   *ballet*
chargé d'affaires   *chanteuse*
chauffeur   *cor anglais*
employee   *corps de ballet*
entrepreneur   *pas de deux*

à la mode   *avant-garde*
chic   *bric-à-brac*
coiffeur   *pied-à-terre*
couture   *savoir-faire*
lingerie   *tête-à-tête*
négligée   *vis-à-vis*

bon vivant   *à la carte*
carte blanche   *apéritif*
déjà vu   *au gratin*
laissez faire   *courgette*
pièce de résistance   *haute cuisine*
rendezvous   *hors d'oeuvre*

… and some English words regularly used in French:

club   **baby-sitter**
golf   **camping**
hockey   **hot dog**
sport   **parking**
squash   **shopping**
tennis   **weekend**

chat room   **e-commerce**
internet   **leader**
mail   **manager**
networking   **marketing**
spamming   **sponsoring**
web-cam   **start-up**

Sounds and spelling

The pronunciation and spelling of French can seem a bit daunting at first:

- The sound of some letters is unexpected, for example, **oi** sounds like wa: **moi**.

- There are sounds in French that don't exist in English, such as **r**, which is a guttural sound pronounced in the throat, and nasal vowels, where the air is expelled through the nose as well as the mouth.

- Some letters are silent: **h** is always silent, while other consonants are silent only when they appear at the end of words.

- One sound can have several different spellings: **parler**, **parlez**, **parlé**, **parlais**, **parlait** and **parlaient** are all pronounced more or less the same.

Don't be put off by these features; there are consistent rules governing French pronunciation, and a knowledge of these rules, plus frequent and regular practice, will soon have you speaking French with confidence.

However good your knowledge of grammar is, however wide your vocabulary, you won't learn to speak French just by reading and writing. You need to listen too – so take every opportunity to listen to native French speakers. Even if at first you don't understand a great deal of what they're saying, you can focus on how French sounds and watch people's faces as they speak.

pronunciation

vowel sounds

French has many different vowel sounds, including some that don't exist in English. The sound of a vowel can change when it has an accent or when it's combined with another vowel.

These are the basic guidelines:

a	like *a* in *bad*: **Paris**
	an accent makes no difference: **voilà**
e	without an accent e sounds like *er* in *mother*: **je**, **le**
	unless it's followed by two consonants, when it sounds like *e* in *bed*: **merci**, **cette**
è, ê	like *e* in *bed*: **crème**, **être**, **fête**
é	like *ay* in *day* but stopping short of pronouncing the *y*: **café**,
i	like *ea* in *peace*: **ici**, **Nice**
o	like *o* in *hot*: **homme**
	unless it's at the end of a word or has a circumflex (^), when it sounds like *over*: **vélo**, **hôtel**
u	this sound doesn't exist in English. Position your lips to say *oo* but say *ee* instead without moving your lips: **tu**, **vue**
ai	like *ay* in *day* but stopping short of pronouncing the *y*: **maison**
ei	like *e* in *bed*: **treize**
eu	like *i* in *girl*: **peux**
ou	like *oo* in *ooze*: **vous**
oi	like *wa* in *wag*: **moi**
au/eau	like *o* in *over*: **château**
ui	like *we*: **cuisine**

y is usually a vowel in French, sounding like *y* in *happy*: **Yves**, **lycée**. But when it's at the beginning of words like **yoga** and **yeux**, it's a consonant and it's pronounced like *y* in *yellow*.

Some vowels are nasal, as in words like **temps** *time*, **change**, **vin** *wine*, **pain** *bread*, **faim** *hunger*, **point** *full stop*. To produce a nasal vowel, say the English word *sang* or *song* but stop short before the *ng*. You'll notice that your tongue doesn't touch the roof of your mouth and that you can feel the build-up of air in your nostrils.

Nasal vowels occur before m and n unless:
- there's another vowel following the m or n as in **cinéma**
- the m or n is doubled as in **pomme** *apple* and **Cannes**

consonants

Most consonants sound very similar in French and English. The only ones to look out for are **c**, **g**, **h**, **j**, **q** and **r**, plus the combinations **ll** and **th**.

c	like *c* in *cat* before **a**, **o**, **u**: **carte**, **coton**
	like *s* in *sat* before **e**, **i**, **y**: **glace**, **Nancy**
ç	like *s* in *sat*: **français**
ch	like *sh* in *shop*: **château**
g	like *g* in *golf* before **a**, **o**, **u**: **garçon**, **baguette**
	like *s* in *leisure* before **e**, **i**, **y**: **général**
gn	like *ny* in *canyon*: **champagne**, **montagne**
h	always silent: **hôtel**
j	like *s* in *leisure*: **je**, **jardin**
ll	sometimes the same as English: **village**
	sometimes like *y* in *day*: **fille**, **bouteille**, **Marseille**
qu	like *c* in *cat*: **quatre**, **quiche**
r	rolled at the back of the throat: **rouge**
th	like *t* in *tea*: **théâtre**

liaison

Usually the final consonant of a word isn't pronounced: **ballet**, **petits fours**, **grand prix**, **froid**, **restaurant**. But when the following word begins with a vowel, you do pronounce that final consonant and run the two words together. It's called liaison:

les_enfants *the children* – the **s** of **le͟s** is pronounced like **z**
vous_êtes *you are* – the **s** of **vou͟s** is pronounced like **z**
aux_autres *to the others* – the **x** of **au͟x** is pronounced like **z**
elle est_allée *she went* – the **t** of **es͟t** is pronounced
en_Angleterre *in England* – the **n** of **e͟n** is pronounced

Most words beginning with **h** are also liaised:
deux_heures, **trois_hommes** – the **x** and **s** sound like **z**.

But a few words beginning with **h** are not liaised. These are mainly (but not all) words of foreign origin like **le hockey** and **le hamster**. The **h** in these words is called an aspirated **h**, and with words beginning with an aspirated **h**, **le** isn't shortened to **l'** and there's no liaison:
les haricots is pronounced lay-arrico.

stress and intonation

English has a tum-ti-tum rhythm, where certain syllables are stressed more than others: *I wandered lonely as a cloud*; *Our Father, who art in heaven*. French has a rat-a-tat rhythm; in other words, each syllable of a word, and each word in the sentence, is given equal emphasis.

French sentences are made up of rhythmic groups, or groups of related words e.g. **Maman et papa | m'ont visité | hier soir** *Mum and Dad visited me yesterday* and **Mon mari Luc | est cuisinier | à l'Hôtel Montmartre** *My husband Luc is a chef at the Hotel Montmartre*. The last syllable of each rhythmic group, apart from the final one, has a rising intonation, i.e. it is pronounced at a higher pitch. The final syllable of the final rhythmic group has a falling intonation, i.e. it's pronounced at a lower pitch. When asking a question the final syllable of the sentence is also given a rising intonation.

accents

It's useful to know what the various accents are called in French for spelling out or taking down accented words.

[ʹ] **L'accent aigu** *acute accent* appears only over **é** and changes the sound to *ay*, as in words like **communiqué**, **exposé**, **lamé**, **café**, **résumé**, which keep the accent in English.

[ˋ] **L'accent grave** *grave accent* can appear over **à**, **è** and **ù**. There's no difference in pronunciation between **à** and **a** or **ù** and **u**; the accent mainly distinguishes between two words: **la** *the*, **là** *there*; **ou** *or*, **où** *where*. **e** without an accent sounds like *er* in *father* whereas **è** is longer and stronger, like *e* in *end*: **père** *father*; **bière** *beer*.

[ʌ] **L'accent circonflexe** *circumflex* can appear over **â**, **ê**, **î**, **ô** and **û** and doesn't influence pronunciation. It often indicates that the word was once spelt with an **s**: **forêt** *forest*, or it can distinguish between two words: **mur** *wall*, **mûr** *ripe*.

[ͻ] **La cedille** *cedilla* only ever appears below **ç** and shows that it's pronounced *s*, not *k*. When followed by **e** or **i**, **c** is always pronounced *s*, so it doesn't need a cedilla.

[··] **Le tréma** *diaeresis* can appear over **ë** or **ï** to show that the vowel is pronounced separately and distinctly, not combined with the preceding vowel: **Noël**, **naïf** *naive*.

the French alphabet

When spelling words out, the letters of the alphabet sound like the English sounds in the middle column. The names in the right-hand column are used when clarification is needed, in the same way as the UK uses: *alpha*, *bravo*, *charlie* … *x-ray*, *yankee*, *zulu*.

a	ah	Anatole
b	bay	Bérthe
c	say	Célestin
d	day	Désiré
e	euh	Eugène
f	eff	François
g	zhay	Gaston
h	ash	Henri
i	ee	Irma
j	zhee	Joseph
k	ka	Kléber
l	el	Louis
m	em	Marcel
n	en	Nicolas
o	oh	Oscar
p	pay	Pierre
q	koo	Quintal
r	ehr	Raoul
s	es	Suzanne
t	tay	Thérèse
u	oo	Ursule
v	vay	Victor
w	doo-bluh-vay	William
x	eeks	Xavier
y	ee-grek	Yvonne
z	zed	Zoé

spelling things out

When using **Anatole**, **Bérthe** etc. the link word is **comme** *as/like*:
Inès? Comment ça s'écrit? *Inès? How do you spell it?*
**i comme Irma, n comme Nicolas, e avec accent grave comme Eugène,
s comme Suzanne**

Double is **double**. *Emma* would be: euh, **double** em, ah

punctuation marks

*   **astérisque**
@   **arobase** (or **at**)
/   **barre oblique** (or **slash**)
\   **barre oblique inversée** (or **anti-slash**, or **back slash**)
.   **point**
-   *(hyphen)* **trait d'union**
–   *(dash)* **tiret**
_   *(underscore)* **trait de soulignement**
,   **virgule**
(symbole) dièse
ABC upper case **majuscule**
abc lower case **minuscule**
(in brackets) **entre parenthèses**
"in inverted commas" **entre guillemets**
space **espace**

It's useful to know the French for punctuation marks and keyboard symbols
if you want to spell out, for example, your **adresse courriel/e-mail**
email address.

And when spelling out a **site internet/site web** *website* or a **page web** *web
page*, you need *www*, which would be doo-bluh vay, doo-bluh vay, doo-bluh
vay or **trois** doo-bluh vay.

www.bbcactive.com would sound like this:
trois doo-bluh vay, **point**, bay bay say ah say tay ee vay euh **point com**
… and if you add /languages:
barre oblique el, ah, en, zhay, oo, ah, zhay, euh, es

Have a go at saying it out loud, then try spelling your own name and
email address.

capital letters

French uses **majuscules** *capital letters* less than English. They're used at the beginning of a sentence but they're not used for:

- **je** *I* (unless it starts a sentence)

- names of days or months (see page 30):
  jeudi *Thursday*; **mars** *March*

- languages or adjectives of nationality:
  Il parle anglais. *He speaks English.*
  Je suis écossais. *I'm Scottish.*
  un pays européen *a European country*

- geographical words such as *ocean* or *mountain* and also words like *street*:
  l'océan Atlantique, la rivière Mersey, la mer Méditerranée, le mont Everest, rue Rimbaud, avenue Victor Hugo

- religions and their adherents:
  le christianisme, le bouddhisme, l'hindouisme, le catholicisme, le judaïsme but **l'Islam**
  les chrétiens, les bouddhistes, les hindous, les catholiques, les juifs *Jews*, **les musulmans**

- names of organisations of which more than one exist – although a proper name within it ***does*** take a capital:
  le ministère de la Culture *Ministry of Culture*; **la bibliothèque Mazarine** *Mazarine Library*

- adjectives as part of the name of an organisation of which there's only one – unless the adjective comes before the noun:
  l'Académie française *French Academy*; **l'Assemblée nationale** *National Assembly*; **la Haute Cour de justice** *High Court of Justice*

Capital letters *are* used:

- for names of people:
  Monsieur et Madame Hubert; Jean-Marc
- places:
  towns: **Paris, Marseille, Lyon, Grenoble, Lille, Nice**

  countries: **l'Allemagne** *Germany*, **l'Angleterre** *England*, **l'Autriche** *Austria,* **la Belgique, le Canada, le Danemark, l'Ecosse** *Scotland,* **l'Espagne** *Spain*, **les Etats-Unis** *United States*, **la Finlande, la France, la Grande Bretagne** *Great Britain*, **la Grèce, la Hongrie** *Hungary*, **l'Irlande, la Norvège** *Norway*, **le Pays de Galles** *Wales*, **la Pologne** *Poland*, **le Portugal, les Pays-Bas** *Netherlands*, **la Roumanie, le Royaume-Uni** *United Kingdom*, **la Russie, la Slovaquie, la Suède** *Sweden*, **la Suisse** *Switzerland*, **l'Ukraine**

  although the adjective is lower case in countries whose name consists of unhyphenated noun + adjective(s): **la République tchèque** *Czech Republic*, **la République dominicaine** *Dominican Republic*, **l'Arabie saoudite** *Saudi Arabia*, **les Emirats arabes unis** *United Arab Emirates*

  continents: **l'Afrique, l'Amérique du Nord/Sud, l'Asie, l'Antarctique, l'Australie, l'Europe**

- nationalities when used as nouns:
  Les Français aiment leur langue. *The French love their language.*
  Les Anglais aiment faire la queue. *The English like standing in queues.*

Accents can be missed off capital letters, but it's not wrong to include them, particularly if the accent affects the sound of the letter. A cedilla is never missed off a capital **C**:
les États-Unis or **les Etats-Unis** *United States*; **Ça, c'est fait.** *That's* done.

word power

There's a pattern to the way some consonants in letter combinations in English and French correspond. These are only broad guidelines and there are plenty of exceptions.

🇬🇧	🇫🇷	
c	que	*Arctic* **Arctique**, *classic* **classique**, *ethnic* **ethnique**, *logic* **logique**, *music* **musique**
dv	v	*advance* **avance**, *advantage* **avantage**, *Advent* **Avent**, *adventure* **aventure**, *advocate* **avocat**
ni	gn	*companion* **compagnon**, *onion* **oignon**, *pinion* **pignon**
ory	oire	*glory* **gloire**, *history* **histoire**, *ivory* **ivoire**, *memory* **mémoire**, *victory* **victoire**
ous	eux	*amorous* **amoureux**, *copious* **copieux**, *joyous* **joyeux**, *nervous* **nerveux**
words beginning with s	é	*spell* **épeler**, *stallion* **étalon**, *star* **étoile**, *state* **état**, *study* **étudier**
v	f	*active* **actif**, *evasive* **évasif**, *expansive* **expansif**, *naive* **naïf**, *positive* **positif**

checkpoint 1

1 In which of these phrases would you hear the s of les?
les rues, les oignons, les hindous, les soirs, les chaussures,
les wagons, les haricots, les Européens

2 In which of these words is c pronounced like *k*?
citron, leçon, glace, comme, société

3 When spelling words out, what names are used for the letters
f, l, n and t?

4 How is *www* pronounced?

5 How can you say @ in an email address, apart from using the
English *at*?

6 l'adresse de l'académie française est 23, quai de conti,
75006 paris. Which of the words in this sentence need a
capital letter?

7 What happens to the pitch of your voice at the end of
a question?

8 What's the sixth vowel in French?

9 Pick out the word that doesn't rhyme: pavé, avais, laver,
ravi, savez

10 Without looking at page 22, name four western European
countries in French.

Once you're comfortable with spelling out your own details,
have a go at spelling out the names and email addresses of
friends and family.

Numbers, time and date

Some aspects of French and English numbers are very different. For example, in French:

- a comma is used where English uses a full stop, and vice versa, so *24,000* would be **24.000** in French and *7.5* would be **7,5**
- *one* has a masculine and a feminine version: **un** and **une**
- 17, 18 and 19 have a different pattern from 11–16
- 71–99 are based on a counting system that's different from 21–69. 70–79 translate literally as *sixty-ten*, *sixty-eleven*, etc; 80 translates literally as *four-twenties* and 81–99 use 80 followed by 1–19.
- French phone numbers are read out in pairs, not single digits:
  93 44 50 08 is said as **quatre-vingt-treize, quarante-quatre, cinquante, zéro huit.**

There are also some interesting differences where time and date are concerned:

- In writing, time using the 24–hour clock (which is widespread in France) includes **h**, short for **heures** *hours* but has no full stop:
  22h15, vingt-deux heures quinze *22.15*
  le train de 13h40 *the 13.40 train* lit. *the train of 13.40*
- The French for a *week* is **huit jours** *eight days*, and a *fortnight* is **quinze jours** *15 days* or **une quinzaine.**

Zero is **zéro** in French. The noun that follows it is in the singular: **zéro faute** *no mistakes*. If you look it up in a dictionary, you'll find it has the following English translations:

zéro (m) **1.** nought, zero: *au-dessous de* ~ below zero; *au-dessus de* ~ above zero; ~ *heure* zero hour, midnight; *partir de* ~ start from scratch **2.** [*sport*] nil: *trois (buts)* à ~ 3–0 **3.** [*tennis*] love: *quinze à* ~ 15-love. **4.** [*telephone*] 0.

cardinal numbers

1	un	11	onze
2	deux	12	douze
3	trois	13	treize
4	quatre	14	quatorze
5	cinq	15	quinze
6	six	16	seize
7	sept	17	dix-sept
8	huit	18	dix-huit
9	neuf	19	dix-neuf
10	dix		

- **Un** changes to agree with the gender (masculine or feminine) of its noun, like *a/an* (see page 44): **un parc, une maison**

- Numbers are masculine and take the definite article **le** (page 46). **Le** doesn't shorten to **l'** before **huit** or **onze**: **le onze novembre**.

20	vingt	27	vingt-sept
21	vingt et un	28	vingt-huit
22	vingt-deux	29	vingt-neuf
23	vingt-trois	30	trente
24	vingt-quatre	40	quarante
25	vingt-cinq	50	cinquante
26	vingt-six	60	soixante

- The numbers 31–69 repeat the pattern 21–29:
  quarante-huit *48*, **soixante-cinq** *65*

- **un** changes to **une** in numbers followed by a feminine noun:
  trente et une filles *31 girls*; **soixante et une pièces** *61 rooms*

- 70 is literally *sixty-ten*, and 71–79 are counted as *sixty-eleven*, *sixty-twelve … sixty-nineteen*:

70	soixante-dix	75	soixante-quinze
71	soixante et onze	76	soixante-seize
72	soixante-douze	77	soixante-dix-sept
73	soixante-treize	78	soixante-dix-huit
74	soixante-quatorze	79	soixante-dix-neuf

- 80 is literally *four-twenties*. This combines with 1–19 for the numbers 80–99:

80	quatre-vingts	90	quatre-vingt-dix
81	quatre-vingt-un	91	quatre-vingt-onze
82	quatre-vingt-deux	92	quatre-vingt-douze
83	quatre-vingt-trois	93	quatre-vingt-treize
84	quatre-vingt-quatre	94	quatre-vingt-quatorze
85	quatre-vingt-cinq	95	quatre-vingt-quinze
86	quatre-vingt-six	96	quatre-vingt-seize
87	quatre-vingt-sept	97	quatre-vingt-dix-sept
88	quatre-vingt-huit	98	quatre-vingt-dix-huit
89	quatre-vingt-neuf	99	quatre-vingt-dix-neuf

- 80 is the only number to have an s on **vingts**.

- 81 and 91 don't include **et** before **un**, as smaller numbers do.

100	cent	1000	mille
101	cent un	1100	mille cent
102	cent deux	1500	mille cinq cents
110	cent dix	2000	deux mille
150	cent cinquante	10 000	dix mille
175	cent soixante-quinze	100 000	cent mille
200	deux cents	500 000	cinq cent mille
201	deux cent un	1 000 000	un million
220	deux cent vingt	2 000 000	deux millions
500	cinq cents	1 000 000 000	un milliard

In the plural:

- **cent** *a hundred* adds an s only in round hundreds:
  300 **trois cents**, but 310 **trois cent dix**; 700 **sept cents**, but
  701 **sept cent un**

- **mille** *a thousand* doesn't change:
  2 000 **deux mille**, 5 500 **cinq mille cinq cents**

- **un million** *a million* and **un milliard** *a billion* have the regular plurals
  millions and **milliards**. They're followed by **de** when used before a noun:
  un million d'euros *1,000,000 euros*
  sept milliards de dollars *7,000,000,000 dollars*
  … but **un million cinq cent mille euros** *1,500,000 euros*

ordinal numbers

Ordinal numbers are formed by adding **-ième** to the cardinal number minus its final vowel:

1st	premier/première	1er (m), 1re (f)
2nd	deuxième/second(e)	2^e
3rd	troisième	3^e
4th	quatrième	4^e
5th	cinquième	5^e
6th	sixième	6^e
7th	septième	7^e
8th	huitième	8^e
9th	neuvième	9^e
10th	dixième	10^e

- The ^{er} of **premier** changes to ^{re} for **première**.
- **Cinquième** adds u before **ième**.
- The f in **neuf** becomes v in **neuvième**.
- *First* in 21, 31, 41, etc. is **unième**: **vingt et unième** *21st*, **cent unième** *101st*.

Ordinal numbers are used much as in English except that:
- they agree in gender (masculine or feminine) and number (singular or plural) with their noun – although only **premier** and **second** have separate feminine forms:
  première (1re) classe *first class*
  les premiers jours *the first days*
  la Seconde Guerre mondiale *the Second World War*
  les troisièmes rencontres *the third meetings*
- they're not used for dates, with the exception of **premier** (page 30).

Premier is also the odd one out when talking about sovereigns and popes. From *second* onwards, cardinal numbers are used:
Charles premier *Charles I*
Elizabeth deux *Elizabeth II*
Napoléon trois *Napoleon III*
Louis quatorze *Louis XIV*
le Pape Benoît seize *Pope Benedict XVI*

---

umpteenth *adj* **énième**: *for the ~ time* **pour la énième fois**

time

- When telling the time in English you generally begin with the minutes: *five (minutes) past nine*. It's the opposite in French: first the hour, then the minutes.
- There's no word for *past*; *to* is **moins** for minutes to the hour.
- **Quart** *quarter* is accompanied by **le** when used for *quarter to* the hour, but not for *quarter past*.

Quelle heure est-il? Il est quelle heure? *What time is it?*
Il est … *It's …*
midday/midnight **midi/minuit**
01.00 **une heure**
02.00 **deux heures**
09.05 **neuf heures cinq**
09.10 **neuf heures dix**
09.15 **neuf heures quinze** or **neuf heures et quart**
09.20 **neuf heures vingt**
09.25 **neuf heures vingt-cinq**
09.30 **neuf heures trente** or **neuf heures et demie**
09.35 **neuf heures trente-cinq** or **dix heures moins vingt-cinq**
09.40 **neuf heures quarante** or **dix heures moins vingt**
09.45 **neuf heures quarante-cinq** or **dix heures moins le quart**
09.50 **neuf heures cinquante** or **dix heures moins dix**
09.55 **neuf heures cinquante-cinq** or **dix heures moins cinq**

A quelle heure …? *(At) what time …?*
à une heure *at one o'clock*
à deux heures, à trois heures, à onze heures *at two o'clock, three o'clock, 11 o'clock*

Half past is **et demie** (f) except with midday and midnight, when it's **et demi** (m):
à huit heures et demie *at half past eight*
à midi/minuit et demi *at half past 12*

The use of the 24-hour clock is widespread in France:
à vingt-trois heures quinze *at 23.15* (**23h15** in French)
de neuf heures à dix-huit heures *from 09.00 to 18.00*
le train de 13h40 *the 13.40 train* lit. *the train of 13.40*

date: days, months, years

Days, months and seasons are all masculine and they're written without a capital letter in French.

- **Les jours de la semaine sont** *The days of the week are*:

lundi	*Monday*	**vendredi**	*Friday*
mardi	*Tuesday*	**samedi**	*Saturday*
mercredi	*Wednesday*	**dimanche**	*Sunday*
jeudi	*Thursday*		

  There's no word for *on* in French with days, but you use **le** when you want to convey that something is a regular event:
  Je travaille lundi. *I'm working on Monday.*
  Je travaille le lundi. *I work on Mondays/every Monday.*

- **Les mois de l'année sont** *The months of the year are*:

janvier	*January*	**juillet**	*July*
février	*February*	**août**	*August*
mars	*March*	**septembre**	*September*
avril	*April*	**octobre**	*October*
mai	*May*	**novembre**	*November*
juin	*June*	**décembre**	*December*

  Je vais à Strasbourg en août. *I'm going to Strasbourg in August.*

- **Les quatre saisons sont** *The four seasons are*:

le printemps	*spring*	**au printemps**	*in spring*
l'été	*summer*	**en été**	*in summer*
l'automne	*autumn*	**en automne**	*in autumn*
l'hiver	*winter*	**en hiver**	*in winter*

- There are various ways of saying the years 18.., 19.. etc., including using **mil**, a special form of **mille**:
  Je suis né(e) *I was born*
  … **en mille/mil neuf cent soixante-quinze** … *in 1975*
  … **en dix-neuf cent soixante-quinze** … *in 1975*
  … **en soixante-quinze** … *in '75*

- With the date, ordinal numbers are used only for the first of the month; cardinal numbers are used after that. *On* isn't translated.
  le premier mai *(on) 1 May*, **le quatorze juillet** *(on) 14 July*
  le huit juin *(on) 8 June*, **le onze mai** *(on) 11 May* (NB **le** not **l'**)

quand? *when?*
à trois heures pile *at three o'clock on the dot*
vers six heures *about six o'clock*
jusqu'à une heure *until one o'clock*
avant sept heures *before seven o'clock*
après trois heures *after three o'clock* (c.f. **trois heures plus tard** *after three hours*)
dans cinq minutes *in five minutes' time*

aujourd'hui *today*
à dix heures du matin/du soir *at ten o'clock in the morning/evening*
à trois heures de l'après-midi *at three o'clock in the afternoon*
ce matin *this morning;* **ce soir** *this evening*
cet après-midi *this afternoon*
tous les jours/mois *every day/month*
tous les deux jours *every two days, every other day*
toutes les semaines *every week*
une fois par semaine/mois *once a week/month*

demain *tomorrow*
demain matin/soir *tomorrow morning/evening*
après-demain *the day after tomorrow*
en deux jours/en moins de deux jours *within two days*
la semaine/l'année prochaine *next week/year*
lundi prochain *next Monday;* **le lendemain** *the following day*

hier *yesterday*
hier matin/soir *yesterday morning/evening*
avant-hier *the day before yesterday*
l'autre jour *the other day*
il y a deux jours/une semaine *two days/a week ago*
la semaine dernière *last week;* **l'année dernière** *last year*
mardi dernier *last Tuesday*

pendant les années soixante *in the '60s*
au vingtième/vingt et unième siècle *in the 20th/21st century*

checkpoint 2

1   What's the French for a) *nil*, b) *comma*?

2   Is cent soixante-dix-neuf greater or smaller than cent quatre-vingt-dix-sept?

3   Write down the French for 8, 18, 28, 78 and 88.

4   Now write deux millions quatre cent mille in numbers, punctuating it the French way.

5   What do these mean?

    a Il est cinq heures.
    b à sept heures du soir
    c après minuit
    d hier soir à sept heures
    e à huit heures et demie
    f le premier août
    g vers une heure
    h vendredi prochain
    i à onze heures pile
    j jusqu'à dix heures

6   ... and how do you say these times in French?

    a *it's 11 o'clock*
    b *at nine am*
    c *at 12 noon*
    d *after 18.00*
    e *at exactly 09.00*
    f *tomorrow at ten o'clock*
    g *yesterday at 10.00*
    h *on Sunday at 16.00*
    i *at seven o'clock every day*
    j *before three o'clock in the afternoon*

7   What are the three different French words for *in* in these phrases: a) *in winter* b) *in ten minutes' time* c) *in the '70s?*

8   What do you think une quinzaine de jours means?

9   In French, write the date of *New Year's Day*, *Christmas Day* and *New Year's Eve*.

10 What time is le train de seize heures quarante-quatre expected?

11 soixante, _____ , quatre-vingts What's missing from the sequence?

12 What are the various ways of saying 1789 in French?

13 Is printemps, été, automne or hiver the French for *spring*?

14 What do you think soixante-quinze pour cent means?

Nouns

Nouns are the words for
- living beings: man, sister, doctor, lion, Anton
- things: table, water, night, lesson, sport
- places: country, town, France, Paris
- concepts: beauty, freedom, time, democracy

Every single French noun – not just the words for people – is either masculine (m) or feminine (f). This is its **gender**, and you need to know a noun's gender because words used with it, such as articles and adjectives, have corresponding masculine and feminine forms.

So, whenever you come across a new noun, make a point of associating it with its gender by learning it with an article – **le** *the* or **un** *a* for a masculine noun and **la** or **une** for a feminine noun.

As in English, most nouns in French add **s** for the plural. Unlike English, the **s** isn't usually pronounced in French. The article, **les** *the* or **des** *some*, shows that the noun is plural.

In an English-French dictionary, abbreviations to look out for include *n* noun, *m* masculine, *f* feminine, *sing* singular, *pl* plural.

If you look up *car* and *horse*, this is what you might find:

car *n* automobile *f*, voiture *f*: *by* ~ en voiture; ~ *park n* parc *m* de stationnement, parking *m*

horse *n* cheval *m* [*gym*] cheval sautoir *m*: ~ *race* course *f* de chevaux; ~ *riding* équitation *f*; *rocking* ~ cheval à bascule; *I could eat a* ~! J'ai une faim de loup!

people: the family

As you might expect, nouns for male family members are masculine and those for females feminine:

m		f	
un père	*father*	une mère	*mother*
un mari	*husband*	une femme	*wife*
un fils	*son*	une fille	*daughter*
un frère	*brother*	une sœur	*sister*
un grand-père	*grandfather*	une grand-mère	*grandmother*
un petit-fils	*grandson*	une petite-fille	*granddaughter*
un oncle	*uncle*	une tante	*aunt*
un cousin	*cousin (male)*	une cousine	*cousin (female)*
un neveu	*nephew*	une nièce	*niece*
un homme	*man*	une femme	*woman*
Monsieur	*Mr*	Madame	*Mrs*
un beau-père	*father-in-law* *stepfather*	une belle-mère	*mother-in-law* *stepmother*
un beau-frère	*brother-in-law*	une belle-sœur	*sister-in-law*
un beau-fils	*son-in-law* *stepson*	une belle-fille	*daughter-in-law* *stepdaughter*
un demi-frère	*stepbrother*	une demi-sœur	*stepsister*
un parrain	*godfather*	une marraine	*godmother*

Enfant *child* can be either masculine or feminine (un enfant or une enfant) but bébé *baby* is always masculine (un bébé).
Chloë est une belle enfant. *Chloe is a beautiful child.*
Chloë est un beau bébé. *Chloe is a beautiful baby.*

A few words are always feminine, even when they refer to a man:
personne *person*, vedette *star*, idole *idol*, victime *victim*

... and the workplace

Many words for occupations have different endings according to whether they refer to a man or a woman. In many cases it's simply a matter of adding **e** for the feminine – but remember that this makes quite a difference to the pronunciation:

-e	un avocat	une avocate	*lawyer*
	un étudiant	une étudiante	*student*
	un employé	une employée	*employee*
-ière	un caissier	une caissière	*cashier, check-out assistant*
	un infirmier	une infirmière	*nurse*
-ienne	un informaticien	une informaticienne	*IT technician*
	un musicien	une musicienne	*musician*
	un pharmacien	une pharmacienne	*pharmacist*
-euse	un serveur	une serveuse	*waiter/waitress*
	un vendeur	une vendeuse	*salesman/woman*
	un chanteur	une chanteuse	*singer*
-trice	un acteur	une actrice	*actor/actress*
	un directeur	une directrice	*manager/ess*
	un rédacteur	une rédactrice	*editor*

Other occupations use the same word for men and women:
un/une **architecte** *architect*   un/une **comptable** *accountant*
un/une **fonctionnaire** *civil servant*   un/une **journaliste** *journalist*
un/une **collègue** *colleague*   un/une **secrétaire** *secretary*

The words for some traditional male roles are masculine even when they refer to a woman: **un médecin** *doctor*, **un ingénieur** *engineer* **un chef** *boss*, **un peintre** *painter*.
Sometimes **femme** is added: **une femme médecin** *a woman doctor*.

French is changing in line with the workplace, and new feminine forms of traditionally male occupations – such as **une chirurgienne** *surgeon* – are becoming commonplace. In Canada and Switzerland you now hear **une professeur**, although it's still the masculine **un professeur** for both men and women in France.

other masculine nouns

Although you can't usually tell from looking at a noun what its gender is, most nouns with the following endings are masculine. Beware of exceptions, though!

-et, -isme, -ment

> un jouet *toy*, un carnet *notebook*, le journalisme *journalism*,
> le terrorisme *terrorism*, un monument *monument*,
> un gouvernement *government*, un appartement *flat*
> Exceptions include **une jument** *mare* and **une forêt** *forest*.

-ège, -age

> un collège *school*, un cortège *procession*, un fromage *cheese*,
> un village *village*
> Exceptions include **la Norvège** *Norway*, **une image** *picture* and many one-syllable nouns such as **une cage, une rage, une plage** *beach*.

-ou, -eau

> un hibou *owl*, un bijou *jewel*, un bateau *boat*, un gâteau *cake*,
> un cadeau *present*, un château *castle*
> Exceptions include **l'eau** *water* and **la peau** *skin*.

-ier, -eur

> un cahier *exercise book*, un pompier *firefighter*, un ascenseur *lift*,
> un aspirateur *vacuum cleaner*
> Exceptions include **la peur** *fear*, **une douleur** *pain*, **la chaleur** *heat*.

-acle, -ail

> un miracle, un obstacle, le travail *work*, l'ail *garlic*
> Exceptions include **une débâcle** *rout*.

The following categories of noun are all masculine:
- days of the week, months and seasons:
  le lundi *Monday*, le printemps *spring*, l'été *summer*,
  l'automne *autumn*, l'hiver *winter*
- metric weights and measures: un litre, un demi-kilo
- languages: le français *French*, le russe *Russian*

other feminine nouns

There are also endings associated with feminine nouns. Many of the words with these endings are identical to the English when you see them written down but not, of course, when you hear them.

-tion, -aison

une question, une situation, une solution, une opération, une nation, l'équitation *horse riding*, la natation *swimming*, l'alimentation *food*, une maison *house*, une saison *season*

-ette, -esse

une fillette *little girl*, une chaussette *sock*, une toilette *wash*, la tristesse *sadness*, la jeunesse *youth*, la vitesse *speed*, la presse *press, newspapers*, une messe *Roman Catholic mass*

-ence, -ance, -ense, -anse

une différence, la violence, la patience, une science, une agence *agency*, la concurrence *competition*, une balance *scales*, une enfance *childhood*, une licence, la défense, une danse *dance*

Exceptions include le silence.

-ure

une chaussure *shoe*, une blessure *wound*, une culture *culture*, la nourriture *food*

-ité

une cité, une activité, la liberté, la sérénité, une université

-ée

une entrée *entrance, first course*, une chaussée *highway*, une employée *female employee*

Exceptions include un musée *museum*, un lycée *secondary school*.

The following categories of noun are all feminine:
- continents: l'Asie, l'Afrique, l'Europe, l'Amérique
- many countries: la France, la Suisse *Switzerland*, la Belgique. But not le Canada, le Japon, le Maroc *Morocco*, le Brésil, le Mexique or les États-Unis *United States*.
- most rivers: la Seine, la Tamise *Thames*, la Loire. But not le Rhône or le Rhin *Rhine*.

nouns that can be masculine or feminine

Some nouns can be either masculine or feminine, and they have different meanings depending on the gender:

m		f	
un aide	*assistant*	l'aide	*assistance*
un boum	*bang*	une boum	*party*
un crêpe	*crepe (material)*	une crêpe	*thin pancake*
un finale	*finale (musical)*	une finale	*final (sport)*
un livre	*book*	une livre	*pound (sterling or weight)*
un mémoire	*memo*	une mémoire	*memory*
un mode	*way, method*	la mode	*fashion*
un mort	*dead (male) body*	la mort	*death*
un page	*page boy*	une page	*page*
un poêle	*stove*	une poêle	*frying pan*
un poste	*job, radio/TV set*	la poste	*post office, mail*
un tour	*tour, turn*	une tour	*tower*
un voile	*veil*	une voile	*sail, sailing*

compound nouns

Compound nouns fall into three categories:

- two nouns together. The gender is the gender of the first noun:
  un wagon-lit *sleeping car*   une porte-fenêtre *French window*
  un chou-fleur *cauliflower*   une pause-café *coffee break*
  … although un **tête-à-tête** is masculine.

- verb + noun. These are masculine:
  un **porte-monnaie** *purse*   un **pare-brise** *windscreen*
  un **gratte-ciel** *skyscraper*

- adjective or preposition + noun. These have the gender of the noun:
  un **grand-père** *grandfather*   une **grande-mère** *grandmother*
  un **après-midi** *afternoon*   une **chauve-souris** *bat*
  un **coffre-fort** *safe*   une **demi-heure** *half (an) hour*

making nouns plural

- Most nouns, masculine and feminine, form their plural by adding **s**:
  un/une enfant → des enfants *children*
  une femme → des femmes *women*
  un hôtel → des hôtels *hotels*

- If the singular ends in **-s**, **-x**, or **-z**, the plural stays the same:
  un fils → des fils *sons*, *children*; un nez → des nez *noses*;
  un prix → des prix *prices*

- **-al** and **-ail** usually change to **-aux**
  un animal → des animaux *animals*; un journal → des journaux
  newspapers; un cheval → des chevaux *horses*; un travail → des travaux
  works
  Exceptions include **un bal** *dance*, **un festival**, **un carnaval** and **un détail**,
  which add **s**.

- **-eu**, **-eau** and some words ending in **-ou** add **x**
  un lieu → des lieux *places*; un cheveu → des cheveux *hair*; un vœu →
  des vœux *wishes*; un gâteau → des gâteaux *cakes*; un château → des
  châteaux *castles*; l'eau (f) → les eaux *waters*; un bijou → des bijoux
  jewels, jewellery; un chou → des choux *cabbages*; un caillou → des
  cailloux *pebbles*
  Exceptions include **un pneu** *tyre*, **un trou** *hole* and **un clou** *nail,* which add **s**.

- A few nouns are irregular in the plural:
  un œil → les yeux *eyes*; monsieur → messieurs *gentlemen*;
  madame → mesdames *ladies*

> There are few hard-and-fast rules for making compound nouns plural,
> and the easiest thing to do is to learn these as you come across them.
> - Two nouns, and a noun + adjective, usually change both parts:
>   **des wagons-lits, des choux-fleurs**
>   **des grands-pères, des chauves-souris**
> - Many don't change at all: **des porte-monnaie, des gratte-ciel, des
>   pare-brise**
> - Some have alternative forms: you'll see **des après-midi** as often as
>   **des après-midis** for *afternoons*. And you'll see **des allers-retours**
>   for *return tickets* whereas you might expect **des aller-retours**.

word power

Literally hundreds of nouns are identical in French and English. These include nouns ending in **-tion**, **-sion**, **-age**, **-nce**, **-nt**, **-ble** and **-acle**:

abdication, abolition, admission, vision, camouflage, bandage, arrogance, assurance, astringent, contingent, spectacle, obstacle, impossible, probable

However, they're only identical when you see them written down. When they're spoken, they sound quite different. In French, for example, **expert** is pronounced *experr*.

There are many other nouns which are nearly the same in both languages. Sometimes the French version has an accent because of the different pronunciation.

🇬🇧	🇫🇷	
ism	isme	le communisme, l'égoïsme (m), le racisme, le réalisme, le tourisme
ist	iste	un/une dentiste, un/une linguiste, un/une optimiste, un/une pessimiste, un/une pianiste
y (abstract concepts)	ie	l'astrologie (f), l'astronomie (f), l'économie (f), la géographie, la philosophie, la sociologie
ty	té	la beauté, l'égalité, la fraternité, la liberté, l'université (f)
ologist	ologue	un/une archéologue, un/une astrologue, un/une cardiologue, un/une psychologue, un/une sociologue But un/une écologiste
our (abstract concepts)	eur	une couleur, une faveur, un honneur, une odeur, une rumeur, une saveur, la valeur
or/er (often people)	eur	un boxeur, un dineur, un docteur, un employeur, un porteur, un tour-opérateur, un vendeur

Look out too for:

- English words beginning with an *s* followed by a consonant. These are often spelt é- or es- in French: *screen* → un écran; *school* → une école; *sponge* → une éponge; *space* → un espace; *Spain* → l'Espagne (f)

- French words with a circumflex, which often indicates the presence of an *s* in English: un hôpital, une forêt, une île, la hâte *haste*, un hôte *host, guest*

false friends

Not all nouns mean what they appear to mean:

l'actualité (f) means *current affairs*	*actuality* is la réalité
un car means *coach*	*car* is une voiture
une casquette means *cap*	*casket* is un coffret
une cave means *cellar*	*cave* is une grotte
la chair means *flesh*	*chair* is une chaise
la chance means *luck*	*chance* (opportunity) is une occasion
le coin means *corner*, *spot*	*coin* is une pièce (de monnaie)
le collège means *school*	*college* is une université
un crayon means *pencil*	*crayon* is un crayon de couleur
la déception means *disappointment*	*deception* is la tromperie
une journée means *day*	*journey* is un voyage
le lard means *bacon*	*lard* is le saindoux
une librairie means *bookshop*	*library* is une bibliothèque
un menu means *set menu*	*menu* is une carte
une pièce means *room* or *play*	*piece* is un morceau
une place means *square*	*place* is un lieu or un endroit
un préservatif means *condom*	*preservative* is un conservateur
une prune means *plum*	*prune* is un pruneau
un raisin means *grape*	*raisin* is un raisin sec
une réunion means *meeting*	as well as *reunion*
un store means *blind*	*store* is un magasin
une veste means *jacket*	*vest* is un maillot de corps
un talon means *heel*	*talon* is une serre
les vacances (f) means *holidays*	*vacancy* is une chambre libre (*hotel*) or un poste (*job*)
un stage means (*training*) *course*	*stage* is une scène (*theatre*) or une étape (*point*)

checkpoint 3

1   Write m, f, or m/f in the boxes depending on whether the noun is masculine, feminine or could be either.

gâteau ☐   chou-fleur ☐   personne ☐

toilette ☐   médecin ☐   pare-brise ☐

collègue ☐   victime ☐   chaussure ☐

cousine ☐   silence ☐   enfant ☐

2   What are these in the plural?

porc ....   neveu ....

cadeau ....   chat ....

souris ....   café ....

chou ....   monument ....

personne ....   œil ....

lieu ....   fonctionnaire ....

prix ....   pneu ....

enfant ....   monsieur ....

cheval ....   hôpital ....

grenouille ....   pays ....

3   Is eau masculine or feminine?

4   What two meanings does livre have?

5   Does musiciennes mean one male musician, one female musician, several male musicians, several female musicians or a mixed group?

6   Think of a word that's feminine even when it refers to a man.

7   Can you work out the French for a) *biology*, b) *inflation*, c) *probability*, d) *criminologist*, e) *obstacle*, f) *absence*, g) *journalism*?

8   What are the two meanings of belle-mère?

9   Does Bonne journée mean *Have a good day* or *Have a good trip*?

10 What do you think tempête is in English?

11 Given that rédacteur is *male editor* and rédactrice *female editor*, what's the female equivalent of traducteur *translator*?

Articles: the, a, some

An **article** is used with a noun to show whether you're talking about something which is specific or defined: ***the*** *house*, ***the*** *houses*, or something which is not: ***a*** *house*, ***some*** *houses*.

Grammatically, articles fall into three categories:

- the definite article: *the*
- the indefinite article: *a/an*
- the partitive article: *some/any*

In French there are four words for *the*, and the one you use depends on whether the following noun is masculine or feminine, singular or plural; whether it begins with a vowel or a consonant. *A/an* can be **un** or **une** and there are several ways of saying *some* and *any*, depending again on the gender of the following noun.

There's a difference too in the way articles are used. French often uses the definite article in sentences where it's not used in English – for instance when generalising, as in **J'aime le chocolat** *I like chocolate* or **L'exercice est important** *Exercise is important*.

On the other hand, French leaves out the indefinite article in some sentences where it's needed in English, for example **Elle est médecin** *She's a doctor*.

a: un, une

Like English, French has two forms of the indefinite article. In English, however, the use of *a* or *an* depends on the initial sound of the following word, whereas in French the use of **un** or **une** depends on the gender (masculine or feminine) of the noun that the article relates to.

- **masculine**
  The word for *a/an* with masculine nouns is **un**:
  un homme *a man*
  un ami *a (male) friend*
  un verre de vin *a glass of wine*
  un petit livre *a little book*
  un euro *a euro*

- **feminine**
  The word for *a/an* with feminine nouns is **une**:
  une femme *a woman*
  une amie *a (female) friend*
  une maison *a house*
  une bouteille de vin *a bottle of wine*
  une bonne idée *a good idea*
  une personne *a person (male or female)*

> In negative sentences *a/an* is always **de**, which shortens to **d'** before a vowel:
> **Je n'ai pas de dictionnaire.** *I haven't got a dictionary.*
> **Je n'ai pas d'excuse.** *I haven't got an excuse.*

- **plural**
  Un and **une** have a plural in French: **des**, which is used whenever you're talking about an unspecific plural noun. The nearest English equivalent is *some* but, whereas *some* is omitted more often than not, **des** can't be omitted:
  J'ai des amis qui ... *I've got (some) friends who ...*
  Nous avons acheté des fleurs. *We bought (some) flowers.*

... and how to use them

Un and **une** are used in pretty much the same circumstances as *a/an* in English, i.e. before a noun that isn't referring to a specific person or thing.

However, unlike English, they're not used:
- with nouns denoting occupation and marital status:
  Je suis étudiant. *I'm a student.*
  Mathis est journaliste. *Mathis is a journalist.*
  Mon mari est cuisinier. *My husband is a cook.*
  Ma grand-mère est veuve. *My grandmother is a widow.*

  unless those nouns have additional information added to them:
  Mon mari est un excellent cuisinier. *My husband is an excellent cook.*

- with nouns denoting nationality and religion (where English has a choice):
  Il est irlandais. *He is Irish* or *He is an Irishman.*
  Vous êtes catholique? *Are you (a) Catholic?*

- before 100 and 1,000 and sometimes before *half*:
  Ça coûte cent euros. *It costs a hundred euros.*
  Je l'ai dit mille fois. *I've said it a thousand times.*
  deux ans et demi *two and a half years*
  But: **un demi-litre** *half a litre*

- after **quel** and **quelle** in exclamations:
  Quel joli nom! *What a lovely name!*
  Quelle bonne idée! *What a good idea!*
  Quel dommage! *What a pity!*
  Quelle coïncidence! *What a coincidence!*

the: le, la, l', les

There are four different words for *the* in French: **le, la, l', les**.
Which one you use depends on three things:

- whether the noun with the article is masculine or feminine
- whether that noun is singular or plural
- the first letter of the word immediately following the article

- **masculine**

  In the singular, the word for *the* is **le** with a masculine noun. It shortens to **l'** when the next word begins with a vowel:

  le directeur *the director*
  le jardin *the garden*
  l'enfant *the child*
  l'autre directeur *the other director*

- **feminine**

  In the singular, the word for *the* is **la** with a feminine noun. It shortens to **l'** when the next word begins with a vowel:

  la femme *the woman*
  la ville *the town*
  l'église *the church*
  l'autre femme *the other woman*

Words beginning with **h** generally take **l'**, except on a few occasions when the **h** acts like a consonant (page 17). These are often words of foreign origin (**le héros, le hamman, le hall**):
le haricot vert *the French bean*; **l'hôtel** (m) *the hotel*;
l'homme *the man*; **la haute cuisine**; **l'herbe** *the grass*

- **plural**

  The word for *the* with all plural nouns is **les**:

  les directeurs *the directors*; **les enfants** *the children*; **les hommes** *the men*; **les haricots verts** *the French beans*; **les femmes** *the women*; **les églises** *the churches*

... and when to use them

Like *the* in English, **le**, **la**, **l'**, **les** are used before a noun referring to a specific person or thing. In French they're also needed:

- when making generalisations:
  Les infirmières ont beaucoup de patience. *Nurses have a lot of patience.*
  Je déteste les escargots. *I hate snails.*
  J'adore la cuisine française. *I love French cooking.*

- with abstract nouns and illnesses:
  C'est la vie. *That's life.*
  L'amour est plus important que l'argent. *Love is more important than money.*
  Il a la rougeole/la varicelle. *He's got measles/chicken pox.*
  However, the article isn't used after **avec** or **sans**: **avec difficulté** *with difficulty*; **sans efforts** *without any effort*.

- with the names of continents, countries, and regions:
  l'Afrique, la Chine, le Canada, les Etats-Unis
  la Corse, le Québec, la Bretagne, le Kent, le Midi de la France

- with languages:
  J'apprends le chinois. *I'm learning Chinese.*
  Vous comprenez l'arabe? *Do you understand Arabic?*
  ... although not immediately after **parler** or **en**:
  Elle parle français. *She speaks French.*
  Comment dit-on en français ...? *How do you say .... in French?*

- when referring to parts of the body where English uses *my*, *his*, *her* etc:
  Fermez les yeux. *Close your eyes.*
  Je vais me laver les cheveux. *I'm going to wash my hair.*
  Il s'est foulé la cheville. *He's sprained his ankle.*

- with some time expressions (pages 30-31):
  la semaine prochaine *next week*; **l'année dernière** *last year*
  J'arrive le vingt mars. *I'm arriving on March 20th.*
  On va à la mosquée le vendredi. *We go to the mosque on Fridays.*

- when talking about prices, where English uses *a* or *per*:
  cinq euros le kilo *5 euros per/a kilo*
  deux euros la tranche *2 euros per/a slice*

the + à, de

When *the* follows à *at, to, in*
                                 de *from, of*
they combine to make the following forms:

	le	la	l'	les
à	au	à la	à l'	aux
de	du	de la	de l'	des

au centre-ville *in/to the town centre*
au Maroc *in/to Morocco*
Nous sommes arrivés au Havre. *We've arrived in Le Havre.*
à la gare *at/to the station*
à l'hôtel *at/to the hotel*
aux Pays Bas *in/to the Netherlands*
J'ai mal aux dents. *I've got toothache.*

la femme du président *the president's wife*
la capitale du Canada *the capital of Canada*
Il vient du Québec. *He comes from Quebec.*
la population de la France *the population of France*
au pied de l'escalier *at the bottom of the stairs*
le charme des petits villages *the charm of the small villages*
Il est rentré des Etats-Unis. *He has come back from the USA.*

When you're speaking French, remember that you need to
sound the final letter of **un**, **les**, **des** and **aux** before a word
starting with a vowel or most words starting with **h**. The **s** and **x**
of **des**, **les** and **aux** sound like a **z**: un ami, aux Etats-unis,
des eglises, les hommes.

some/any

- Du, de la, de l' and des are used in a similar, but not identical, way to *some* and *any* in English.
  Je vais acheter du vin. *I'm going to buy some wine.*
  Je voudrais de l'eau minérale. *I'd like some mineral water.*
  Vous avez des épinards? *Do you have any spinach?*

- They're used in this way even when English might leave them out, and they're repeated before each noun in a list:
  J'ai apporté du pain. *I've brought (some) bread.*
  On a mangé des croissants. *We ate (some) croissants.*
  Donnez-moi des olives, du fromage et de l'huile. *Give me some olives, (some) cheese and (some) oil.*

- In negative sentences de is used instead, regardless of the gender and number of the noun:
  Je n'ai pas de sœurs. *I haven't got any sisters.*
  Il n'y a pas de champagne. *There isn't any champagne.*
  Je n'ai pas acheté de chocolat. *I didn't buy (any) chocolate.*

- There are other ways of translating *some* and *any*.
  When *some* means *a few*, you can use quelques followed by a plural noun:
  Il a dit quelques mots. *He said some (a few) words.*
  il y a quelques jours *some (a few) days ago*

- In the negative, the singular aucun or aucune can be used to express the idea *not a single*. They replace pas, which is the usual negative word:
  Je ne connais aucun de vos collègues. *I don't know any of your colleagues.* (i.e. *I don't know a single one of your colleagues.*)
  Je n'ai aucune idée. *I've got no idea.* (i.e. *not a single idea*)

- When *some* and *any* appear without a noun, they're translated by the pronoun en (see page 83):
  Il y en a qui pensent ... *Some (people) think ...*
  Je n'en ai pas. *I haven't got any.*

checkpoint 4

1 Choose **un** or **une** for these nouns. If in doubt about what gender they are, check with pages 33-38.

chef	infirmière	secrétaire
vedette	université	solution
personne	gâteau	eau minérale
question	musée	chaussette
village	lycée	serveuse

2 Now put **le**, **la** or **l'** in front of the same nouns.

3 How would you combine **à** with *the* to ask directions to the following places? Begin each question with **Pour aller ...?**
   a (la) gare
   b (l')hôtel de ville
   c (Les) Halles
   d (Le) Louvre

   And how would you combine **de** with *the* to ask for some of these items in the market? Begin each sentence with **Je voudrais ...**
   e (l') eau minérale
   f (les) pommes
   g (le) Brie
   h (la) bière

4 How would you ask Hugo, your new acquaintance (use **vous**):
   a if he is French?
   b if he is a student?
   c whether he speaks English?
   d whether he likes Chinese cooking?

Adjectives

Adjectives are words that describe nouns and pronouns:
We have a **small** garden.
The film was **superb**.
She is **French**.
Take the **second** turning.
I prefer **red** wine.

There are two major differences in the way French and English adjectives are used:

- **Position**

  French adjectives generally – though not always – go after the noun: **crème brûlée**, **femme fatale**, **Rive Gauche** *Left Bank,* **Union européenne** *European Union.*

- **Agreement**

  The ending of a French adjective varies depending on the noun it's describing: it has to be masculine or feminine, singular or plural to agree with, i.e. match, that noun: **Royaume-Uni** *United Kingdom,* **Etats-Unis** *United States,* **Nations Unies** *United Nations.*

The dictionary abbreviations for *adjective* are *adj* in English and French (the full word is **adjectif**).

If you look up *clear*, this is what you might find:

clear *adj* **1.** clair, transparent, lucide **2.** manifeste, évident: *as ~ as daylight* clair comme le jour **3.** net: *~ profit* bénéfice clair; *~ conscience* conscience nette **4.** libre: *all~* fin d'alerte

word power

Many adjectives look exactly the same in English and French; many others are only differentiated by having an accent in French. Examples include adjectives ending in **-able**, **-al**, **-ant**, **-ent** and **-ible**, for example:

capable, durable, probable, global, local, général, national dominant, élégant, important, absent, différent, récent incompatible, possible

There are hundreds of other English adjectives which you can easily convert to French – it's simply a matter of recognising and converting the ending.

🇬🇧	🇫🇷	
al	el	artificiel, habituel, sensationnel, traditionnel, universel
ic(al)	ique	classique, diplomatique, économique, érotique, fantastique, islamique, magique, microscopique, politique, romantique, tragique
		and many more ending in -*ological*: archéologique, astrologique, écologique, psychologique
ive	if	actif, aggressif, excessif, impulsif, intensif, négatif
ous	eux	ambitieux, délicieux, furieux, généreux, ingénieux, nombreux, précieux, sérieux

Remember that not one of these adjectives will sound the same in French as it does in English. It's worth making the time to say several of them out loud – as well as fixing the French version in your mind, it's good pronunciation practice. If you're not sure of some of the sounds, have another look at Sounds and Spelling on page 15.

false friends

Some adjectives, however, don't mean what you might think they mean:

actuel means *current*	*actual* is **réel**
effectif means *real*	*effective* is **efficace**
éventuel means *possible*	*eventual* is **ultime**
formidable means *great*	*formidable* is **redoutable**
gentil means *kind*	*gentle* is **doux**
large means *wide*	*large* is **grand**
rude means *tough*	*rude* is **impoli**
sensible means *sensitive*	*sensible* is **sensé**
sympathique means *nice*	*sympathetic* is **compatissant**
gros means *fat*	*gross* is **brut** (profit) or **dégoûtant** *(disgusting)*

Learning words in sets is more effective than learning them individually. This doesn't only mean learning words relating to a particular topic or situation but, for example, learning an adjective together with its opposite or a word with a similar meaning: **grand/petit, vieux/ancien**. Or you could learn some of the above false friends as pairs.

If you have to search for the partner word, so much the better because the more active your learning is, the more your brain will be disposed to remember the words.

Create your own associations. If you were asked to think of a partner for **blanc** *white*, would you choose **noir** *black* or **rouge** (wine connection)? Both? Or another word altogether?

If you use an adjective after **quelque chose** *something* or **rien** *nothing*, you need to put **de** between them. The adjective is in the masculine form:

quelque chose d'important *something important*
quelque chose de terrible *something awful*
rien de sérieux *nothing serious*
rien de spécial *nothing special*

adjective endings and agreement

In a dictionary, adjectives are listed in the masculine singular. But adjectives change their ending, depending on whether the noun being described is masculine or feminine, singular or plural.

- Most adjectives have four possible forms:

m sing	**un livre vert** *a green book*
f sing	**une jupe verte** *a green skirt*
m pl	**des livres verts** *green books*
f pl	**des jupes vertes** *green skirts*

- If the adjective already ends in -e, the feminine form doesn't add another one so is the same as the masculine:

m sing	**un bâtiment moderne** *a modern building*
f sing	**une ville moderne** *a modern town*
m pl	**des bâtiments modernes** *modern buildings*
f pl	**des villes modernes** *modern towns*

- If the adjective already ends in -s, the masculine plural is the same as the masculine singular:

m sing	**un écrivain français** *a French writer*
f sing	**une ville française** *a French town*
m pl	**des écrivains français** *French writers*
f pl	**des villes françaises** *French towns*

An adjective describing more than one noun has the masculine plural ending except when both the nouns are feminine:
Thierry et Nicolas sont français.
Fabienne et Charlotte sont françaises.
Thierry et Fabienne sont français.

spelling changes

- Adjectives ending in **-er** or **-ier** become **-ère** or **-ière** in the feminine:

m sing	f sing	m pl	f pl
cher *expensive*	chère	chers	chères
premier *first*	première	premiers	premières
dernier *last*	dernière	derniers	dernières

le premier jour *the first day*; la semaine dernière *last week*

- Adjectives ending in **-et** become **-ète** in the feminine:

complet *full*	complète	complets	complètes
inquiet *anxious*	inquiète	inquiets	inquiètes

une revue complète *a complete review*; des mères inquiètes *worried mothers*

- Adjectives ending in **-f** change this to **-ve** in the feminine:

actif	active	actifs	actives
neuf *brand new*	neuve	neufs	neuves

une vie active *an active life*; des vêtements neufs *new clothes*

- Adjectives ending in **-c** change this to **-che** in the feminine:

blanc *white*	blanche	blancs	blanches
sec *dry*	sèche	secs	sèches

des vin blancs et secs *dry white wines*; une chemise blanche *a white blouse*

- Adjectives ending **-al** change this to **-aux** in the masculine plural:

local	locale	locaux	locales
national	nationale	nationaux	nationales
digital	digitale	digitaux	digitales

des journaux locaux *local newspapers*; des montres digitales *digital watches*

- Adjectives ending in **-x** change this to **-se** in the feminine and stay the same in the masculine plural:

m sing	f sing	m pl	f pl
heureux *happy*	heureuse	heureux	heureuses
sérieux *serious*	sérieuse	sérieux	sérieuses
jaloux *jealous*	jalouse	jaloux	jalouses

des maris jaloux *jealous husbands*; **des femmes jalouses** *jealous wives*

Except for these:

doux *gentle, soft*	douce	doux	douces
faux *false*	fausse	faux	fausses
roux *red-haired*	rousse	roux	rousses

un billet doux *love letter*; **des faux amis** *false friends*

- Some adjectives ending in **l, n, s** and **t** double the final consonant before adding **e** for the feminine:

bon *good*	bonne	bons	bonnes
gentil *kind*	gentille	gentils	gentilles
mignon *sweet*	mignonne	mignons	mignonnes
italien	italienne	italiens	italiennes
bas *low*	basse	bas	basses
épais *thick*	épaisse	épais	épaisses
gros *fat*	grosse	gros	grosses
net *clear*	nette	nets	nettes

une voix basse *a low voice*; **des filles mignonnes** *sweet girls*

- **Long** adds **u** before the **e** of the feminine to keep the hard **g** sound. Similarly, **c** changes to **qu**.

long	longue	longs	longues
public	publique	publics	publiques

irregular adjectives

- Some adjectives have irregular feminine forms:

m sing	f sing	m pl	f pl
favori	favorite	favoris	favorites
frais *fresh, cool*	fraîche	frais	fraîches

des livres favoris *favourite books*; la crème fraîche

- A few common adjectives have special forms for the feminine and also for the masculine when it's used before a vowel or certain nouns beginning with **h** (page 17).

m sing	m sing before vowel	f sing	m pl	f pl
beau *beautiful*	bel	belle	beaux	belles
fou *mad, foolish*	fol	folle	fous	folles
mou *soft*	mol	molle	mous	molles
vieux *old*	vieil	vieille	vieux	vieilles
nouveau *new*	nouvel	nouvelle	nouveaux	nouvelles

un vieux bâtiment *an old building* but un vieil homme *an old man*
un beau jardin *a beautiful garden* but un bel arbre *a beautiful tree*
le nouveau chef *the new boss* but le nouvel an *the new year*

Some adjectives don't change their ending:
- borrowed or shortened adjectives: **cool, chic, sympa** *nice*
  la musique cool *cool music*; des parents sympa *nice parents*; une boutique chic *a fashionable shop*
- colours that are the names of objects, such as **orange**; **marron** *brown* (n *chestnut*); **argent** *silver*; **turquoise**; **olive**; **kaki** *khaki*
  des chaussures marron *brown shoes*
  des bijoux turquoise *turquoise jewellery*
  But not **rose** and **violet**, which behave like other adjectives:
  des chaussettes roses *pink socks*
- colours using a combination of two words: **bleu marine** *navy blue*; **bleu-vert** *blue-green*; **pomme vert** *apple green*; **vert foncé** *dark green*; **jaune clair** *pale yellow*; **une veste bleu marine** *a navy blue jacket*; **des yeux bleu-vert** *blue-green eyes*; **une robe vert foncé** *a dark green dress*

position of adjectives

When adjectives and nouns are next to each other, the adjective usually goes after the noun:

un document important *an important document*
la musique classique *classical music*
des employés permanents *permanent staff*
les sciences sociales *social sciences*

Some adjectives **always** go after the noun:
- colour
  un chat noir *a black cat*
  des vins rouges *red wines*
- shape
  une table ronde *a round table*
  un gâteau carré *a square cake*
- nationality
  la cuisine française *French cooking*
  le drapeau américain *the American flag*

There are a small number of very common adjectives which go before the noun:

beau* *beautiful*; **bon*** *good*; **court** *short*; **excellent**; **grand** *big*; **gros*** *fat*; **haut** *high*; **jeune** *young*; **joli** *pretty*; **long***; **mauvais** *bad*; **meilleur** *better/best*; **nouveau*** *new*; **petit** *little*; **vague**; **vieux*** *old* and the ordinal numbers **premier*** *first*, **deuxième** *second*, **troisième** *third* etc.
* see pages 55-57 for the irregular endings of these adjectives.

un excellent cuisinier *an excellent cook*
une bonne ambiance *a good atmosphere*
les premiers jours *the first days*
les longs cheveux blonds *long blonde hair*
la meilleure chanson *the best song*
une jolie église blanche *a pretty white church*

> Most adjectives which normally go after the noun can be put beforehand for emphasis, or in set phrases:
> **un important document** *a (particularly) important document*
> **une rude journée** *a hard day*
> **un sacré menteur** *a damn liar*
> **un bref discours** *a (very) brief speech*

adjectives with dual meanings

A few adjectives actually change their meaning depending on whether they go before or after the noun:

un ancien ami *an old friend*	**un ami ancien** *an elderly friend*
un brave homme *a decent man*	**un homme brave** *a brave man*
un cher ami *a dear friend*	**un restaurant cher** *an expensive restaurant*
la dernière semaine *the last (final) week*	**la semaine dernière** *last (preceding) week*
différentes idées *various ideas*	**des idées différentes** *different ideas*
divers problèmes *various problems*	**problèmes divers** *different problems*
une faible probabilité *a remote possibility*	**un homme faible** *a weak man*
un grand homme *a great man*	**un homme grand** *a tall man*
la même chose *the same thing*	**la chose même** *the very thing*
un modeste employé *a humble/ simple employee*	**un employé modeste** *a modest employee*
Pauvre Marie! *Poor Marie!*	**un pays pauvre** *a poor country*
le prochain autobus *the next bus*	**l'année prochaine** *next year*
ma propre maison *my own house*	**une maison propre** *a clean house*
la seule femme *the only woman*	**la femme seule** *the lonely woman*
une simple idée *just an idea*	**une idée simple** *a simple idea*
une vraie histoire *a real story*	**une histoire vraie** *a true story*

In English we use the word *one(s)* with adjectives to avoid repeating a noun: *the red one, the old ones*. In French there's no equivalent of *one(s)* – you simply use the adjective with the ending matching the noun *one(s)* refers to:
le bleu *the blue one*, referring to **le livre** (m) *book*
la première *the first one*, referring to **la rue** *street*
les petits *the little ones*, referring to **les enfants** (m) *children*
les blanches *the white ones*, referring to **les chemises** (f) *shirts*

checkpoint 5

1   The adjectives in brackets are in their dictionary form. Where
    necessary, change the endings so that they agree with the
    nouns – then work out what the phrases mean:
    a le (premier) ministre   b la Maison (Blanc)
    c un centre (sportif)   d la musique (populaire)
    e une carte (vert)   f les grandes villes (français)
    g Les Nations (Uni)   h une coïncidence (heureux)
    i (deuxième) classe   j les femmes (fatal)
    k l'art (moderne)   l la communauté (local)

2   Find adjectives in this unit with the opposite meaning from these:
    a difficile   b court
    c premier   d bas
    e vrai   f insignifiant
    g privé   h foncé

3   Guess the French for the following. There are no false friends
    among them.
    a *accessible*   b *brutal*
    c *ethnic*   d *stagnant*
    e *biological*   f *copious*
    g *radical*   h *portable*
    i *susceptible*   j *prestigious*

4   Would the adjective go before or after the noun in these
    phrases? Have a go at translating them into French.
    a *fatal attraction*
    b *a dear colleague*
    c *the only person*
    d *French films*

5   How would you say in French:
    a) *the white one* (wine); *the big ones* (houses); *the old one*
    (a man); *the dark green one* (jacket); b) *something impossible*;
    something different; *nothing new*; *nothing special*?

Adverbs and comparisons

Adverbs are words that add an extra dimension to:

- adjectives:
  Our garden is **very** *small*.
  I'm **really** *tired*, **too** *tired* to go out.

- verbs:
  They *cooked* it **perfectly**.
  He's *walking* **quickly**.

- other adverbs:
  They cooked it **absolutely** *perfectly*.
  He's walking **extremely** *quickly*, **rather** *quickly* for me.

- whole sentences:
  Unfortunately *we have to leave*.
  They would be here **otherwise**.

Just as many English adverbs end in *-ly*, many French ones end in **-ment**. They're easy to use because their endings never have to change, and they fit within a sentence in much the same way as their English equivalent. However, they don't usually go between the subject and its verb as they do in English in a sentence like *I sincerely hope*. In French the order is *I hope sincerely*.

The dictionary abbreviations for *adverb* are *adv* in both English and French (the French is **un adverbe**). If you look up *clearly* and *nicely*, this is what you might find:

clearly *adv* **1.** clairement, d'une manière claire **2.** [*after* voir, parler] clair **3.** [*obviously, without doubt*] évidemment, sans aucun doute

nicely *adv* **1.** bien: *everything was ~ done* tout était bien fait **2.** [*politely, kindly*] poliment, gentiment **3.** [*in a pleasant way*] agréablement

word power

- Many adverbs are formed by adding -ment to the feminine singular form of an adjective:
  autre (m adj) → autre (f adj) → autrement (adv) *otherwise*
  doux → douce → doucement *gently, softly*
  exacte → exacte → exactement *exactly*
  extraordinaire → extraordinaire → extraordinairement *extraordinarily*
  facile → facile → facilement *easily*
  franc → franche → franchement *frankly*
  habituel → habituelle → habituellement *usually*
  heureux → heureuse → heureusement *happily*
  immédiat → immédiate → immédiatement *immediately*
  sérieux → sérieuse → sérieusement *seriously*
  sincère → sincère → sincèrement *sincerely*
  soudain → soudaine → soudainement *suddenly*

- Sometimes the e of the feminine ending becomes é:
  énorme → énorme → énormément *enormously*
  précis → précise → précisément *precisely*
  profond → profonde → profondément *profoundly*

- Adjectives that end in -i or -u add -ment to the masculine singular:
  absolu → absolument *absolutely*
  poli → poliment *politely*
  résolu → résolument *resolutely*
  vrai → vraiment *really*

- Most adjectives that end in -ant or -ent become -amment or -emment:
  abondant → abondamment *abundantly*
  brillant → brillamment *brilliantly*
  courant → couramment *fluently*
  évident → évidemment *evidently*
  récent → récemment *recently*
  But not lent → lente → lentement *slowly*

- Some adverbs are not derived from adjectives and don't end in **-ment**. These are often adverbs of position, place, quantity and time:

  bien *well*, **mal** *badly*, **vite** *quickly*
  assez *quite*, **si** *so*, **plutôt** *rather, quite,* **trop** *too*
  très *very*, **peu** *little*, **ensemble** *together*
  aussi *also*, **peut-être** *perhaps*, **presque** *almost*
  maintenant *now*, **déjà** *already*, **souvent** *often,* **bientôt** *soon*
  toujours *always*, **surtout** *especially*, **même** *even*
  encore *still,* **près** *near,* **loin** *far*

  Vous parlez bien le français, très bien. *You speak French well, very well.*
  La maison est trop petite. *The house is too small.*
  Je suis plutôt sportif. *I'm quite sporty.*
  Ils sont toujours en retard. *They're always late.*
  Il parle peu en classe. *He doesn't say much in class.* lit. *He speaks little.*

  Just as in English, a few French adjectives are used as adverbs:
  Elle travaille dur. *She works hard.*
  Il parle fort/bas. *He speaks loudly/in a low voice.*
  Ça coûte cher. *It costs a lot.* lit. *It costs dear.*

- Phrases can be used as alternatives to adverbs:
  avec soin *carefully*; **avec enthousiasme** *enthusiastically*
  avec impatience *impatiently*
  d'une manière différente *differently*; **d'un ton poli** *politely*
  d'une façon élégante *elegantly*
  sans effort *effortlessly*; **sans difficulté** *easily*
  en hâte *hastily*; **en colère** *angrily*
  tout de suite *immediately*; **tout à coup** *suddenly*

false friends

actuellement means *currently*
éventuellement means *if need be*
finalement means *eventually*
forcément means *inevitably*

actually is **en fait**
eventually is **finalement**
finally (= lastly) is **enfin**
forcefully is **vigoureusement**

adverbs of quantity

The following adverbs, which all refer to quantity, are always followed by
de + noun without an article:

assez de *enough*

beaucoup de *a lot of, many*

moins de *less, fewer*

plus de *more*

trop de *too much, too many*

autant de *as much/many*

combien de *how many*

pas mal de *quite a bit/few*

tant de *so much, so many*

J'ai mangé trop de bonbons. *I've eaten too many sweets.*

Il a pas mal d'argent. *He's got quite a bit of money.*

Il y a autant de femmes que d'hommes ici. *There are as many women as men here.*

But **encore de** *more* and **la plupart de** *most* are followed by **de** + noun with its definite article:

encore de la glace *more ice cream*

encore du vin *more wine*

la plupart du temps *most of the time*

la plupart des gens *most people*

Some of these adverbs of quantity can be used before verbs. If this is the case, use **que**:

Repose-toi autant que tu peux. *Rest as much as you can.*

position of adverbs

The position of adverbs isn't as flexible in French as it is in English. In most cases the adverb goes after the verb, and where there's more than one verb the adverb goes after the first verb.

Je mange bien. *I eat well.*

J'ai bien mangé. *I ate well.*

Je vais vite faire les devoirs. *I'm going to do my homework quickly.*

plus and moins

Plus and moins are used in several ways:

- *plus* and *minus*, with numbers (the s of plus is pronounced when it's used in this sense):

  deux plus deux font quatre *2 + 2 = 4*
  dix moins quatre font six *10 - 4 = 6*
  les personnes qui ont soixante-cinq ans et plus *people aged 65+*
  Il fait plus douze (degrés). *It's plus 12 (degrees).*
  Il fait moins cinq (degrés) dehors. *It's minus five outside.*

- *more* and *less* or *fewer*, followed by de + noun:

  Tu as plus d'énergie que moi. *You've got more energy than me.*
  Ils ont moins d'argent que nous. *They've got less money than us.*
  Je connais moins de gens que toi. *I know fewer people than you.*
  plus de vingt personnes *more than 20 people*

- moins is used when telling the time:

  deux heures moins dix *ten to two*
  une heure moins le quart *quarter to one*

Plus and moins also feature in many everyday phrases:
en plus *extra, in addition*
au moins *at least*
x fois plus grand *x times bigger*
moi non plus *me neither*
plus ou moins *more or less*
de plus *furthermore*
(une heure) de plus *(one hour) more*
(une heure) au plus *(an hour) at the most*
de plus en plus (difficile) *more and more (difficult)*
plus ... plus ... *the more ... the more ...*
Plus ça change ... plus c'est la même chose. *The more things change ... the more they stay the same.*

comparisons: plus, moins

- When making comparisons, **plus** *more* and **moins** *less* are the key words; this corresponds to English in certain cases, but there's no equivalent of the English *-er* ending, as in *faster, cheaper, nicer* or *bigger*.
  Cette méthode est plus facile. *This method is easier.* lit. *more easy*
  Voulez-vous perdre du poids plus facilement? *Do you want to lose weight more easily?*
  Il y a un train plus lent. *There's a slower train.*
  Ce train va plus lentement. *This train is going more slowly.*

- *Than* is **que**:
  Anna est plus sportive que Stéphanie. *Anna is more sporty than Stephanie.*
  Glasgow est moins cher que Paris. *Glasgow is less expensive (cheaper) than Paris.*
  Ils sont plus riches que nous. *They are richer than us.*
  Il pleut moins souvent que l'année dernière. *It rains less often than last year.*

superlatives: le plus, le moins

- To say *the most/least* … you use **le/la/les** + **plus/moins**. There's no equivalent of the English *-est* as in *fastest, cheapest* or *biggest*.
  Ce livre est le plus intéressant. *This book is the most interesting.*
  C'est la chambre la moins chère. *It's the least expensive room.*
  Les films français sont les plus intéressants. *French films are the most interesting.*
  Rachel parle français le moins couramment. *Rachel speaks French the least fluently.*
  Robert parle le plus vite. *Robert speaks the most quickly.*

- If the adjective is one that comes before the noun (page 58), it comes before the noun in the superlative too:
  la plus belle ville *the most beautiful town*

- *In* after a superlative is **de**:
  le plus petit portable du monde *the smallest laptop in the world*
  le politicien le plus populaire de la France *the most popular politician in France*

irregular comparatives and superlatives

- As in English, the adjective **bon** *good* and the adverb **bien** *well* have irregular comparatives and superlatives, *better* and *best*. Beware of translating *better* and *best*, as in English they can be both an adjective and an adverb, but in French the words are not interchangeable:

  bon *good*   **meilleur** *better* (adj)   **le meilleur** *the best* (adj)
  bien *well*   **mieux** *better* (adv)   **le mieux** *the best* (adv)
  la meilleure équipe de la ligue *the best team in the league*
  l'équipe qui joue le mieux *the team that plays the best*

- The adverbs **peu** *little* and **beaucoup** *a lot* also have an irregular comparative and superlative:

  peu *little*   **moins** *less*   **le moins** *the least*
  beaucoup *a lot*   **plus** *more*   **le plus** *the most*
  Mathilde parle peu en classe, Océane parle plus mais Ilona parle le plus. *Mathilde speaks little in class, Océane speaks more but Ilona speaks the most.*

- The adjective **mauvais** *bad* and the adverb **mal** *badly* have both a regular form and an irregular form (**pire**) in the comparative and superlative:

  mauvais *bad*   **plus mauvais/pire** *worse* (adj)
  le plus mauvais/le pire *worst* (adj)
  mal *badly*   **plus mal/pire** *worse* (adv)
  le plus mal/le pire *worst* (adv)
  Once again, be careful when translating *worse* and *worst*, as in English they are both adjective and adverb, while in French the adverb and adjective have different forms when they are regular.
  les plus mauvais films du vingtième siècle/les pires films du vingtième siècle *the worst films of the 20th century*
  Il chante le plus mal/le pire de tous. *He sings the worst of all.*

- **Moindre** is a special comparative and superlative form of **petit** meaning *lower, lowest* or *lesser, least*:

  des produits de moindre qualité *lower-quality products*
  la moindre suspicion *the least suspicion*

as ... as: aussi ... que

Montréal est aussi joli que Toronto. *Montreal is as pretty as Toronto.*
On mange aussi bien ici que dans un restaurant plus cher. *You can eat as well here as in a more expensive restaurant.*

checkpoint 6

1 What's the masculine singular of the adjective these adverbs come from?

a absolument   b simplement
c constamment   d récemment
e vraiment   f précisément
g lentement   h couramment
i complètement   j effectivement
k brillamment   l doucement

2 And what's the adverb from these adjectives?

a autre   b sérieux
c scientifique   d général
e fréquent   f malheureux
g actuel   h évident
i franc   j agressif
k poli   l énorme

3 Find the opposites of these adverbs. They're all in this unit.

a approximativement   b pire
c lentement   d bien
e rarement   f doucement

4 Fill the gaps by translating the words in brackets.

a Marianne travaille _____ . (harder)

b Je pense que ces chaussures sont _____ . (better)
Elles sont _____ . (less expensive)

c A mon avis, ce livre est _____ . (the most interesting)

d Théo est plus âgé _____ Florian. (than)

e Le train de 9h00 est _____ . (the slowest)

f C'est le _____ film que j'ai jamais vu. (worst)

g Luca joue bien mais Joël joue _____ . (better)

h Le Sahara est le _____ désert _____ .
(the largest desert in the world)

i Le Havre est _____ grand _____ Reims. (as big as)

Demonstratives and possessives

Demonstratives are words like *this*, *that one*, *those*, which you use to point things out.

The English *this* and *that* have two functions. They can be:

- demonstrative adjectives, used with a noun: I'm going to buy **this** house, not **that** bungalow.
- demonstrative pronouns, taking the place of the noun: I'm going to buy **this (one)**, not **that (one)**.

In French there's a different set of words for each of these two grammatical categories. The words in both sets start with **ce** and they all have to agree with the noun they're describing (adjectives) or replacing (pronouns).

When you're talking about possession, the most striking difference between French and English is that there's no French equivalent of *'s*. Instead you have to use **de** *of*: **la maison de Paul** *Paul's house*.

But in both English and French, possessive adjectives and possessive pronouns are separate sets of words:

- adjectives: **mon** *my*, **votre** *your*
- pronouns: **le mien** *mine*, **le vôtre** *yours*

French possessive adjectives and pronouns have to agree with the noun they're describing or replacing.

demonstrative adjectives

The demonstrative adjectives *this, that, these* and *those* are used with a noun. The French demonstrative adjective **ce** means both *this* and *that*. Like all adjectives in French, it changes its ending to agree with the noun that follows. There are two masculine singular forms, with **cet** being used before a vowel or **h** (in most cases; see page 17).

	this/that	*these/those*
m	ce/cet	ces
f	cette	ces

ce livre *this/that book;* **en ce moment** *at this moment*
cet enfant *this/that child;* **cet homme** *this/that man*
cette femme *this/that woman;* **cette semaine** *this week*

un de ces livres *one of these/those books*
J'aime bien ces chaussures. *I like these shoes very much.*

You repeat a demonstrative adjective before each noun in a list:
ces hommes et ces femmes *these/those men and (these/those) women*

As in English, you can also use **ce**, **cet**, **cette** and **ces** before adjectives and numbers:
ce grand chien *this/that big dog*
cet ancien château *this/that former palace*
cette ancienne église *this/that former church*
ces chaussures vertes *these/those green shoes*
ces deux femmes *these/those two women*

If you want to highlight the difference between something that's nearby and something that's further away, you can tag **-ci** *this* or **-là** *that* to the noun:
ce livre-ci *this book*
en ce moment-là *at that moment*

Cet enfant-ci est plus sage que cet enfant-là. *This child (here) is better behaved than that child (over there).*
J'aime bien ces chaussures-ci mais je n'aime pas ces bottes-là. *I like these shoes, but I don't like those boots.*

demonstrative pronouns

The demonstrative pronouns *this (one)*, *that (one)*, *these* and *those* replace a noun. In French they agree with the noun they replace:

	this one/that one	these/those
m	celui	ceux
f	celle	celles

They're often used with a preposition, e.g. **à, de, dans**:
Mon portable coûte moins cher que celui de Paul. *My mobile phone costs less than Paul's.*
Je préfère ces T-shirts-ci que ceux à dix euros. *I prefer these T-shirts to the ones costing 10 euros.*
Je pense que les cerises au marché sont plus fraîches que celles dans le supermarché. *I think that the cherries in the market are fresher than those in the supermarket.*

They're also used with **qui** or **que** *who, which* (page 92):
Les gens qui connaissent une langue étrangère sont plus intéressants que <u>ceux qui</u> ne parlent qu'anglais. *People who know a foreign language are more interesting than those who only speak English.*
Tu aimes ces chemises? Dis-moi <u>celles que</u> tu veux essayer. *Do you like these shirts? Tell me which ones you want to try on.*

You can add **-ci** for *this (one)*, *these (ones)* or **-là** for *that (one)*, *those (ones)*:
J'ai lu ce livre-ci, mais je n'ai pas encore lu celui-là. *I've read this book, but I haven't read that one.*
J'aime bien ces chaussures-ci, mais je n'aime pas du tout celles-là. *I like these shoes very much, but I don't like those (ones) at all.*
Tu préfères quelle robe? Moi, je préfère celle-ci. *Which dress do you prefer? I prefer this one.*
Je ne veux pas ces oignons-là; je voudrais ceux-ci. *I don't want those onions, I want these.*

---

cela, ça, ceci, ci, ce

- **Cela** *that*, and its shortened form **ça**, are used very frequently in spoken French to refer to an idea or situation rather than to a specific noun:
  Cela ne m'étonne pas. *That doesn't surprise me.*
  Je n'aime pas ça. *I don't like it/that.*
  C'est ça! *That's right.*
  Ça te plaît? *Do you like it?* lit. *Does it to you please?*
  Qu'est-ce que ça veut dire? *What does it/that mean?*

- **Ceci** *this* is used far less than **cela/ça**:
  A cause de ceci j'ai raté le train. *Because of this, I missed the train.*
  Et avec ceci? *Anything else?* This is something you'll hear said in a shop. It literally means *And with this?*

- **Ci** on its own means *this* but only appears in a few idioms:
  comme ci, comme ça *so-so*

- **Ce** on its own means *this, that* or *it* and is usually used with **être** *to be*.
  Ce is shortened to **c'** before a vowel: **c'est, c'était.**

  When the noun following **ce** is plural, then the verb is plural too:
  Ce sont mes collègues. *These are my colleagues.*
  C'étaient elles. *It was them* (f).

  Ce can also go before **qui** or **que** (page 92).

C'est has a number of uses, including:
- defining or identifying things and people:
  Qu'est-ce que c'est? C'est un ordinateur. *What is it? It's a computer.*
  C'est qui? C'est ma femme. *Who is it? She's my wife.*
  C'est David. *It's David.* **C'est moi.** *It's me.*
- expressing a view:
  C'est vrai. *That's true.*
  Ce n'est pas grave. *It doesn't matter.* lit. *It's not serious.*

c'est or il est?

As a general rule of thumb:

- with an adjective, you use **il/elle est** to describe a person and **c'est** to describe a situation:
  Il est tres gentil. *He's very kind.* **C'est bizarre.** *It's strange.*
- with an adverb, you use **il est** if it's unmodified, i.e. has no extra information added to it, and **c'est** if it is modified:
  Il est tard. *It's late.* **C'est tres tard.** *It's very late.*
- with a noun, you use **il/elle est** if it's unmodified and **c'est** if it is modified: **Elle est chanteuse.** *She's a singer.* **C'est une bonne chanteuse.** *She's a good singer.*
- in impersonal phrases where *it* doesn't refer back to something already mentioned, you use **il est**; when *it* refers back to something that has already been identified, use **c'est**. **Il est** is followed by **de** and **c'est** by **à**:
  Il est difficile de savoir que faire. *It's hard to know what to do.*
  La casse-tête? C'était facile à faire. *The brain-teaser? It was easy to do.*

checkpoint 7

1 Match up the noun with **ce, cet, cette** or **ces**.

a	église	b	gens
c	hôtel	d	ville
e	restaurant	f	arbre
g	personne	h	choses
i	ancien bâtiment	j	ancienne église
k	vêtements	l	haut bâtiment

2 Place the correct form of **celui** in the gap to mean *the one(s)* or *this/that/those one(s)*:

a Quelle maison? .... au coin de la rue.

b Quels livres? .... qui sont sur la table.

c Quel appartement? .... au deuxième étage.

d Quelles chaussures? .... à 60 euros.

e Quel bâtiment? .... que nous avons vu hier.

f Tu préfères quel portable? Moi, je préfère .... -ci.

g Tu préfères quelles lunettes? Moi, je préfère .... -là.

possessive adjectives

- There's no French equivalent of the English apostrophe -s ('s) as in *Paul's house* or *the company's address.* Neither is there the equivalent of two nouns together as in *company address* or *telephone number.*
  Instead, you always say *the house of Paul; the address of the company.*
  Of is **de**, changing to **du**, **des**, etc. (page 48) when followed by *the*:
  la maison de Paul *Paul's house;* **l'adresse de la société** *the company's address;* **le numéro de téléphone** *the phone number.*

- Possessive adjectives, which are used with a noun, are:

	my	*your*	*his/her/its*	*our*	*your*	*their*
m	mon	ton	son	notre	votre	leur
f	ma	ta	sa	notre	votre	leur
pl	mes	tes	ses	nos	vos	leurs

  The possessive adjective that goes with **on** is **notre/nos**:
  On a perdu notre chien. *We've lost our dog.*

- Possessive adjectives agree with what's owned, not with the owner.
  My house is **ma maison**, regardless of whether it's a man or woman talking: **notre enfant** *our child;* **nos enfants** *our children;* **leurs enfants** *their children;* **un de mes amis** *one of my friends;* **une de tes amies** *one of your girlfriends*
  It's particularly important to bear this in mind with **son/sa/ses**, which can mean *his* or *her*:
  son épouse *his/her spouse;* **sa sœur** *his/her sister*
  Robert a nettoyé sa voiture. *Robert has cleaned his car.*
  Camilla a nettoyé sa voiture. *Camilla has cleaned her car.*

- **Mon**, **ton** and **son** are used with feminine nouns when the following word begins with a vowel or before most words beginning with **h**:
  mon amie *my girlfriend;* **ton adresse** *your address;* **son autre sœur** *his/her other sister*

- You use the definite article, not the possessive adjective, with parts of the body when it's clear who the owner is:
  Les enfants se brossent les dents. *The children are brushing their teeth.*

possessive pronouns

Possessive pronouns, i.e. *mine, yours, theirs,* etc. are used without a noun, but they agree with the noun they stand for.

	mine	*yours* (**tu**)	*his/hers/its*
m sing	**le mien**	**le tien**	**le sien**
f sing	**la mienne**	**la tienne**	**la sienne**
m pl	**les miens**	**les tiens**	**les siens**
f pl	**les miennes**	**les tiennes**	**les siennes**

	ours	*yours* (**vous**)	*theirs*
m sing	**le nôtre**	**le vôtre**	**le leur**
f sing	**la nôtre**	**la vôtre**	**la leur**
m pl	**les nôtres**	**les vôtres**	**les leurs**
f pl	**les nôtres**	**les vôtres**	**les leurs**

La mienne est ici. *Mine is here.* (referring to something feminine)
Les passeports? Voici le mien. Où est le tien? *The passports? Here's mine. Where's yours?*
Et les billets? Les nôtres sont avec les leurs. *And the tickets? Ours are with theirs.*

The **le** and **les** of the possessive pronouns follow the usual rules when following **à** or **de**, becoming **au**, **aux**, **du**, **des** (page 48):
Leurs coutumes sont plutôt différentes des vôtres. *Their customs are rather different from yours.*
En général je n'ai pas peur des chiens, mais j'ai peur du sien. *Usually I'm not afraid of dogs, but I'm afraid of his/hers.*
Je préfère tes chaussures aux miennes. *I prefer your shoes to mine.*

à moi, à toi

You can also say who something belongs to with **être** + **à** + noun or emphatic pronoun (**moi, toi, lui, elle, nous, vous, eux, elles** page 87):
À qui est ce manteau? *Whose is this coat?*
C'est à Valérie. *It's Valérie's.*
C'est à moi = C'est le mien. *It's mine.*
Les bagages sont à eux. *The luggage is theirs.*

checkpoint 8

1   Underline the correct possessive adjective:

a Il a expliqué [son, sa, ses] idée.

b [leur, leurs] chef est très sympa.

c Où sont [votre, vos] enfants?

d Nous avons oublié [notre, nos] appareil photo.

e Où se trouve [ton, ta, tes] sac?

f Quel est [votre, vos] film préféré?

g [leur, leurs] enfants sont étudiants.

h [mon, ma, mes] amie va arriver ce soir.

i On a visité [notre, nos] parents.

j [mon, ma, mes] parents habitent en Ecosse.

2   Answer the question using the possessive pronoun in the brackets:

a A qui est ce livre? C'est _____ (*mine*)

b A qui sont ces chaussures? Ce sont _____ (*his*)

c A qui est cette voiture? C'est _____ (*hers*)

d A qui sont ces bagages? Ce sont _____ (*ours*)

e A qui sont ces jouets? Ce sont _____ (*yours*, tu form)

f A qui est ce vélo? C'est _____ (*yours*, vous form)

g A qui est ce portable? C'est _____ (*hers*)

h A qui est ce chien? C'est _____ (*theirs*)

There may be lots of rules in French grammar but there are patterns to them, and learning one rule helps when you come across a new grammar point.

You can see, for example, that the endings of the demonstrative pronouns **celui** (masculine singular), **ceux** (masculine plural), **celle** (feminine singular) and **celles** (feminine plural) are identical to the stressed pronouns **lui** (masculine singular), **eux** (masculine plural), **elle** (feminine singular) and **elles** (feminine plural).

Pronouns

Pronouns are words like *I*, *she*, *we*, *us*, *him*, *them*, *your*, *mine* and *those*, which you use to save repeating a noun:
The plumber called – **he**'s going to be late.
Have you seen **the children**? I can't find **them**.
Where's **my key**? I've lost **it**.

Personal pronouns can be:
- the subject of a verb: *I, we, you, he, she, they*
- the direct object of a verb: *me, us, you, him, her, them*
- the indirect object of a verb: *(to/for) me, (to/for) us, (to/for) you, (to/for) him, (to/for) her, (to/for) them.* French has single words for these.

Subject pronouns are used in a similar way in English and French.

Object pronouns usually go before the verb in French, as in the phrase
s'il <u>vous</u> plaît *please*, literally *if it pleases <u>you</u>.* When there's more than one object pronoun, there's a strict word-order pattern that they must follow.

For demonstrative pronouns (e.g. *this one, those*) see page 71, for possessive pronouns (e.g. *mine, yours*) see page 75, and for the interrogative pronouns (e.g. *which one?*) see page 125.

subject pronouns

je (**j'** before a vowel) *I*	**nous** *we*
tu *you*	**vous** *you*
il *he, it*	**ils** *they* (m)
elle *she, it*	**elles** *they* (f)
on *one, we, you, they*	

- Unlike *I* in English, **je** isn't written with a capital letter, except when it starts a sentence.

- The English *it* is **il** or **elle**, depending on the gender of the noun it refers to. **Où est la voiture? Elle est ici.** *Where's the car? It's here.* In impersonal expressions (i.e. when not referring to a particular noun) it is **il**: **Il pleut.** *It's raining.*

- The English *they* is **ils** or **elles**, depending on the gender of the noun *they* refers to. **Elles sont jolies, tes chaussures.** *Your shoes are lovely* (**chaussures** are feminine). **Ils** is used for a mixed group, even if there's just one male in a big group.

- There are two words for *you*, each using a different verb ending:
  tu: a friend, a family member or a child; young people usually call one another **tu** from the start.
  vous: a person you don't know well or who is older than you. If in doubt, use **vous** rather than **tu**. **Vous** is also the plural of **tu** and is used when talking to more than one person, whether they're friends or strangers.

- When the subject of a verb is nobody in particular, *on* is often used. It can mean *we*, *you*, *they* or *one*.
  On ne peut pas stationner ici. *You can't park here.*
  Ici on parle anglais. *English is spoken here.* lit. *Here we speak English.*
  Comment dit-on ça en français? *How do you say that in French?*
  On ne sait jamais. *You never know.*
  On dit que c'est un bon film. *They say it's a good film.*

- The verb with **on** has the same ending as with *he/she*.

- **On** is often used in informal spoken French instead of **nous**.
  On vient de rentrer. *We've just come back.*
  Où est-ce qu'on va ce soir? *Where shall we go this evening?*
  On se rencontre ce soir? *Shall we meet this evening?*

- The possessive adjectives (page 74) used with **on** are **notre** or **nos** *our*:
  Où est-ce qu'on peut laisser nos bagages? *Where can we leave our luggage?*
  On voudrait louer notre maison. *We'd like to let our house.*

- Although the endings of verbs are the same as for *he/she*, adjectives and past participles (page 154) that follow **on** have a plural ending – masculine or feminine, as appropriate:
  On est prêts. *We're ready.* (group of men, or mixed group)
  On est prêtes. *We're ready.* (group of women)
  On est arrivés hier./On est arrivées hier. *We arrived yesterday.*

object pronouns

Object pronouns (*me, us, you, him, her, it, them*) can either be:

- the direct object of a verb: *Anne knows <u>me</u>, the children saw <u>him</u>, I've invited <u>them</u>*
- or the indirect object of a verb: *Anne writes <u>to me</u>, the children listened <u>to him</u>; I've made a cake <u>for them</u>*

In French, there's no distinction made between these four direct and indirect object pronouns:

me (m') *me, to/for me*	**te (t')** *you, to/for you* **(tu)**
nous *us, to/for us*	**vous** *you, to/for you*

Anne me/nous connaît. *Anne knows me/us.*
Anne m'/nous écrit. *Anne writes to me/to us.*

However, the pronouns *him, her, it, them* are entirely different words from *to/for him, to/for her, to/for them*.

direct	**indirect**
le (l') *him, it* (m)	**lui** *to/for him*
la (l') *her, it* (f)	**lui** *to/for her*
les *them* (m and f)	**leur** *to/for them* (m and f)

Anne le/la connaît. *Anne knows him/her.*
Anne lui écrit. *Anne writes to him/to her.*
Je les ai invité(e)s. *I've invited them.*
Je leur ai fait un gâteau. *I've made a cake for them.*

Me, te, le and **la** usually shorten to **m', t'** and **l'** before a vowel:
Je t'aime. *I love you;* **Nous l'adorons.** *We adore him/her/it.*

direct or indirect object?

In general, the same verbs take a direct or indirect object in English and French. However, there are some to look out for.

- With some verbs it's not immediately obvious that the object is indirect because there are two ways of using them in English – with or without a preposition before the pronoun:

  Je **lui** ai donné de l'argent. *I gave him some money./I gave some money to him.*

  Je **lui** ai acheté une glace. *I bought an ice cream for her./I bought her an ice cream.*

  Je vais **leur** envoyer les photos. *I'm going to send them the photos./I'm going to send the photos to them.*

- Unlike English, the following have an indirect object in French:

convenir *to suit*	dire *to say, tell*
demander *to ask*	faire mal *to hurt*
faire confiance *to trust*	obéir *to obey*
plaire *to please*	resister *to resist*
ressembler *to resemble*	téléphoner *to phone*

  These verbs all need à before a noun.

  Je ne veux pas téléphoner à ma mère. *I don't want to phone my mother.*

  Je ne veux pas lui téléphoner. *I don't want to phone her.*

  Tu vas demander à tes professeurs? *Are you going to ask your teachers?*

  Tu vas leur demander? *Are you going to ask them?*

- In English, these verbs are followed by a preposition before a noun whereas in French they have a direct object:

attendre *to wait for*	chercher *to look for*
demander *to ask for*	écouter *to listen to*
payer *to pay for*	regarder *to look at*

  J'aime écouter la musique de Bizet. *I like to listen to Bizet's music.*

  On attend l'autobus. *We're waiting for the bus.*

  On l'attend. *We're waiting for it.*

y

Y is a pronoun meaning *there* (or *here*, depending on the context). Like other pronouns, it comes before the verb.

- Y replaces a phrase referring to a place.
  Vous habitez à Paris? Oui, j'y habite depuis dix ans. *Do you live in Paris? Yes, I've been living there/here for ten years.*
  Vous connaissez l'Ecosse? Oui, j'y suis allé l'année dernière. *Do you know Scotland? Yes, I went there last year.*
  On s'amuse très bien chez elle. Oui, c'est vrai, on s'y amuse très bien. *We have a good time at her house. Yes, that's true, we have a very good time there.*

- Y is the pronoun used with verbs that are followed by à, such as **répondre à** *to reply to*, **penser à** *to think about* (page 196), when you're talking about **something** rather than **someone**. It can't be left out in French:
  Tu as répondu à sa lettre? Oui, j'y ai répondu hier. *Have you replied to his letter? Yes, I replied to it yesterday.*
  Il y pense tout le temps. *He thinks about it all the time.*

- Y is often used after **aller** when no specific place is referred to:
  On y va? *Shall we go?*
  Allons-y! *Let's go, off we go!*
  Vas-y! *Go ahead!*

Y appears in the following phrases:
il y a *there is/there are; ago*
Ça y est! *That's it!*
Nous y voilà./On y est. *Here we are.*
y compris *including*
le Royaume-Uni, y compris les îles Anglo-Normandes et l'île de Man *the UK including the Channel Islands and the Isle of Man*
Il faut y réfléchir. *We'll have to give it some thought.*

---

en

En is a pronoun which replaces nouns accompanied by **du**, **de la**, **de l'** and **des**. Like other pronouns it comes before the verb.

- **En** translates *of it/them*, *with it/them* etc. when used with verbs and adjectives that are followed by **de**, such as **avoir besoin de** *to need*, **se souvenir de** *to remember*, **ravi de** *delighted with*. It cannot be omitted in French:

  Je n'en ai pas besoin. *I don't need it/them.*
  Tu t'en souviens? *Do you remember (it)?*
  J'en ai marre. *I'm fed up (with it).*
  J'en suis sûr/certain. *I'm sure/certain (of it).*
  Elle en est fière. *She's proud of it.*
  Ils n'en sont pas capables. *They're not capable of it.*
  Nous en sommes ravis. *We're delighted (with it/them).*

> **En** isn't used to replace a person. You use an emphatic pronoun (page 87) instead:
> **Elle est fière de lui.** *She's proud of him.*
> **Je me souviens de lui.** *I remember him.*

- **En** corresponds to *of it*, *of them* in phrases involving quantity and numbers:

  Vous en voulez combien? *How much/many (of it/them) do you want?*
  J'en prends deux kilos. *I'll take two kilos (of them).*
  Des enfants? J'en ai trois. *Children? I've got three (of them).*
  Il y a combien de banques dans cette ville? Il y en a beaucoup.
  How many banks are there in this town? There are a lot.
  Et combien de cinémas? Il y en a un. *And how many cinemas?*
  (There's) one.
  Encore du vin? Non merci, j'en ai eu assez. *More wine? No thank you,*
  I've had enough.

- **En** can also replace a place in a phrase beginning with **de** *from*:
  Votre mari est rentré des Etats-Unis? Oui, il en est rentré hier soir.
  Has your husband come back from the United States? Yes, he came back (from there) last night.
  Vous êtes allé au travail? Oui, j'en viens. *Have you been to work? Yes, I've just come from there.*

- **En** means *some* or *any*:
  J'en ai./Je n'en ai pas. *I've got some./I haven't got any.*
  Tu en veux? *Do you want some?*
  Tu voudrais en avoir? *Would you like to have some?*

- **En** is an integral part of the verbs **s'en aller** *to go away* and **s'en faire** *to worry*:
  Va-t-en!/Allez-vous-en! *Go away!*
  Je m'en vais. *I'm going (away)./I'm off.*
  Ne t'en fais pas./Ne vous en faites pas. *Don't worry.*

checkpoint 9

Fill the gaps with **y** or **en**.

1   Comment allez vous au travail? J'_____ vais par le train.
2   Vous connaissez le restaurant Chez Nico? Oui, on _____ dîne souvent.
3   Vous avez des sœurs? Oui, j'_____ ai une.
4   On est prêts? Allons-_____.
5   Tu peux me donner de l'argent? Non, je ne peux pas t'_____ donner.
6   Quel est son nom? Je ne m'_____ souviens pas.
7   Tu as lu son dernier roman? J'_____ ai lu quelques pages.
8   Tu sais que c'est mon anniversaire demain? Oui, j'_____ pensais ce matin.
9   Le train arrivera à Waterloo à quelle heure? Il _____ arrivera à 14h56.
10 Vous connaissez les frères de Martin? J'_____ connais un.

position of object pronouns

- All object pronouns (direct, indirect, **y** and **en**) generally go before a verb:
  Vous me comprenez? *Do you understand me?*
  Je te crois. *I believe you.*
  J'y vais demain. *I'm going there tomorrow.*
  Je ne les connais pas. *I don't know them.*

- When there are two verbs, the object pronoun comes before the verb it belongs to:
  Je vais lui téléphoner demain. *I'm going to phone him tomorrow.* (i.e. *him* goes with *phone*, it's *phone* him, not *go* him)
  Tu peux m'écrire. *You can write to me.*
  Je veux y passer deux jours. *I want to spend two days there.*

- When there's more than one object pronoun belonging to the same verb, they appear in the following order (except in positive imperatives – see opposite):

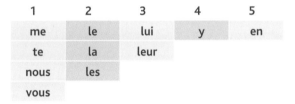

1	2	3	4	5
me	le	lui	y	en
te	la	leur		
nous	les			
vous				

Je vous la passe maintenant. *I'll transfer you to her now.*
Je vais le lui envoyer demain. *I'll send it to him/her tomorrow.*
Je leur y en ai donné. *I gave them some there.*

When **le** and **les** are object pronouns and not articles (page 48) they don't combine with **à** or **de** to become **au**, **aux**, **du** or **des**:
Je lui ai demandé de le faire tout de suite. *I asked him/her to do it immediately.*
Il a réussi à les voir. *He succeeded in seeing them.*

---

object pronouns and the imperative

- When you're telling somebody ***not to*** do something (page 171), the order of pronouns is the same as in ordinary sentences:
  Ne me les donnez pas. *Don't give them to me.*
  Ne la lui envoyez pas. *Don't send it* (f) *to her.*

- But when you're telling somebody ***to*** do something (page 170), object pronouns come after the verb and are joined to it with a hyphen. **Me** changes to **moi** or **m'** if followed by **y** or **en**. The order of pronouns is:

1	2	3	4	5
le	lui	moi	y	en
la	leur	nous		
les				

Prends-le. *Take it.* **Apportez-le-leur.** *Bring it to them.*
Laissez-nous en paix. *Leave us in peace.*
Donnez-les-moi. *Give them to me.*
Donnez-m'en. *Give me some.* This is quite formal, and you'll also hear
Donnez-en-moi in everyday speech.

object pronouns and the past tense

In the past tense, object pronouns go before the auxiliary verb **avoir/être** (pages 158,159). For verbs taking **avoir**, the past participle has to agree with the noun represented by the direct pronoun, but there's no agreement necessary with indirect pronouns or with **y** and **en**. These agreement endings only make a difference to pronunciation in the few past participles that end in a consonant e.g. **fait** *done*, **écrit** *written*, **mis** *put*.
Où est la voiture? Je l'ai laissée sur le parking près de la cathédrale.
Where's the car? I've left it in the car park near the cathedral.
Les billets! Il les a oubliés. *The tickets! He's forgotten them.*
Les lettres? Je les ai mises à la poste. *The letters? I've posted them.*
(The middle **s** of **mises** is pronounced.)
On nous a invités à une soirée. *We've been invited to a party.*

There's no agreement with indirect object pronouns:
On nous a téléphoné hier. *They phoned us yesterday.*
Vous leur avez écrit? *Have you written/did you write to them?*

reflexive pronouns

subject	reflexive
je	me (m') *myself*
tu	te (t') *yourself*
il/elle	se (s') *himself, herself, itself*
nous	nous *ourselves*
vous	vous *yourselves*
ils/elles	se (s') *themselves*

- These pronouns are an integral part of reflexive verbs (page 116), and as such are generally not translated into English:
  Elle se maquille. *She's putting on (her) make-up.*
  Nous nous sommes biens amusés. *We had a good time.*
  Vous vous êtes mariés quand? *When did you get married?*
  Je ne me souviens pas. *I don't remember.*

- The reflexive pronoun that goes with **on** is **se**:
  On s'amuse bien. *We're having a good time.*
  On se retrouvera bientôt. *We'll meet up again soon.*

- **Nous, vous** and **se** or **s'** (plural) can mean *each other* or *one another*:
  Nous nous comprenons. *We understand each other.*
  Vous vous connaissez depuis longtemps? *Have you known each other long?*
  Ils s'aiment. *They love each other.*

- **Te** becomes **toi** in positive imperatives, except when followed by **en** (page 171). All other reflexive pronouns stay the same:
  Dépêchez-vous! *Hurry up!*
  Lève-toi! *Get up!*

If you want to say *myself*, *yourself* etc, you can use the emphatic pronouns (see next page) attached to **-même(s)**: **moi-même** *myself*, **toi-même** *yourself*, **eux-mêmes** *themselves*.
Je l'ai fait moi-même. *I did it myself.*
Ils l'ont vu eux-mêmes. *They saw it themselves.*

emphatic pronouns

These emphatic (or stressed) pronouns have a variety of uses in French.

moi *I, me*	**nous** *we, us*
toi *you*	**vous** *you*
lui *he, him*	**eux** *they, them* (m)
elle *she, her*	**elles** *they, them* (f)

- One of their uses is to add emphasis to the subject pronoun:
  Moi, je sais. *I know.*
  Toi, tu peux venir. *You can come.*
  Lui, il a dix-sept ans, et elle, elle a dix-neuf ans. *He's 17 and she's 19.*
  Eux, ils ont raison. *They're right.*

- They can also go at the end of the sentence:
  Je ne sais pas, moi. *I don't know.*
  On est américains, nous. *We're American.*

- They are used after prepositions:
  Je vais avec eux. *I'm going with them.*
  Grâce à lui, je suis contente. *Thanks to him, I'm happy.*
  C'est pour toi. *It's for you.*

- They are used after **être** *to be*:
  C'est moi. *It's me.*
  C'était qui? C'étaient eux. *Who was it? It was them.*

- They can stand alone without a verb:
  Qui veut le faire? Pas moi! *Who wants to do it? Not me!*
  Toi aussi? *You too?*

> **Nous** is the emphatic pronoun used with **on**:
> **Nous, on va rester à la maison.** *We're going to stay at home.*

checkpoint 10

1 How would you say *Hello, it's me* in French?

2 Would you use **tu** or **vous** for these people?
   a a six-year-old child
   b an elderly neighbour
   c the person on the hotel reception desk
   d two friends

3 Match the underlined pronoun in these sentences with the noun or phrase it replaces. There's one extra phrase.
   a Vous <u>lui</u> avez téléphoné?   i **les questions**
   b Je <u>les</u> ai déjà faits.   ii **à Paris**
   c Il m'<u>en</u> a donné.   iii **votre ami**
   d On <u>y</u> va.   iv **du chocolat**
   e Je <u>les</u> ai finies.   v **les devoirs**
   vi **à votre mari**

4 Fill the gap with the correct object pronoun.
   a Tu ___ connais? *him*
   b Tu ___ crois? *me*
   c Je ___ ai parlé. *to them*
   d Vous ___ avez écrit? *it*
   e Il va ___ inviter. *us*
   f On ___ a demandé. *(to) her*
   g Je ___ aime. *them*
   h On ___ a dit. *(to) us*

5 Replace **le concert** and **les billets** with *it* and *them*.
   Vous voulez écouter <u>le concert?</u> Il faut acheter <u>les billets</u>.

6 Translate these into French. If you need to check up on prepositions, they're on pages 97-107.
   a *with them* (f)
   b *for me*
   c *without them* (m)
   d *except you* (to a friend)
   e *after us*
   f *at his place*

7 What do you think **Elles se connaissent** means?

8 To emphasise that you've made something yourself, what could you add to **Je l'ai fait?**

9 Which of these sentences means *I've already asked them?*
   a **Je lui ai déjà demandé.**
   b **Je les ai déjà demandés.**
   c **Je leur ai déjà demandé.**

10 Talking about a masculine noun, how would you say *He gave it to us?*

Sentence structure

The more French you learn, the more you'll progress from simple, short phrases to longer sentences which express your needs and opinions in more detail. The two main things to consider when constructing more complex sentences are word order and how to join together the various parts of the sentence.

- Word order is broadly similar in English and French although there are some fundamental differences, such as the position of adjectives after nouns, the position of pronouns (e.g. *us*, *him*, *them*) before verbs and the variety of ways you can ask a question in French.

- To join together the various elements of what you want to say, you can use conjunctions – words like *and*, *but*, *since*, *so*, *however*. You also need words that save you having to repeat nouns or phrases when you're giving additional information about them: words like **qui** and **que** *who*, *which*, **dont** *whose*, and **lequel** *which*.

Progressing isn't simply about more and more grammatical rules. If you listen to native speakers of any language, you'll find that they use words like *well then*, *let's see*, *anyway*, *furthermore*, which bring a sense of continuity to what they say and take it beyond the strictly functional. When you learn a new language, it's an effort at first to remember to use these words as well as everything else – but when you get used to them, you'll find not only that they make you sound more fluent, but also that they give you useful thinking time when you're stuck for a word.

word order

English and French word order is broadly similar – but there are some differences between the two languages.

- When a noun and an adjective are used together, the noun often comes first in French, whereas in English the adjective practically always comes first: **une décision importante** *an important decision*. Interestingly, French has the flexibility to change the position of the adjective for emphasis: **une importante décision** *a (truly) important decision*. (see page 58)

- To ask a yes/no question, English brings in words like *do/does* or reverses the order of the subject and verb. *Do you work here? Is she ill?* French either puts **Est-ce que** at the beginning of a statement or makes it sound like a question. **Est-ce que vous travaillez ici?/Vous travaillez ici?** *Do you work here?*

  A question word is sometimes found at the end of a French question: **Vous travaillez où?** *Where do you work?* (lit. *You work where?*). French can also reverse the order of subject and verb: **Où travaillez-vous?** but this option is usually kept for short, simple questions. (see pages 122-123)

- When the object of a verb is a pronoun (*me*, *us*, *you*, *him*, *her*, *it*, *them*) it generally goes in front of the verb in French and after it in English:
  Elle me téléphone tous les jours. *She phones me every day.*
  Je l'ai laissé dans le train. *I left it on the train.*

- Adverbs go after the verb in French:
  Je vais souvent au cinéma. *I often go to the cinema.*

- In English you make a verb negative with *not*, while in French you put the words **ne** and **pas** round the verb:
  Nous ne sommes pas touristes. *We are not tourists.*
  Je n'habite pas à Londres. *I don't live in London.*

- When two nouns are linked together, they're in the opposite order in French to that in English: **la maison de mon oncle** *my uncle's house*; **une tasse à thé** *a teacup*; **mon numéro de téléphone** *my phone number*; **un pull en laine** *a woollen pullover*.

joining parts of a sentence

The words on this page will help you join together the various elements of what you say, and bring logic and continuity to your sentences.

- Draw things together with **et** *and*, **aussi** *also*.

- Express reservation with **mais** *but* or one of several words for *however*: **cependant**, **pourtant** or **toutefois**. If you disagree strongly you could say **au contraire** *on the contrary*.

- Introduce alternatives with **ou** *or*, **autrement** *otherwise*, **plutôt** *instead, rather*.

- Contrast two elements with **d'une part** *on the one hand* and **d'autre part** *on the other hand*.

- Show you're about to infer a conclusion with **donc** *so, therefore*.

- Reinforce or clarify what you've said with **c'est-à-dire** *that is, i.e.,* **en fait** *in fact*, **en effet** *indeed*, **par exemple** *for example*.

- Provide detail with **où** *where*, **quand** *when*, **tandis que** *while, whereas*.

- Introduce an explanation with **parce que** or **car*** *because*, **puisque** *since*, **étant donné que** *given that*.

- Show there's a consequence with **alors** *then*, **par conséquent**, **en conséquence** *as a result*.

- Introduce a condition with **si** *if*.

- Introduce further information about something you've just said with **qui** *who, whom, which*; **que** *who, which, that*; or **dont** *whose, of which*.

*In written and formal French, **car** is used, while **parce que** is used in everyday language.

> **Or** means *however, yet* – not the English *or*, which is **ou**.
> **Effectivement** means *really, indeed* – not *effectively*, which is **efficacement** or **en realité** *in effect*.

who, whom, which, that

que

Que, which shortens to **qu'** before a vowel and most words beginning with **h**, has several meanings. It can mean *than* (page 66), *what?* (page 124) and it has two other important meanings:

- *that*, which is never left out in French as it often is in English:
  Je sais que tu es très occupé. *I know (that) you are very busy.*
  Il dit qu'il ne peut pas venir. *He says (that) he can't come.*

- *whom, which, that*, referring to a person or thing. **Que** can't be omitted here either:
  l'homme que je connais depuis longtemps *the man (whom) I've known for a long time*
  le nouveau manteau que j'ai acheté hier *the new coat (which) I bought yesterday*
  C'est la bleue que tu préfères? *Is it the blue one (that) you prefer?*

qui

In the above examples **que** is the object of **je connais, j'ai acheté** and **tu préfères**. When *who/which* refer to the subject, you use **qui**:
mon frère qui habite en Suisse *my brother who lives in Switzerland*
le bâtiment qui se trouve au coin de la rue *the building which is on the corner of the street*
C'est nous qui avons tort. *We are the ones who are wrong.* lit. *It's we who are wrong.*

ce qui, ce que

When referring to an idea rather than to a particular noun, *which* is **ce qui** (subject) or **ce que** (object). English often uses *and this*.
Il dit que c'est impossible, ce qui n'est pas vrai. *He says it's impossible, which isn't true.*
Il n'est pas allé, ce qui m'étonne. *He didn't go, and this surprises me.*
Ma fille fume, ce que je n'aime pas. *My daughter smokes, which I don't like.*

Ce qui and **ce que** also translate the English *what*:
Je fais ce que je veux. *I do what I want.*
Je ne sais pas ce qu'il a fait. *I don't know what he has done.*
Ce qui m'embête, c'est ton attitude. *What annoys me is your attitude.*

lequel, laquelle

You can use **qui** after a preposition (pages 97-107) to refer to a person:
les gens avec qui je travaille *the people with whom I work*
ma tante, chez qui je vais habiter *my aunt, with whom I'm going to live*

But for a thing or an idea, you use the appropriate form of **lequel** *which*:

	singular	plural
m	**lequel**	**lesquels**
f	**laquelle**	**lesquelles**

les outils avec lesquels je travaille *the tools with which I work*
la maison derrière laquelle on propose de construire un hypermarché
the house behind which they're planning to build a hypermarket

Parmi and **entre** are followed by **lesquels** or **lesquelles**, not **qui**, even when referring to people:
deux copains entre lesquels il faut choisir *two boyfriends who you must choose between*
de nombreuses victimes, parmi lesquelles plusieurs enfants *numerous victims, among whom several children*

Lequel and **laquelle** combine with **à** and **de**:

à + lequel → **auquel**	de + lequel → **duquel**
à + lesquels → **auxquels**	de + lesquels → **desquels**
à + lesquelles → **auxquelles**	de + lesquelles → **desquelles**

À laquelle and **de laquelle** don't change.

le bâtiment en face duquel on propose de construire un hypermarché
the building opposite which they're planning to build a hypermarket
des associations caritatives auxquelles je donne de l'argent *the charities to which I donate money*

> **Quoi** means *what* when no specific preceding noun is being referred to:
> **Je ne sais pas quoi préparer pour mes invités.** *I don't know what to cook for my guests.*

dont

Dont stands for **de qui** and means *whose*, *of whom*, *of which*. Unlike the English, **dont** always follows the word it refers to. Also unlike English, the word order after **dont** is subject + verb + object:

la femme dont j'ai acheté la voiture *the woman whose car I bought;*
des chambres dont la plupart sont occupées *bedrooms, most of which are occupied*

Dont is used as an alternative to **duquel**, **de laquelle** etc. (page 93) with verbs which are followed by **de**, e.g. **avoir besoin de** *to need*, **avoir envie de** *to feel like*, **parler de** *to talk about,* **se souvenir de** *to remember* (pages 198-199). Very often it's not translated into English:

Voici l'argent dont tu as besoin. *Here's the money you need.*
Je ne connais pas la femme dont vous parlez. *I don't know the woman you're talking about.*
C'est la femme dont je me souviens. *It's the woman I remember.*

> When **dont** doesn't refer to a specific noun, it's preceded by **ce** or **tout ce**, and usually expressed in English as *what*:
> **Tu sais très bien ce dont je te parle.** *You know very well what I'm talking to you about.*
> **Je mange ce dont j'ai envie.** *I eat what I feel like.*

où

Où refers back to a place, and is often not translated in English:
Voici la maison où elle est née. *Here's the house where she was born.*
les pays d'où viennent nos étudiants *the countries our students come from*

où means *when* after a noun referring to time. Again, it's often not translated in English:
C'était le jour où tu es arrivé. *It was the day (when) you arrived.*
Août est le mois où on part généralement en vacances. *August is the month (when) we usually go on holiday.*
C'était le moment où j'ai compris que ... *That was the moment (when) I understood that ...*

making conversation flow

Words that help the flow of conversation, such as *well*, are difficult to translate exactly – making it more effective to focus on the context they're used in.

- **Alors** can convey *Well then ..., So ..., Right then ...* at the start of a sentence. Other words used in the same way include **eh bien**, **donc**.

- **Bah** and **ben**, also meaning *well*, suggest a bit of uncertainty or hesitation.

- **Bof** shrugs something off, conveying *I don't care* or *Whatever!*

- **Pourtant** and **néanmoins** mean *however, nevertheless*, indicating that you're about to offer an alternative viewpoint. You could also use **quand-même** or **de toute façon** *anyway*.

- **N'est-ce pas?** *Isn't that so?* (see page 123 for more on this handy expression), **tu sais/vous savez** *you know* and **tu vois/vous voyez** *you see* can be used to reinforce what you're saying and ask for agreement.

- **Dis donc!** expresses surprise, like the English *No!, Wow!,* or *You don't say!*

opinions

When giving your opinion, you can start with **moi, je pense que** *I think* or **à mon avis** *in my opinion*. To strengthen your argument you can use **bien sûr** *of course* or **évidemment** *obviously*. As you get into your stride you can punctuate what you're saying with **d'abord** or **en premier lieu** *first of all,* **en second lieu** *secondly,* and summarise with **en bref** *in short*. And you can show that you're coming to a conclusion with **alors** or **eh bien** *so then* or **enfin** *finally*.

Et toi, qu'est-ce que tu en penses?/Et vous, qu'est-ce que vous en pensez? *What do you think about it?* will bring others into the discussion. Or you can ask for someone's opinion by beginning **selon toi/vous** *according to you* or **à ton/votre avis** *in your opinion* instead.

To agree with someone you can say **Je suis d'accord** *I agree* or **Tu as/Vous avez raison** *You're right,* and when you disagree you use **Je ne suis pas d'accord** or, to make it a little less strident, **Je ne suis pas tout à fait d'accord** *I don't quite agree with you*.

checkpoint 11

1   Which of these would you use:

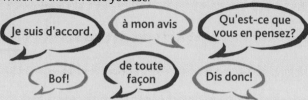

Je suis d'accord.   à mon avis   Qu'est-ce que vous en pensez?

Bof!   de toute façon   Dis donc!

   a to express surprise?
   b when asking someone for their opinion?
   c if you don't know and don't much care?
   d when offering your opinion?
   e to say you agree with someone?
   Which one is left over and what does it mean?

2   Choose the correct form of **lequel** to fit in the blank.
   a Où est le sac dans _____ j'ai mis mes choses?
   b C'est la raison pour _____ j'ai acheté un chien.
   c C'est un outil sans _____ je ne peux pas faire mon travail.
   d Les associations avec _____ nous travaillons.
   e Les arbres derrière _____ on construit une maison.

3   Does qui, que or où belong in the gap in this sentence?
   Le jour _____ j'ai rencontré ma femme.

4   Fill these gaps with qui, que or dont.
   a Mes amis _____ habitent à Londres.
   b L'argent _____ je t'ai donné hier.
   c C'est vous _____ m'avez téléphoné?
   d Les étudiants _____ les noms sont sur la liste.
   e La maison _____ la porte est blanche.
   f Je pense _____ vous avez fait une erreur.

5   What's the opposite of d'une part?

6   Parce que, plutôt, car, puisque: which is the odd one out?

Prepositions

Prepositions are words like *at, in, on, of, with, to, between*:
I'm **at** home.
He's going **to** France, **with** her.
It's **in** the office, **by** the phone.

French prepositions usually have a noun or a pronoun after them; they never go at the end of a sentence or question as they often do in English:
À qui appartient ce portable? *Who does this mobile phone belong to?*
lit. *To whom belongs this mobile phone?*
Vous travaillez pour quelle société? *Which company do you work for?*
lit. *You work for which company?*

Many French and English prepositions correspond directly, such as:
après *after*, **avant** *before*, **avec** *with*, **pendant** *during* and **sauf** *except*.
But this isn't the case for the widely used **à**, **de** and **en**. For example:

- In French **en** is used where English uses *in*, *on* and *by*; **à** can be translated by the English *at*, *to*, *in*, *on* or *with*.

- Certain verbs are always followed by **à** or **de**. They're not translated into English, they're simply part of that verb: **assister à une réunion** *to attend a meeting*; **jouer de la guitare** *to play the guitar*.

It's therefore often more effective to associate a preposition with the way it's used rather than look for a straight translation.

à

which becomes **au** when followed by **le**, and **aux** when followed by **les**, is used for:

- *to* + a person:
  J'ai écrit à Vincent. *I've written to Vincent.*
  Elle a donné des livres aux étudiants. *She gave some books to the students.*

- *at, to, in* + a place – except continents, regions and feminine countries, which all use **en** (page 37):
  à la maison, au lit, à l'école *at home, in bed, at/in school*
  à l'ombre, au soleil *in the shade, in the sun*
  Il est à l'aéroport. *He's at the airport.*
  Elle est allée à la gare. *She's gone to the station.*
  Je vais à Grenoble. *I'm going to Grenoble.*
  Ils habitent à Bruxelles. *They live in Brussels.*
  au Canada, au Maroc, aux Antilles *in/to Canada, in/to Morocco, in/to the West Indies.*

- *on*:
  à la télé *on the TV*, **aux infos/informations** *on the news*
  à la guitare/batterie *on the guitar/drums*
  à grande échelle *on a large scale*; **à l'heure** *on time*
  à l'arrivée du chef *on the boss's arrival*
  au mur *on the wall*; **au téléphone** *on the phone*
  à genoux *on one's knees*
  au menu *on the menu*; **à l'ordre du jour** *on the agenda*
  au premier/deuxième étage *on the first/second floor*
  Except when *on* means *on top of/on the surface of,* which is usually **sur** (page 104). Compare *on the ground floor* **au rez-de-chaussée** with *on the floor* which is **sur le plancher** or **par terre.**

- *at, in* + time and occasions:
  Le train arrive à quelle heure? *What time does the train arrive?*
  à midi/minuit *at 12 noon/midnight*
  à une heure *at one o'clock*
  à dix heures et demie *at half past ten*
  à Noël/à Pâques *at Christmas/at Easter*
  À demain. *See you tomorrow.*
  À l'année prochaine à Paris. *See you next year in Paris.*

- *a/per* + speed:
  cent kilomètres à l'heure *100 kilometres per hour*

- *with* + features or characteristics:
  l'homme à la barbe blanche *the man with the white beard*
  la fille aux yeux bleus *the girl with blue eyes*
  la maison aux volets verts *the house with green shutters*

- when talking about direction, distance and location:
  la première rue à gauche *the first street on the left*
  Mon village est situé à cent kilomètres/deux heures de Paris.
  My village is 100 kilometres/two hours from Paris.
  Nancy est situé à l'ouest de Strasbourg. *Nancy is (to the) west
  of Strasbourg.*

- when describing food flavours and styles of cooking:
  un sandwich au jambon/à la dinde *a ham/turkey sandwich*
  une glace à la vanille/au chocolat *vanilla/chocolate ice cream*
  des crêpes au citron *pancakes with lemon*
  pommes de terre à la lyonnaise *potatoes cooked in the Lyonnaise style*
  poulet à la Kiev *chicken Kiev;* **pomme au four** *baked apple*

- with prices to show value:
  un timbre à cinquante cents *a 50-cent stamp*
  un appartement à cent mille euros *a 100,000-euro flat*

- to describe the purpose of an object:
  une tasse à thé *teacup* (cf. **une tasse <u>de</u> thé** *a cup of tea*)
  un sac à dos *backpack,* **une machine à laver** *washing machine*

- after certain verbs (see page 197 for a list):
  Les enfants apprennent à lire. *The children are learning to read.*
  Il commence à neiger. *It's starting to snow.*
  Je n'arrive pas à vendre ma voiture. *I can't manage to sell my car.*

Some common expressions use **à**:
à pied *on foot;* **à point** *medium-rare;* **peu à peu** *little by little;* **avoir mal
à** *to hurt;* **C'est à qui?** *Whose is it?* **C'est à moi/à eux.** *It's mine/theirs.*
Attention au chien! *Beware of the dog!*

de

which becomes **du** when followed by **le**, and **des** when followed by **les**

- *of*:

  un verre de vin *a glass of wine;* **un kilo de pommes** *a kilo of apples;*
  une tasse de thé *a cup of tea*

- *'s*:

  la maison de nos amis *our friends' house* lit. *the house of our friends*
  le frère de Sébastien *Sebastian's brother*
  le journal d'aujourd'hui *today's paper;* **l'arrivée du train** *the train's arrival*

- *from*:

  de Paris à Bordeaux *from Paris to Bordeaux*
  de neuf heures à onze heures *from nine to 11 o'clock*
  du lundi au vendredi *from Monday to Friday*
  du 17 jusqu'au 27 mai *from the 17th to 27th of May*
  Je viens de Londres/du Québec. *I come from London/Quebec.*
  C'est loin de la mer. *It's a long way from the sea.*
  C'est à quelle distance du centre-ville? *How far is it from the town centre?*
  une lettre de mon père *a letter from my father*

- *by* denoting authorship:

  les poèmes de Rimbaud *the poems of Rimbaud*
  un film de Laurent Cantet *a film by Laurent Cantet*
  C'est de qui? *Who's it by?*

- *by* + amounts:

  Les impôts ont augmenté de 20%. *Taxes have risen by 20%.*
  Les prix ont baissé de moitié. *Prices have dropped by a half.*

- *some, any* (combines with **le, la, l', les** except in negative sentences):

  Je voudrais du vin/de la bière. *I'd like some wine/beer.*
  Tu veux des légumes? *Do you want any vegetables?*
  Nous n'avons pas d'enfants. *We haven't got any children.*
  Il n'a plus d'argent. *He hasn't got any more money.*

- *than*, after **plus** *more* and **moins** *less, fewer* with quantities (page 64):

  moins de cinquante euros *less than 50 euros*
  plus de vingt personnes *more than 20 people*

- *in* after superlatives (page 66):
  la plus grande ville de France *the largest town in France*

- *in, within, from, of* with some expressions relating to time:
  à sept heures du matin/du soir *at seven in the morning/evening*
  à trois heures de l'après-midi *at three in the afternoon*
  de temps en temps *from time to time;* **d'ici une semaine** *within a week*

- *in, with* to indicate manner:
  d'une manière étrange *in a strange way* lit. *manner*
  d'une autre façon *in another way*
  d'un air fâché *with an angry expression, angrily*

- *made from*:
  un jus d'orange *orange juice* (i.e. juice made from oranges)
  la soupe de tomates *tomato soup* (soup made primarily from tomatoes)
  But you use **à** if you're talking about a flavour or variety:
  une glace à l'orange *orange ice cream*
  le pain au chocolat *chocolate croissant*

- where English uses two nouns together:
  une maison de famille *a family house;* **un film d'épouvante** *a horror film*
  un bulletin d'informations *a news report*
  le zeste de citron *lemon peel;* **la peau de banane** *banana skin*
  des numéros de téléphone *phone numbers*
  le train de onze heures cinq *the 11.05 train*

- after **quelque chose** *something* and **rien** *nothing*:
  quelque chose d'amusant *something amusing*
  rien de nouveau *nothing new;* **rien de personnel** *nothing personal*

- after some adjectives:
  couvert de neige *covered in snow;* **content d'être ici** *pleased to be here*
  fatigué de bloguer *tired of blogging*
  Il est certain d'être élu. *He's sure to be elected.*

- after some verbs (see page 199 for a list):
  J'ai décidé d'acheter une nouvelle voiture. *I've decided to buy a new car.*
  J'ai besoin d'argent. *I need money.*
  Il faut changer de train à Lille. *You need to change trains at Lille.*

en

En is almost always used directly before a noun, without an article:

- *in, to* + feminine countries, continents and regions:
  en France; en Angleterre *in/to England*; **en Italie; en Irlande;**
  en Bretagne *in/to Brittany*; **en Provence; en Corse** *in/to Corsica*;
  en Bavière *in/to Bavaria*
  Masculine countries and regions use **au:**
  au Liban *in/to Lebanon*; **au Tyrol**
  English counties use **dans** + article: **dans le Kent; dans le Yorkshire**

- *in* + years, months, seasons:
  Je suis venu ici en 2009. *I came here in 2009.*
  Je vais en France en juillet. *I'm going to France in July.*
  en été *in summer;* **en automne** *in autumn;* **en hiver** *in winter* – but **au printemps** *in spring*

- *by* + means of transport:
  en avion *by plane*; **en vélo** *by bike*; **en autobus** *by bus*; **en voiture** *by car*;
  en train *by train*
  You can also say **par le train** *by train* and **à vélo** *by bike*.

- *in* indicating time taken to do something, i.e. *within* or *within the space of*:
  gagner mille euros en cinq jours *to earn 1,000 euros in five days*
  Les piles se rechargent en deux heures. *The batteries take two hours to recharge.*
  In when it means *after* or *in … time* is **dans** (page 104).

- *in* with languages:
  en français; en espagnol; en arabe
  Comment dit-on … en français? *How do you say … in French?*

- *in* with colours and clothes:
  le même en bleu *the same in blue*
  Elle est sortie en pyjama. *She went out in her pyjamas.*
  des pommes de terre en robe de chambre *jacket potatoes* lit. *potatoes in dressing gown*

- to describe what something is made of:
  une écharpe en soie *a silk scarf*
  des chaussettes en coton *cotton socks*
  une tasse en plastique *a plastic cup*
  des jouets en bois *wooden toys*

- *by, while* with the present participle (page 168):
  J'ai perdu cinq kilos en faisant du vélo et en ayant une bonne alimentation. *I've lost five kilos by cycling and having a good diet.*
  la chanson de Disney 'Sifflez en travaillant' *the Disney song 'Whistle while you work'*

Very many common expressions use **en**:
en arrière *behind*
en avance *early, in advance*
en avant *forwards*
en bas *downstairs*
en bon état *in good condition*
en bonne forme *in good shape*
en bonne santé *in good health*
en bref *in brief*
(une pièce) en désordre *(an) untidy (room)*
(couper) en deux *(cut) in half/in two*
en face *opposite*
en fait *in fact, indeed*
en haut *upstairs*
en même temps *together*
en outre *besides, moreover*
en plein air *in the fresh air*
en route
en tout cas *in any case*
en vacances *on holiday*
en ville *in town*

The phrase **être en train de** means *to be in the process/in the middle of doing something*:
J'étais en train de lire l'article. *I was in the middle of reading the article.*

dans

- physically *in* or *inside*:
  dans la cuisine *in the kitchen;* **dans la rivière** *in the river*

- *in* with regions, English counties and French départements:
  dans le Nord *in the North;* **dans le Sud-Ouest** *in the South-West*
  dans le Suffolk; dans le Calvados

- *in* with time expressions meaning *after*, *at the end of*:
  J'arriverai dans cinq minutes. *I'll arrive in five minutes.*
  Il va rentrer dans deux jours. *He's going to go home in two days.*

- after **entrer** *to enter* where English has no preposition:
  Il est entré dans la pièce. *He entered the room.*

- *out of*:
  boire dans la même bouteille *to drink out of the same bottle*
  J'ai pris des livres dans la boîte. *I took some books out of the box.*
  Some common expressions use **dans**:
  dans l'ensemble *on the whole;* **dans l'intention de** *with the intention of;*
  dans la mesure où *in so far as;* **dans les environs** *in the vicinity*

sur

- *on*, literally *on top of*, *on the surface of*:
  sur la table *on the table;* **sur le toit** *on the roof*
  sur le pont d'Avignon *on Avignon bridge*

- *on*, *about*:
  un guide sur le Portugal *a guide book on Portugal*
  un livre sur la philosophie *a book about philosophy*

- *in*, *out of* indicating proportion and with time expressions:
  neuf sur dix *nine out of ten;* **un enfant sur cinq** *one child in five;*
  vingt-quatre heures sur vingt-quatre *round-the-clock;* **une semaine**
  sur deux *every other week*

  The phrase **être sur le point de** means *to be on the point of, about to*:
  J'étais sur le point de sortir. *I was on the point of going out./I was just*
  about to go out.

pour

- *for* indicating intention or destination:
  C'est pour toi. *This is for you;* **le train pour Paris** *the train for Paris*
  Nous partons demain pour les montagnes. *We're leaving tomorrow for the mountains.*
  Nous y allons pour une semaine. *We're going (there) for a week.*

- *for, in favour of:*
  Vous avez voté pour Sarkozy? *Did you vote for Sarkozy?*
  une association pour la légalisation du cannabis *an organisation in favour of the legalisation of cannabis*

- *in order to* + infinitive - often translated in English simply as *to:*
  Je travaille simplement pour survivre. *I work merely (in order) to survive.*
  Je l'ai fait pour t'amuser. *I did it (in order) to amuse you.*
  Il est trop fatigué pour marcher. *He's too tired to walk.*

par

- *by:*
  par téléphone; par hasard *by chance;* **par avion** *by airmail*
  Il est allé par le train. *He went by train.*
  Ils ont été attaqués par une bande. *They were attacked by a gang.*

- *out of, for:*
  Il l'a fait par amour/par jalousie. *He did it for love/out of jealousy.*

- *through, by, via:*
  On peut entrer par les portes-fenêtres. *You can enter through the French windows.*
  Il est sorti par la porte arrière. *He left by the back door.*
  passer par le périphérique de Paris *to go via the Paris ring road*

- *a, per:*
  trois fois par jour *three times a/per day;* **deux fois par mois** *twice a month;* **par an** *per annum;* **cinq euros par personne** *5 euros per person*

Some common expressions include **par** or **pour**: **par-là** *that way;*
par terre *on the ground;* **par conséquent** *as a result;* **par rapport à** *compared with;* **pour l'instant** *for the time being;* **Pour quoi faire?** *What for?*

sans

sans usually translates the English *without*. When followed by a noun there's usually no article:

Je vais sortir sans toi. *I'm going to go out without you.*
Il est venu sans argent. *He came without any money.*
Elle est partie sans payer. *She left without paying.*

depuis

Depuis means *since, for*:
cinq cents morts depuis janvier *500 deaths since January*
depuis le début *since the beginning*

When talking about something that started in the past and is still going on, you use **depuis** with the present tense:

On habite ici depuis trente ans. *We've been living here for 30 years.*
J'apprends le français depuis trois mois. *I've been learning French for three months.*

However, in negative sentences the verb is in the past tense – just as it is in English:

Je ne t'ai pas vu depuis longtemps. *I haven't seen you for a long time.*
On n'a pas eu d'électricité depuis lundi. *We haven't had electricity since Monday.*

There's more on **depuis** with the past and present tenses on pages 139 and 149.

If you want to talk about something that happened in the past and is completed, use **pendant** *for*:
J'ai habité à Londres pendant cinq ans. *I lived in London for five years.*
And for something that's going to happen in the future:
Et maintenant je vais habiter à Paris pendant six mois. *And now I'm going to live in Paris for six months.*
Another useful expression to talk about when something happened is **il y a** *ago*:
Je suis arrivé il y a une heure. *I arrived an hour ago.*
… not to be confused with the much-used *there is/there are*:
Il y a beaucoup de restaurants ici. *There are many restaurants here.*

other common prepositions

devant *in front of*
derrière *behind*
entre *between*
sous *under*
vers *towards* (direction),
    about (time)
envers *towards, in relation to*
parmi *among*

chez *at somebody's house/place*
malgré *in spite of*
avec *with*
sauf *except*
selon *according to*
voici *this is, here is*
voilà *there is, that is*
contre *against*

J'ai passé deux semaines chez mes parents. *I spent two weeks with my parents (at my parents' house).*
Nous sommes arrivés vers sept heures. *We arrived at about seven o'clock.*

compound prepositions

Some prepositions are made up of two or more words, one of which is **à** or **de** – which change to **au**, **du**, **aux** or **des** when followed by **le** or **les** and a masculine noun.

à cause de *because of, due to*
à côté de *next to*
à propos de *about, concerning*
à travers *across*
au-dessous de *below*
au-dessus de *above*
au bout de *at the end of*
au fond de *at the bottom of, at the end of*
au lieu de *instead of*

au milieu de *in the middle of*
autour de *around*
en face de *opposite*
grâce à *thanks to*
hors de *outside*
jusqu'à *up to, until*
le long de *along*
près de *near*
pret à *ready to*
quant à *as for*

à côté du cinéma *next to the cinema*
au-dessous de l'équateur *below the equator*
Le séminaire a été annulé à cause de la grève. *The seminar has been cancelled because of the strike.*
Quant à moi, j'ai fini. *As for me, I've finished.*

checkpoint 12

1 Choose one of the following prepositions to fill the gaps (each can only be used once): à, aux, avec, pour, en, du, par, depuis, dans.

a Je vais fêter mon anniversaire .... juin.

b Nous partons demain pour aller en Suisse .... deux semaines.

c Il faut prendre le médicament trois fois .... jour.

d Tu vois la femme .... lunettes?

e Elle apprend l'anglais .... l'année dernière.

f Le spectacle commence .... onze heures .... matin.

g Aujourd'hui c'est lundi; nous partons pour New York jeudi, c'est-à-dire .... trois jours.

h Tu peux venir .... moi?

2 How are the following houses described?

a une maison au bord de la mer b la maison de mon oncle

c une maison aux murs blancs d une maison à l'ombre

e une maison à deux millions d'euros f une maison de Sir Christopher Wren

g une maison en bois h une maison sans garage

i une maison à trois étages j une maison sous le pont

k la maison en face l la maison au bout de la rue

3 Translate these into French.

a *Michelle's sister* b *a phone number*

c *tomato juice* d *a bottle of wine*

e *see you* (i.e. *until*) *Tuesday* f *it's mine*

g *tomorrow's article* h *something different*

4 Is *a champagne glass* un verre à champagne or un verre de champagne?

5 What's the difference between <u>sur la</u> and <u>à la</u> télévision?

6 How do you say *opposite the car park* in French?

7 Decide which prepositions are missing from un sandwich .... fromage *a cheese sandwich*; un roman .... amour *a love story*; .... été *in summer*; and .... nylon *made of nylon*.

Verbs: overview

Verbs are the words we use to say
- what people and things are and have: *be*, *exist*, *have*
- what happens to them: *live*, *die*, *become*, *change*, *break*
- what they do physically: *breathe*, *eat*, *run*, *wait*, *arrive*
  and mentally: *like*, *believe*, *decide*, *respect*, *dream*, *analyse*

In a dictionary you find the **infinitive** of a verb. In English, this is the basic verb, which can have *to* in front of it: *(to) arrive, (to) finish, (to) descend.* In French, infinitives are identified by their ending, which can be **-er**, **-ir** or **-re**: **arriver, finir, descendre**.

When you remove **-er**, **-ir** or **-re**, you're left with the stem of the verb: **arriv-, fin-, descend-**. A range of other endings can now be added to this stem, each of them conveying precise information about
- how the verb is being used = **mood**
- when it's happening: present, past or future = **tense**
- who/what is doing it = **person**

Each of the -er, -ir and -re verb groups has sets of regular endings, and most verbs use these endings. However, some verbs are irregular and need to be learnt individually.

A group of verbs called *reflexive verbs* always have **se** or **s'** in front of the infinitive: **s'amuser** *to enjoy oneself*, **s'appeler** *to be called*, **se marier** *to get married*.

Although they have the same endings as other verbs, reflexive verbs always have to be accompanied by a reflexive pronoun, e.g. **me**, **te**, **se** (page 117).

moods and tenses

Mode *mood* refers to how the verb is being used.

Infinitive	the name of the verb, i.e. the basic dictionary form: *(to) work*.
Indicative	indicating that facts are being talked about: *I work, they were working, he doesn't work, do you work?*
Conditional	referring to a hypothetical situation, often involving conditions: *we would work if… /but …*
Subjunctive	conveying that the verb is not fact but is subject to opinion, speculation, attitude or emotion: *if you were to work, should I ever work, if only I'd worked.*
Imperative	giving an instruction: *Work! Let's work!*

Temps *tense* refers to when the verb is happening: in the past, present or future. Tenses have names, e.g. present, perfect, imperfect. English has

- two simple one-word tenses: *I work, I worked*

- many compound tenses which use extra words with the basic verb, e.g. *I am working, I will work, I was working, I have worked, I have been working, I had worked.*

French too has simple and compound tenses but, as you see from the table opposite, the balance is different. In French there are far more simple tenses, where the ending of the verb supplies all the necessary information without the need for any extra words.

You'll find it much easier to use French tenses correctly if you make a point of remembering that the only extra words you'll use relate to *have* and *had*.

You can then concentrate on endings. Even if you think these look complicated at first, you'll find that you soon start to make subconscious associations. For example, there's always an r before the endings for the future tense and the present conditional.

Infinitive	travailler *to work*
Stem	travaill-
Perfect infinitive	**avoir travaillé** *to have worked*

Indicative

Present	**je travaille**	*I work, I'm working*
Future	**je travaillerai**	*I will/shall work*
Imperfect	**je travaillais**	*I was working, I used to work*
Past historic*	**je travaillai**	*I worked*
Perfect	**j'ai travaillé**	*I have worked, I worked*
Future perfect	**j'aurai travaillé**	*I will have worked*
Pluperfect	**j'avais travaillé**	*I had worked*

Conditional

Present	**je travaillerais**	*I would work*
Perfect	**j'aurais travaillé**	*I would have worked*

Subjunctive

Present	**je travaille**	*I work*
Imperfect**	**je travaillasse**	*I worked*
Perfect	**j'aie travaillé**	*I worked*
Pluperfect**	**j'eusse travaillé**	*I had worked*

Imperative

	Travaille! Travaillez!	*Work!*
	Travaillons!	*Let's work!*

Verbs also have participles:

Present participle	**travaillant**	*working*
Past participle	**travaillé**	*worked*

*The past historic is used only in formal written French, e.g. literature, essays, newspaper articles.
**The imperfect and pluperfect subjunctive are all but obsolete in modern French.

person

The **personne** *person* of a verb refers to who/what is making the verb happen.

A verb has three persons in the singular and three in the plural:

1st person singular	**je**	*I*
2nd person singular	**tu**	*you*
3rd person singular	**il, elle**	*he, she, it*

1st person plural	**nous**	*we*
2nd person plural	**vous**	*you*
3rd person plural	**ils, elles**	*they*

This is the order verbs are set out in, with each major group of verbs (**-er**, **-ir** and **-re**) having a specific ending for each of these six persons in each of the various moods and tenses.

In English there's only one word for *you*, while French has two:
tu: a friend or family member
vous: someone you don't know well, someone older than you. You also use **vous** when speaking to more than one person. The ending of the verb (usually **-ez**) is the same whether you're speaking to one person or several people.

Il *he* and **elle** *she* are also used to mean *it*. **Il** refers to a masculine object and **elle** to a feminine object.

One ending for each of six persons in each of the moods and tenses sounds like a huge number of endings to learn – but in reality you'll find that the various endings for each person have a similarity across the tenses that makes most of them instantly recognisable. For example, in all simple tenses the **nous** ending virtually always finishes with **-ons** and the **vous** ending **-ez**.

verb groups and irregular verbs

Many English verbs follow predictable patterns. These verbs are called regular verbs and once you know the patterns you can apply them to all regular verbs:

to work	*I work*	*I worked*	*I have worked*
to believe	*I believe*	*I believed*	*I have believed*

Irregular verbs are verbs that deviate from the regular patterns:

to be	*I am*	*I was*	*I have been*
to go	*I go*	*I went*	*I have gone*
to hide	*I hide*	*I hid*	*I have hidden*

French verbs divide into three groups, according to whether the infinitive ends in **-er**, **-ir** or **-re**. Each group has a set of endings for each of the tenses and moods. Once you know a set of endings you can apply them to all the regular verbs in that group. Each group also includes some irregular verbs which have to be remembered separately.

- **-er** verbs form the largest group and nearly all of them are regular. However, **aller** *to go* is completely irregular and so needs to be treated as a one-off. And **envoyer** *to send* is irregular in the future tense and the present conditional.

- Some **-ir** verbs are irregular in the present tense only e.g. **partir** *to leave*; some are irregular across the board e.g. **venir** *to come*. Many common verbs ending in **-oir** are irregular and need to be learnt individually: **pouvoir** *to be able*, **vouloir** *to want*, **savoir** *to know*, **devoir** *to have to*.

- Alongside regular **-re** verbs, there are many widely-used irregular verbs that end in **-re** which need to be learnt individually: **faire** *to do*, **dire** *to say*, **prendre** *to take*.

Several verbs have regular endings but incur a spelling change in the stem to keep the sound consistent. For example, verbs that end in **-cer** add a cedilla (**ç**) before certain endings to maintain the soft pronunciation of the **c** (page 18): **nous commençons** *we begin*.

the infinitive

The infinitive is the basic form of a verb that you find in a dictionary, ending in **-er**, **-ir** or **-re**: **visiter** *to visit*, **dormir** *to sleep*, **vendre** *to sell*.

It corresponds to both *to …* and *… ing* in English, and is used:

- after another verb, sometimes separated by **à** or **de** (pages 196-200):
  J'aime aller en France. *I like going to France.*
  Je vais continuer à aller en France. *I'm going to continue going to France.*
  J'ai décidé d'aller en France. *I've decided to go to France.*

- after adjectives, either directly or linked by **à** or **de**:
  L'équipe est incapable de gagner. *The team is incapable of winning.*
  C'est possible de perdre un kilo en une semaine. *It's possible to lose a kilo in a week.*
  Etes-vous prêt à nous aider? *Are you ready to help us?*
  C'est difficile à croire. *It is difficult to believe.*

- as a noun, where in English we use *… -ing*:
  Vivre ici est un plaisir. *Living here is lovely.*
  Apprendre le russe n'est pas facile. *Learning Russian isn't easy.*
  Voir, c'est croire. *Seeing is believing.*

- after some prepositions:
  au lieu de/avant de partir *instead of/before leaving*
  Il ne faut pas entrer sans frapper. *You can't come in without knocking.*
  Je suis venu pour aider ma mère. *I've come to help my mother.*

French has a present participle which ends in **-ant** and also translates as *-ing* (page 168). But it cannot be used in any of the above circumstances.

- The infinitive can also be used for instructions:
  Pousser. *Push.* **Tirer.** *Pull.* **Déchirer ici.** *Tear here.*
  Attacher votre ceinture de sécurité. *Fasten your safety belt.*
  Remplir ce formulaire. *Fill out this form.*

- And it's used in general questions like these:
  Que faire? *What shall we do?*
  Comment préparer les escargots? *How do you cook snails?*

Some sentences that use an infinitive in English, e.g. *I want you to go …*, can't be translated using a French infinitive. This is because the subjects of the verbs *want* and *go* are different. Such sentences require a subjunctive in French (page 178).

negative infinitive

When an infinitive is negative, both parts of the French negative, e.g. **ne** and **pas**, **ne** and **rien**, **ne** and **jamais** (page 128), go before the infinitive:

J'ai décidé de ne pas aller. *I've decided not to go.*

Il m'a demandé de ne rien dire. *He asked me to say nothing.*

Ne pas marcher sur les pelouses. *Don't walk on the grass.*

past infinitive

French has a past or perfect infinitive, used after the preposition **après** *after*. It's formed by combining **avoir** *to have* or **être** *to be* with the past participle. For **être** verbs (page 159), the past participle agrees with the subject:

Après avoir frappé, nous sommes entrés. *After knocking/having knocked, we entered.*

Après être entrés, nous nous sommes assis. *After entering/having entered, we sat down.*

verbs in a dictionary

In a dictionary, *v* stands for **verbe** *verb*. Next to the *v*, you'll find further information:

irr: irregular

pp: past participle (included if this is irregular)

rfl: reflexive

i: intransitive, needing only a subject; does not have a direct object: *go*, *laugh*

t or *tr*: transitive, needing a subject and a direct object: *give*, *use*

Many verbs can be both transitive and intransitive: *he's reading*, *he's reading a book*; *I continued*, *I continued the story*.

If you look up *wash*, this is what you might find:

wash 1. *vt* laver [*person*], nettoyer [*thing*]: *to ~ one's hands/face* se laver les mains/le visage; *to ~ the dishes* faire la vaisselle; *to ~ one's hands of sth/s.o.* se laver les mains de qch/qn **2.** *vi* [= *have a wash*] se laver [*person*], faire sa toilette [*cat*] **3.** *vi* [*do laundry*] faire la lessive **4.** *vt* [*of sea*] baigner une côte: *waves ~ing against the cliffs* vagues qui baignent les falaises

5. *n* lavage *m* lessive *f*: *car ~* lave-auto *m* **6.** [*waves*] embruns *mpl*: *the ~ of the sea* les embruns marins

reflexive verbs

Reflexive verbs have **se** in front of the infinitive. The **se** refers to *oneself*, which only occasionally features in the English translation:

> **s'amuser** *to have a good time* lit. *to amuse oneself*
> **s'appeler** *to be called* lit. *to call oneself*
> **s'arrêter** *to stop* lit. *to stop oneself*
> **s'asseoir** *to sit (oneself) down*
> **se coucher** *to go to bed* lit. *to put oneself to bed*
> **se demander** *to wonder* lit. *to ask oneself*
> **se dépêcher** *to hurry*
> **s'en aller** *to go away*   **se plaindre** *to complain*
> **s'endormir** *to fall asleep*   **se promener** *to go for a walk*
> **s'ennuyer** *to get bored*   **se rappeler** *to remember*
> **s'habiller** *to get dressed*   **se renseigner** *to enquire*
> **s'inquiéter** *to worry*   **se reposer** *to rest*
> **se laver** *to get washed*   **se réveiller** *to wake up*
> **se lever** *to get up*   **se souvenir (de)** *to remember*
> **s'occuper (de)** *to deal with*   **se tromper** *to be mistaken*

Reflexive verbs use the same endings as non-reflexive verbs, and **se** changes depending on who/what the subject is:

se laver *to get washed (to wash oneself)*

present	je me lave	*I get washed*
	tu te laves	*you get washed*
	il/elle se lave	*he/she gets washed*
	nous nous lavons	*we get washed*
	vous vous lavez	*you get washed*
	ils/elles se lavent	*they get washed*
future	je me laverai	*I will get washed*
conditional	je me laverais	*I would get washed*
imperfect	je me lavais	*I used to get washed*
past historic	je me lavai	*I got washed*

Je me souviens du jour où … *I remember the day when …*
Nous nous reposerons demain. *We'll rest tomorrow.*
Il se levait à dix heures. *He used to get up at ten o'clock.*

In compound tenses, reflexive verbs use **être**, and the past participle usually agrees with the subject:

perfect	**je me suis lavé(e)**	*I got washed*
	tu t'es lavé(e)	*you got washed*
	il s'est lavé	*he got washed*
	elle s'est lavée	*she got washed*
	nous nous sommes lavé(e)s	*we got washed*
	vous vous êtes lavé(e)(s)	*you got washed*
	ils se sont lavés	*they* (m) *got washed*
	elles se sont lavées	*they* (f) *got washed*
pluperfect	**je m'étais lavé(e)**	*I had got washed*
future perfect	**je me serai lavé(e)**	*I will have got washed*
conditional perf.	**je me serais lavé(e)**	*I would have got washed*

Elle s'est couchée tard. *She went to bed late.*
Nous nous étions trompés. *We had made a mistake.*
Je me serais dépêché mais … *I would have hurried but …*

You use a reflexive verb when you do something to a part of the body, with the possessive replaced by *the* (page 47):
Il s'est cassé la jambe. *He broke/has broken his leg.*
Je me suis foulé les doigts. *I've sprained my fingers.*

In these sentences, **s'** and **me** are indirect – not direct – objects and so the past participle doesn't agree with them. The direct objects are **la jambe** and **les doigts**. However, the past participle follows the normal rule (page 161) by agreeing with a preceding direct object pronoun:
Il se l'est cassée. *He's broken it.*

> Many verbs can be reflexive and non-reflexive. You can have **elle se lave** *she's washing (herself)* and **elle lave le bébé** *she's washing the baby*; **je me réveille à 7h** *I wake (myself) up at 7.00* and **je réveille les enfants à 7h** *I wake the children at 7.00*. And in the plural, **se** can be used to mean *each other*: **ils s'aiment beaucoup** *they love each other very much*; **nous nous écrivons souvent** *we write to each other often*.

word power

Hundreds of verbs are very similar in English and French. Some convert from English to French simply by adding **-er**. Many others replace the final letter/syllable with **-er**. But don't forget that they sound very different in the two languages.

🇬🇧	🇫🇷	
_	-er	abandonner, boycotter, calmer, confirmer, consulter, contrôler, détester, informer, insulter, inventer, mériter, passer, présenter, téléphoner, tester, visiter
-e	-er	accuser, adorer, arriver, baser, causer, combiner, comparer, conserver, continuer, diffuser, imaginer, inviter, massacrer, poser, préserver, voter
-ate	-er	célébrer, collaborer, consacrer, créer, dicter, élever, éliminer, émigrer, illuminer, intégrer, motiver, pénétrer
-ise/ -ize	-iser	angliciser, criminaliser, fraterniser, marginaliser, moderniser, monopoliser, naturaliser, neutraliser, organiser, privatiser, terroriser, utiliser but not *fantasise* fantasmer or rêver, *recognise* reconnaître or *apologise* s'excuser
-ify	-ifier	amplifier, certifier, clarifier, falsifier, horrifier, justifier, liquéfier, modifier, notifier, pacifier, pétrifier, signifier, simplifier, terrifier, unifier, vérifier but not *classify* classer, *typify* caractériser

Remember to take French spelling rules into account when 'converting' from one language to the other (page 23). For example:

- English hard *c* usually becomes **qu** in French: **communiquer** *to communicate*, **fabriquer** *to fabricate*, **impliquer** *to implicate*. Similarly, *to click* (with a mouse) is **cliquer**.

- If an English verb ending in *g* is adopted into French, **u** is inserted after the **g** to keep the sound hard as in the original pronunciation: **bloguer** *to blog*, **déléguer** *to delegate*, **draguer** *to dredge, drag* (canal), also *to flirt*.

  But other verbs have been assimilated into French and so keep the soft pronunciation: **interroger** *to question*.

false friends

assister means *to attend*	*to assist* is **aider**
attendre means *to wait for*	*to attend* is **assister**
blesser means *to wound*	*to bless* is **bénir**
décevoir means *to disappoint*	*to deceive* is **tromper**
demander means *to ask for*	*to demand* is **exiger**
disposer means *to arrange*	*to dispose of* is **se débarasser de**
embrasser means *to kiss*	*to embarrass* is **embarrasser**
ignorer means *to be unaware of*	as well as *to ignore*
importer means *to be important*	as well as *to import*
passer means *to sit* (exams)	*to pass* (exams) is **réussir**
prétendre means *to claim*	*to pretend* is **faire semblant**
réaliser means *to realise/fulfil* (a dream/project)	*to realise (become aware)* is **se rendre compte de**
rester means *to stay*	*to rest* is **se reposer**

checkpoint 13

1   Two of these words are not verbs. Can you identify them?*
    know, negotiate, applaud, arrival, disintegrate, play, depend,
    deep, realise, depart.

2   Which of these words can be a verb and a noun in English?
    disturb, describe, deny, distribute, deliver, dream.

3   What are the infinitive endings for the three groups of French
    verbs? Which is the largest group?

4   Does *mood* or *tense* refer to the time something takes place?

5   Who's doing something when a verb is in the first person
    singular? And the third person plural?

6   Which tense is only used in written texts?

7   If *He decided to stay here* is **Il a décidé de rester ici**, what is
    He decided not to stay here?

8   If you saw **Tirer** on a door, would you push or pull?

9   What does *v irr* signify next to a word in a dictionary?
    And *v rfl*?

10 What's the English for **embrasser**?

11 Work out the French for *to dominate, to illustrate, to isolate,*
    to simulate, and for *to commercialise* and *to maximise*.

12 Given that the prefix **dés-** can signify an opposite meaning,
    and a **u** is often inserted after a **g** to keep the sound hard,
    guess what these verbs mean: **désinfecter, irriguer,**
    subjuguer, désarmer, se désintégrer, réléguer.

*If ever you're not sure, remember that you can put *to* in front of
a verb and *the* in front of a noun.

Questions and negatives

French has more than one way of asking a question. While **Vous habitez ici** means *You live here*, the question *Do you live here?* can be:
- **Vous habitez ici?** with the voice rising towards the end
- **Est-ce que vous habitez ici?** lit. *Is it that you live here?*
- **Habitez-vous ici?**

The one thing that French does ***not*** do is start a question with *do, does, did* like English does.

Question words such as **quand** *when* or **comment** *how* can go at the beginning of the question or at the end: **Vous allez à Paris quand? Quand est-ce que vous allez à Paris?** *When are you going to Paris?* Most question words don't change. But **quel** *which/what* has to agree with the noun it relates to.

In English the single word *not* (often abbreviated to *n't*) indicates a negative, but in French a negative consists of two words, for example **ne ... pas** *not*, **ne ... jamais** *never*, **ne ... rien** *nothing*. They go round the verb:
Je ne suis pas en retard. *I'm not late.*
Je ne suis jamais en retard. *I'm never late.*

asking questions

There are three ways of askin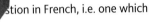stion in French, i.e. one which expects the answer *yes* or *no*.

- Use the same word order as a statement, but raise your voice on the final syllable, i.e. make it sound like a question:
  Vous habitez ici? *Do you live here?*
  Elle est infirmière? *Is she a nurse?*
  Vos parents sont déjà arrivés? *Have your parents arrived yet?*

- Use the same word order as a statement, but place **est-ce que** (lit. *is it that*) at the beginning, which indicates that what follows is a question:
  Est-ce que vous habitez ici?
  Est-ce qu'elle est infirmière?
  Est-ce que vos parents sont déjà arrivés?

- If the sentence is short and simple, particularly if the subject is a pronoun, you can reverse the order of the subject and the verb and link the two with a hyphen. This is less common than the other two ways:
  Habitez-vous ici?
  Est-elle infirmière?
  Voulez-vous venir avec moi? *Do you want to come with me?*
  Êtes-vous sûr? *Are you sure?*

In the **il** and **elle** form, if the verb ends in a vowel, you insert **t** to aid pronunciation:
Habite-t-elle à Paris? *Does she live in Paris?*
Ira-t-il à l'étranger? *Will he go abroad?*
Y a-t-il des étudiants ici? *Are there any students here?*

In compound (two-word) tenses, only the **avoir** or **être** part of the tense is reversed with the subject; the past participle stays at the end:
As-tu fini? *Have you finished?*
Êtes-vous allé au travail hier? *Did you go to work yesterday?*

N'est-ce pas can be tagged on to a sentence to turn it into a yes/no question. It corresponds to all English question tags like *isn't it, is he, don't we, aren't you, did she, have you, won't they*, so it's really easy to use.

Vous habitez ici, n'est-ce pas? *You live here, don't you?*

Elle est infirmière, n'est-ce pas? *She's a nurse, isn't she?*

Elle n'est pas infirmière, n'est-ce pas? *She isn't a nurse, is she?*

Open-ended questions, using question words such as **où** *where* or **quand** *when*, are formed in the same three ways as closed questions:

- Use the statement word order and put the question word at the end of the sentence:

  Vos parents arrivent quand? *When are your parents arriving?*

  Vous allez où? *Where are you going?*

- Start the question with the question word followed by **est-ce que**:

  Quand est-ce que vos parents arrivent?

  Où est-ce que vous allez?

- Start the question with the question word and reverse the order of subject and verb:

  Où allez-vous? *Where are you going?*

  Quand êtes-vous arrivé? *When did you arrive?*

  Combien coûte cette montre? *How much does this watch cost?*

  Comment vous appelez-vous? *What is your name?*

French question words include:

où *where*	**d'où** *from where*
quand *when*	**pourquoi** *why*
comment *how*	**combien** *how much/how many*
qui *who*	**que** *what* (**qu'** before a vowel)

qui? que? quoi?

Qui? means *who?* or *whom?*:
Qui a téléphoné? *Who phoned?*
Qui veut gagner des millions? *Who wants to win millions?*

- When *who* is the subject of the verb, an alternative to **qui** is
  qui est-ce qui:
  Qui est-ce qui a téléphoné?
  Qui est-ce qui veut gagner des millions?

- When *who* or *whom* is the object of the verb, an alternative to **qui** is
  qui est-ce que:
  Qui est-ce que vous avez vu? *Whom did you see?*

- **Qui** can also be used after prepositions:
  Vous allez avec qui? *Who are you going with?*
  Chez qui allez-vous rester? *Who are you going to stay with?*
  Selon qui? *According to whom?*

- *Whose?* is **à qui?**:
  À qui est ce sac? *Whose is this bag?*
  Ces bagages sont à qui? *Whose is this luggage?*

Que? means *what?*:
Que faites-vous? *What are you doing?*
Que manges-tu? *What are you eating?*

- When *what* is the subject of the verb, an alternative to **que** is
  qu'est-ce qui:
  Qu'est-ce qui vous intéresse? *What interests you?*

- When *what* is the object of the verb, an alternative to **que** is
  qu'est-ce que:
  Qu'est-ce que ça veut dire? *What does that mean?*
  Qu'est-ce que c'est? *What is it?*

Quoi? is *what* after prepositions?:
Avec quoi allez-vous payer? *What are you going to pay with?*

quel? lequel?

Quel? *what?, which?, what ... like?* is an adjective and always accompanies a noun, which it must agree with.

	singular	plural
masculine	quel	quels
feminine	quelle	quelles

Quel temps fait-il? *What's the weather like?*
Quelle heure est-il? *What time is it?*
Tu préfères quels bonbons? *Which sweets do you prefer?*
Vous allez prendre quelles chaussures? *Which shoes are you going to take?*

Quel isn't always next to its corresponding noun:
Quel est votre passe-temps préféré? *What is your favourite hobby?*
Quels sont les meilleurs films du cinéma français? *What are the best films in French cinema?*
Quelle est la plus grande ville de la Suisse? *Which is the largest town in Switzerland?*

Lequel? *which (one)?* is a pronoun, used in place of a noun. It must agree with the noun it replaces.

	singular	plural
masculine	lequel	lesquels
feminine	laquelle	lesquelles

Voici des bonbons; tu voudrais lequel? *Here are some sweets; which one would you like?*
Voici des chaussures; lesquelles préférez-vous? *Here are some shoes; which (ones) do you prefer?*

Lequel, lesquels and **lesquelles** combine with **à** or **de** and change in the usual way (page 48):
Auquel pensez-vous? *Which one are you thinking about?* (talking about a masculine object)
Auxquels de vos amis avez-vous écrit? *To which of your friends have you written?*
Tu as peur de certains animaux? Desquels? *You're afraid of certain animals? Which ones?*

exclamations

As in English, **que** *what*, **quel** *what* and **comme** *how* are all used in exclamations as well as questions.

que

Que …! + adjective or adverb means *How …!* in exclamations containing the words *so, such, really,* etc. The verb in these sentences is usually **être** *to be*:

Que c'est joli! *How pretty it is! It's so/really pretty!*
Ouah, que c'est chic! *Wow, that's so cool/trendy!*
Que c'est bien! *How great! That's really great!*
Qu'il est craquant! *He's so cute/sexy!*

In very colloquial French **qu'est-ce que** can replace **que**:

Qu'est-ce qu'il est craquant!

que de

Que de …! is followed by a noun and means *What a lot of …!:*

Que de monde! *What a lot of people!*
Que de réponses! *What a lot of replies!*

comme

Comme …! + verb also means *How …!* or *What …!* It's more formal than **que**:

Comme tu as grandi! *How you've grown!*
Comme elle a de belles dents! *What beautiful teeth she has!*

quel

Quel …! + noun means *What (a) …!* **Quel** must agree with the noun:

Quel beau temps! *What lovely weather!*
Quelle coïncidence! *What a coincidence!*
Quelles jolies fleurs! *What lovely flowers!*

negatives: ne ... pas

To say something negative in French the key words are **ne** (**n'** before a vowel) and **pas**, which go around the verb. You don't translate the English words *do, does, did*.

Je suis français. *I'm French.*
Je ne suis pas français. *I'm not French.*
Je parle français. *I speak French.*
Je ne parle pas français. *I do not/don't speak French.*
Tournez à droite, ne tournez pas à gauche. *Turn right, don't turn left.*

The **ne** is often omitted in colloquial speech:
Je (ne) sais pas. *I don't know.*

- **Du, de la, de l'** and **des** change to **de** in most negative sentences:
  Nous n'avons pas d'argent. *We haven't got any money.*
  Je ne vends pas de vêtements sur l'internet. *I don't sell clothes on the internet.*

  However, when there's a distinction being made between two nouns, **du, de la, de l'** and **des** don't change:
  Ce n'est pas du vin mais de la bière. *This is not wine, but beer.*

- In compound (two-word) tenses, **ne** and **pas** go around **avoir** or **être** (page 158):
  J'ai fini. *I finished./I have finished.*
  Je n'ai pas fini. *I didn't finish./I haven't finished.*
  Elle est arrivée. *She arrived./She has arrived.*
  Elle n'est pas arrivée. *She didn't arrive./She hasn't arrived.*
  Vous n'avez pas acheté de pain. *You didn't buy (any) bread.*

- When there's more than one verb, **ne** and **pas** go round the first one:
  Je ne peux pas venir. *I can't come.*
  Il ne va pas jouer. *He's not going to play.*
  Nous ne voulons pas rester ici. *We don't want to stay here.*
  Ne laisse pas tomber le ballon. *Don't drop the ball.*
  Il ne faut pas rire. *You mustn't laugh.*

- **Ne** normally goes before reflexive and object pronouns (page 85):
  Il ne se lève pas tôt. *He doesn't get up early.*
  Nous ne nous sommes pas très bien amusés.
  We didn't have a very good time.
  Ça ne me plaît pas. *I don't like it.*
  Vous ne m'avez pas écrit. *You didn't write to me./*
  You haven't written to me.
  Je ne le lui ai pas donné. *I didn't give it to him./I haven't given it to him.*
  Il n'y en a pas beaucoup. *There isn't much./There aren't many.*

- **Ne ... pas du tout** means *not at all.*
  Je ne l'aime pas du tout. *I don't like it/him/her at all.*
  Vous ne me convainquez pas du tout. *You don't convince me at all.*

- **Pas** can be left out when **savoir** *to know* is followed by a question word or **si** *if*:
  Je ne sais que faire. *I don't know what to do.*
  Je ne sais s'il est là. *I don't know if he's there.*

  And in formal written French, you'll also find **ne** without **pas** after **cesser** *to stop*, **pouvoir** *to be able* and **oser** *to dare*:
  Je n'ose le regarder. *I daren't watch it.*

  The most common negatives are:

ne ... pas	*not*
ne ... rien	*nothing, not anything*
ne ... jamais	*never*
ne ... personne	*no one, nobody, not anyone*
ne ... aucun(e)	*no, not any, none*
ne ... guère	*hardly*
ne ... ni ... ni	*neither ... nor*
ne ... nulle part	*nowhere*
ne ... que	*only*
ne ... plus	*no more, not any more, no longer, not any longer*

other negatives

- **Ne ... plus** *no longer, not any more*, **ne ... jamais** *never* and **ne ... rien** *nothing* behave like **ne ... pas**:
  Nous n'habitons plus à Londres. *We don't live in London any more.*
  Il ne reste plus de vin. *There's no more wine left.*
  Il ne me téléphone jamais. *He never phones me.*
  Je ne me lève jamais tôt. *I never get up early.*
  Vous n'avez rien fait. *You haven't done anything.*

- The second part of **ne ... personne** *nobody, no-one* and **ne ... nulle part** *nowhere* goes after the past participle (see page 158):
  Je ne vois personne. *I can't see anyone.*
  Je n'ai vu personne. *I didn't see anyone.*
  On ne le voit nulle part. *We can't see him anywhere.*
  On ne l'a trouvé nulle part. *We didn't find him anywhere.*

- The second part of **ne ... guère** *hardly* and **ne ... que** *only* comes before the word it refers to:
  Nous n'avons guère le choix. *We've hardly any choice.*
  Nous n'avons eu guère le choix. *We had hardly any choice.*
  Je n'ai que cinq euros. *I've only got 5 euros.*
  Je n'ai eu que cinq euros. *I only had 5 euros.*

  When *only* refers to a verb, use **ne faire que**:
  Ils ne font que se disputer. *They only argue. They do nothing but argue.*
  Il ne fait que chanter. *He only sings. He does nothing but sing.*

- **Ne ... ni ... ni** *neither ... nor* is made up of three parts. **Ne** comes before the verb, as usual, and each **ni** comes before the word it refers to:
  Je ne mange ni porc ni bœuf. *I don't eat pork or beef./
  I eat neither pork nor beef.*
  Il ne m'a dit ni oui ni non. *He didn't tell me yes or no.*
  Je ne peux ni chanter ni danser. *I can't sing or dance.*

- **Ne ... aucun(e)** *no, not a, not one, not any* agrees with the noun following it:
  Je n'ai aucune idée. *I've no idea.*
  Je n'ai lu aucun de ses livres. *I haven't read any of his/her books.*

- The second part of most negative expressions can be used without **ne** in sentences without a verb:
  Vous allez souvent au cinéma? Non, jamais. *Do you often go to the cinema? No, never.*
  Qu'est-ce que vous avez vu? Rien d'intéressant. *What did you see? Nothing interesting.* (See page 53 for adjectives after **rien**.)
  Qui est-ce que tu as vu à la réunion? Personne. *Whom did you see at the meeting? No-one.*
  Tu y as été combien de fois? Aucune. *How many times have you been there? None.*

  These words can also begin a sentence as the subject of the verb, with the **ne** coming afterwards:
  Personne n'est venu. *Nobody came.*
  Rien ne m'étonne. *Nothing surprises me.*
  Rien ne s'est passé. *Nothing (has) happened.*
  Aucun animal ne pourrait y survivre. *No animal could survive there.*

  If there's more than one negative expression in the sentence, they go in this order: **plus, jamais, rien, personne, que, nulle part**:
  Je n'y vais plus jamais. *I never go there any more.*
  Elle n'a jamais embrassé personne. *She's never kissed anyone.*
  On n'a jamais bu que du vin français. *We've only ever drunk French wine.*
  Je n'achète plus rien. *I'm not buying anything any more.*

Sans *without* can be followed by the second part of negative expressions (without **ne**) and an infinitive:
Il est parti sans rien dire. *He left without saying anything.*
Tout ce que vous avez toujours voulu savoir sur le sexe, sans jamais oser le demander. *Everything you've always wanted to know about sex and never dared to ask.*

---

negative questions, imperatives and infinitives

- In questions where the subject and verb are reversed, **ne** and **pas** go round the whole lot:
Peux-tu venir? *Can you come?*
Ne peux-tu pas venir? *Can't you come?*

- For one-word verbs, the rules for the negative imperative (page 171) are the same as for ordinary sentences i.e. the **ne** and **pas** etc go round the verb. Where there's an object or a reflexive pronoun, these come after **ne** and before the verb:
Faites vos devoirs. *Do your homework.*
Ne faites pas vos devoirs. *Don't do your homework.*
Asseyez-vous. *Sit down.*
Ne vous asseyez pas. *Don't sit down.*
Dépêche-toi. *Hurry.*
Ne te dépêche jamais. *Never hurry.*

- Both parts of **ne pas**, **plus**, **rien**, **jamais** and **guère** come before the infinitive and any pronouns:
Il espère ne pas voir son chef. *He hopes not to see his boss.*
Il a décidé de ne plus me visiter. *He's decided not to visit me any more.*
Elle m'a demandé de ne rien faire. *She asked me to do nothing.*

But **personne** and **nulle part** come after the infinitive:
J'espère ne voir personne. *I hope not to see anyone.*
Ils ont décidé de ne le chercher nulle part. *They decided not to look anywhere for it.*

Si is used instead of **oui** to mean *yes* in response to a negative question or statement:
Tu n'as pas fini? Si, j'ai fini. *Haven't you finished?*
Yes, I've finished.
Tu ne m'aimes pas. Mais si, je t'aime. *You don't love me.*
Yes, I do love you.

checkpoint 14

1　Write the negative of these sentences using ne ... pas:
　a Il est étudiant.　　　　　　b C'était bien.
　c Je le connais.　　　　　　 d On y va souvent.
　e Nous nous sommes　　　　f J'ai bu du vin.
　 promenés sur la plage.

2　Which of the words in brackets belongs in the gap?
　a Je n'ai ___ d'argent (rien, plus).
　b Il n'a ___ eu de succès (personne, guère).
　c Je ne connais ___ cinq personnes ici (que, aucune).
　d Je ne connais ___ personne ici (pas, aucune).

3　Which words are missing from this sentence:
　Je ___ joue ___ au tennis ___ au golf.

4　What's the negative expression for *nowhere*?

5　Rearrange these words to form three sentences:
　a ne téléphoné personne m'a
　b jamais personne visite ne elle
　c n'ai aucun amis je de vu mes

6　Which expression turns a statement into a question?

7　Which of these words doesn't mean *what*?
　que　quel　qui　quoi

8　Match the questions with the answer:
　a Elle n'est pas arrivée?　　　 i Oui, elle est arrivée.
　b Est-ce qu'elle est déjà arrivée? ii Si, elle est arrivée.
　c Quand est-elle arrivée?　　　iii Elle est arrivée ce matin.

9　What's the French for *isn't it*? And for *haven't we*?

10　Complete these sentences using the correct form of **quel** or
　lequel:
　a _____ est votre actrice préférée?
　b _____ villes voudriez-vous visiter?
　c J'ai deux gâteaux; tu voudrais _____ ?
　d Je ne peux pas choisir entre ces deux jupes; _____
　tu préfères?

Verbs: simple tenses

The following pages guide you through the tenses of French verbs, showing you how to choose the one you need and which endings are involved.

You need to be familiar with the information on pages 109-110. Briefly:

- Verb endings tell you a) how the verb is being used, b) when it's happening, and c) who/what is doing it. The endings fit on to the stem of the verb, which you find by removing **-er**, **-ir** or **-re** from the end of the infinitive: **travailler** *to work* → **travaill-**, **finir** *to finish* → **fin-**, **vendre** *to sell* → **vend-**.

  There are many similarities between verb endings across all groups; the **vous** form almost always ends in **-ez** and the **nous** form in **-ons**; **tu** forms almost always end in **-s** and the **je** form usually ends in **-e** or **-s**. Irregular verbs deviate from the standard patterns in some way, but even most of these have endings that are similar to regular verb patterns.

- The balance of simple (one-word) and compound (two-word) tenses is different in English and French, with French verb endings doing away with the need for support words like *am*, *is*, *are*, *will*, *was*, *would*.

On the whole it's easy to relate French and English tenses, but there are two things to watch out for. The French past historic tense, which translates the simple past tense in English (*I worked, I ate*), is largely used only in formal writing. What you use instead in all other situations is the perfect tense: *I have worked, I have eaten*.

Secondly, English uses the word *would* in two senses: *We would buy it if we had the money*, which is the conditional, and *We would go back every year when we were little*, which is the imperfect.

present tense

	travailler *to work*	finir *to finish*	vendre *to sell*
je	travaill**e**	fin**is**	vend**s**
tu	travaill**es**	fin**is**	vend**s**
il/elle	travaill**e**	fin**it**	vend
nous	travaill**ons**	fin**issons**	vend**ons**
vous	travaill**ez**	fin**issez**	vend**ez**
ils/elles	travaill**ent**	fin**issent**	vend**ent**

- All **-er** verbs except **aller** *to go* have the same endings as **travailler**. However, some undergo minor spelling changes within the stem to keep the overall sound consistent (pages 136-137).

- A small group of **-ir** verbs use **-er** endings. These include **ouvrir** *to open*, **couvrir** *to cover*, **découvrir** *to discover*, **offrir** *to offer*, **souffrir** *to suffer*, **accueillir** *to greet*, **cueillir** *to pick*.

  ouvrir: **j'ouvre, tu ouvres, il/elle ouvre, nous ouvrons, vous ouvrez, ils/elles ouvrent**

- Another group of common **-ir** verbs drops the consonant before **-ir** in the singular and doesn't add **-iss** in the plural. These include **partir** *to leave*, **sortir** *to go out*, **dormir** *to sleep*, **mentir** *to lie*, **sentir** *to feel*, **servir** *to serve*.

  partir: **je pars, tu pars, il/elle part, nous partons, vous partez, ils/elles partent**

  Courir *to run* is similar, except that it keeps the r throughout: **je cours, tu cours, il/elle court, nous courons, vous courez, ils/elles courent**

- **-re** verbs are the smallest group, of which the most common regular examples include: **attendre** *to wait (for)*, **défendre** *to defend*, **descendre** *to descend*, **entendre** *to hear*, **perdre** *to lose*, **rendre** *to give back*, **répondre** *to answer*.

common irregular verbs

Some of the most widely used verbs in French are irregular. Their irregularities are minor in some tenses but in the present tense some parts of these verbs look very different from the infinitive.

	être *to be*	**avoir** *to have*	**aller** *to go*
je/j'	suis	ai	vais
tu	es	as	vas
il/elle	est	a	va
nous	sommes	avons	allons
vous	êtes	avez	allez
ils/elles	sont	ont	vont

	faire *to do/make*	**devoir** *to have to*	**savoir** *to know*
je/j'	fais	dois	sais
tu	fais	dois	sais
il/elle	fait	doit	sait
nous	faisons	devons	savons
vous	faites	devez	savez
ils/elles	font	doivent	savent

	pouvoir *to be able*	**vouloir** *to want*	**venir** *to come*
je/j'	peux	veux	viens
tu	peux	veux	viens
il/elle	peut	veut	vient
nous	pouvons	voulons	venons
vous	pouvez	voulez	venez
ils/elles	peuvent	veulent	viennent

Être is the only French verb to have a present tense **nous** form that doesn't end in **-ons**: **nous sommes** *we are*.

Être, faire and dire are the only verbs to have present tense **vous** forms that don't end in **-ez**: **vous êtes, vous faites, vous dites**.

present tense spelling variations

The following groups of verbs incur a spelling change in the stem to keep the overall sound consistent:

- verbs ending in **-cer**, e.g. **commencer** *to begin*, **annoncer** *to announce*, **avancer** *to advance*, **grimacer** *to grimace*, **lancer** *to throw*, **menacer** *to threaten*, **pincer** *to pinch*, **rincer** *to rinse*

  c changes to **ç** in the **nous** form to maintain the soft *s* sound:
  nous commençons *we begin*

- verbs ending in **-ger**, e.g. **manger** *to eat*, **arranger** *to arrange*, **bouger** *to move*, **(re)charger** *to (re)charge, to (re)load*, **envisager** *to envisage*, **nager** *to swim*, **partager** *to share*, **protéger** *to protect*, **rédiger** *to edit, to write up*, **soulager** *to relieve*.

  e is added after the **g** in the **nous** form to maintain the soft *zh* sound:
  nous mangeons *we eat*

- verbs ending in **-oyer** and **-uyer**, e.g. **employer** *to use*, **appuyer** *to press*, **envoyer** *to send*, **essuyer** *to wipe*, **nettoyer** *to clean*, **s'ennuyer** *to be bored*

  y changes to **i** in the **je**, **tu**, **il/elle** and **ils/elles** forms:
  j'emploie, tu emploies, il/elle emploie, nous employons, vous employez, ils/elles emploient

- verbs ending in **-ayer**, e.g. **payer** *to pay*, **effrayer** *to frighten*, **essayer** *to try*

  These have two equally correct versions for the **je**, **tu**, **il/elle** and **ils/elles** forms:
  je paie or **paye, tu paies** or **payes, il/elle paie** or **paye, nous payons, vous payez, ils/elles paient** or **payent**

- verbs with unaccented **e** in the syllable before **-er**, e.g. **acheter** *to buy*, **achever** *to complete*, **amener** *to bring*, **élever** *to raise*, **emmener** *to take (away)*, **geler** *to freeze*, **peler** *to peel*, **peser** *to weigh*, **se lever** *to get up*, **se promener** *to go for a walk*

  e changes to **è** in the **je**, **tu**, **il/elle** and **ils/elles** forms – because **e** without an accent is a weak vowel sound in French (page 16) and can't be the final sound in a verb:
  j'achète, tu achètes, il/elle achète, nous achetons, vous achetez, ils/elles achètent

- some verbs with **é** in the syllable before **-er**, e.g. **espérer** *to hope*, **céder** *to give way*, **considérer** *to consider*, **exagérer** *to exaggerate*, **libérer** *to free*, **posséder** *to possess*, **préférer** *to prefer*, **protéger** *to protect*, **répéter** *to repeat*

  é changes to **è** in the **je**, **tu**, **il/elle** and **ils/elles** forms:
  j'espère, tu espères, il/elle espère, nous espérons, vous espérez, ils/elles espèrent

- a small group of verbs with **l** or **t** immediately before **-er**, e.g. **appeler** *to call*, **rappeler** *to recall*, **épeler** *to spell*, **grommeler** *to grumble*, **jeter** *to throw*, **renouveler** *to renew*

  The consonant doubles up in the **je**, **tu**, **il/elle** and **ils/elles** forms:
  j'appelle, tu appelles, il/elle appelle, nous appelons, vous appelez, ils/elles appellent
  je jette, tu jettes, il/elle jette, nous jetons, vous jetez, ils/elles jettent

- verbs ending in **-aindre**, **-eindre** or **-oindre**, e.g. **peindre** *to paint*, **atteindre** *to achieve*, **craindre** *to fear*, **éteindre** *to extinguish*, **joindre** *to enclose*, **se plaindre** *to complain*.

  The plural stem ends in **-gn**:
  je peins, tu peins, il/elle peint, nous peignons, vous peignez, ils/elles peignent

when to use the present tense

- The present tense is used in French where in English you say both *I do something* and *I'm doing something*:
  Je travaille à Londres. *I work in London.*
  Nous travaillons aujourd'hui. *We're working today.*
  Je finis mon travail à cinq heures. *I finish work at five o'clock.*
  Et vous, vous finissez à quelle heure? *What time do you finish?*
  Matthieu vend sa maison. *Matthieu is selling his house.*
  Les agents immobiliers vendent des maisons. *Estate agents sell houses.*

- As in English, the present tense can be used to talk about the future:
  Ils travaillent demain. *They're working tomorrow.*
  Je vais au Japon l'année prochaine. *I'm going to Japan next year.*

- For questions and negatives, you don't need extra words like *do*, *does*, *am*, *is*, *are* (although you can add **est-ce que**, page 122):
  Vous travaillez ici? *Do you work here?*
  Vous travaillez demain? *Are you working tomorrow?*
  Je ne travaille pas. *I'm not working./I don't work.*
  Elle va à l'école? *Does she go to school?/Is she going to school?*
  Est-ce que Matthieu vend sa maison? *Is Matthieu selling his house?*

- The phrase **être en train de** + infinitive can be used to stress that something is happening at the moment:
  Ne la dérange pas. Elle est en train de faire les devoirs. *Don't disturb her. She's (busy) doing her homework.*
  Je suis en train de regarder la télé. *I'm (in the middle of) watching TV.*

- The present tense of **venir** *to come*, followed by **de** + infinitive means *to have just (done)*:
  Il vient de partir. *He's just left.*
  Nous venons de le voir. *We've just seen him/it.*
  Je viens de mettre la lettre à la poste. *I've just posted the letter.*
  Elles viennent d'arriver. *They've just arrived.*

After **depuis** *for, since*, French uses the present tense where English uses the form *has/have been doing*. The logic is that although the activity started in the past it's still going on in the present:

J'habite ici depuis dix ans. *I've been living here for ten years.*

Il travaille en France depuis janvier. *He's been working in France since January.*

Depuis quand existe l'internet? *How long has the internet been in existence?*

checkpoint 15

1   Write the present tense of these verbs:

dire	vous	
arriver	ils	
finir	elles	
nager	nous	
offrir	il	
espérer	elles	
partir	je	
menacer	nous	
nettoyer	elle	
craindre	vous	

2   Translate the following into French:

a *We're going to Paris tomorrow.*

b *He's in the middle of speaking.*

c *She's just been here.*

d *I've been working here for five years.*

3   Which of these verbs has an **il/elle** form that ends in **-e**?
dormir   entendre   courir   offrir   aller

future tense

Instead of **replacing** the infinitive ending as other tenses do, the future tense **adds** endings to the infinitive, with -re verbs dropping the -e first. This means that in the future tense every single verb has an **r** immediately before the ending.

	travailler *to work*	**finir** *to finish*	**vendre** *to sell*
je	travaille**rai**	fini**rai**	vend**rai**
tu	travaille**ras**	fini**ras**	vend**ras**
il/elle	travaille**ra**	fini**ra**	vend**ra**
nous	travaille**rons**	fini**rons**	vend**rons**
vous	travaille**rez**	fini**rez**	vend**rez**
ils/elles	travaille**ront**	fini**ront**	vend**ront**

Some of the verbs which incur spelling changes in certain forms of the present tense (pages 136-137) incur these changes in all forms of the future:

- Verbs like **appeler** *to call* double the consonant: **j'appellerai, tu appelleras** etc.

- Verbs like **acheter** *to buy* add a grave accent to the **e**: **j'achèterai, tu achèteras** etc.

- Verbs like **employer** *to use* and **essuyer** *to wipe* change **y** to **i**: **j'emploierai** *I will use*, **tu emploieras** etc; **j'essuierai** *I will wipe*, **tu essuieras** etc.

  Envoyer *to send* is an exception. It has the irregular future **j'enverrai, tu enverras** etc.

- Verbs like **payer** *to pay* can form their future tense with either **i** or **y**: **je paierai, tu paieras** or **je payerai, tu payeras** etc.

However, verbs like **espérer** – which change **é** to **è** in some forms of the present tense – keep **é** throughout in the future tense: **j'espérerai** *I will hope*, **je préférerai** *I will prefer*.

when to use the future tense

- The future tense is used in French where in English you'd say *I will/shall do something*:
  Je lui demanderai de me téléphoner. *I'll ask him to phone me.*
  Les cours commenceront demain. *Lessons will start tomorrow.*
  Je ne sais pas quelle carte il choisira. *I don't know which card he'll choose.*
  Nous mangerons à l'aéroport. *We'll eat at the airport.*

- As in English, you can use the future tense to make assumptions:
  J'ai entendu une voiture. Ce sera mon mari. *I heard a car. That will be my husband.*

- Unlike English, the future tense is used after **quand/lorsque** *when*, **aussitôt que/dès que** *as soon as*, **pendant que/tant que** *while*, **une fois que** *once*, when the other verb in the sentence is in the future:
  Je vous dirai quand ils arriveront. *I'll tell you when they arrive.*
  Aussitôt qu'il te téléphonera, je partirai. *As soon as he rings you, I'll leave.*
  Tant qu'il ne pleuvra pas, on fera un barbecue. *As long as it doesn't rain we'll have a barbecue.*

- When **si** means *whether*, the future tense is used as it is with **quand**, **aussitôt que**, etc (above):
  Je ne sais pas s'il viendra. *I don't know whether he's coming.*

  But when **si** means *if*, the present tense is used, just as in English:
  S'il pleut, on restera à la maison. *If it rains we'll stay at home.*
  On visitera le Louvre, si on a le temps. *We'll visit the Louvre if we've got time.*

Be careful of the word *will* in English; it's not always a future tense. Sometimes it's concerned with being willing to do something, and you use the verb **vouloir** *to want* in these instances:
Voulez-vous passer le sel, s'il vous plaît? *Will you pass the salt please?*

irregular future tense forms

- Some verbs that are irregular in the present tense are regular in the future:
  boire *to drink* **je boirai, tu boiras** etc.
  dire *to say* **je dirai, tu diras** etc.
  prendre *to take* **je prendrai, tu prendras** etc.
  connaître *to know* **je connaîtrai, tu connaîtras** etc.
  lire *to read* **je lirai, tu liras** etc.
  vivre *to live* **je vivrai, tu vivras** etc.

- In the irregular future tense verbs, it's the stem that's irregular, not the endings, which are always the same.

- The common, very irregular verbs in the present tense (page 135) are irregular in the future too:
  être *to be* **je serai, tu seras** etc.
  avoir *to have* **j'aurai, tu auras** etc.
  aller *to go* **j'irai, tu iras** etc.
  faire *to do* **je ferai, tu feras** etc.
  pouvoir *to be able* **je pourrai, tu pourras** etc.
  vouloir *to want* **je voudrai, tu voudras** etc.
  savoir *to know* **je saurai, tu sauras** etc.
  devoir *to have to* **je devrai, tu devras** etc.
  s'asseoir *to sit down* **je m'assiérai, tu t'assiéras** etc.

- Other verbs can be grouped according to patterns in their endings:
  venir *to come* **je viendrai, tu viendras** etc.
  tenir *to hold* **je tiendrai, tu tiendras** etc.

  voir *to see* **je verrai, tu verras** etc.
  envoyer *to send* **j'enverrai, tu enverras** etc.
  acquérir *to acquire* **j'acquerrai, tu acquerras** etc.

  recevoir *to receive* **je recevrai, tu recevras** etc.
  décevoir *to disappoint* **je décevrai, tu décevras** etc.

accueillir *to greet* **j'accueillerai, tu accueilleras** etc.
cueillir *to pick* **je cueillerai, tu cueilleras** etc.

courir *to run* **je courrai, tu courras** etc.
mourir *to die* **je mourrai, tu mourras** etc.

- The impersonal verbs **falloir** *to be necessary*, **valoir** *to be worth* and **pleuvoir** *to rain* are used in the third person singular only:
  il faudra *it will be necessary*
  il vaudra *it will be worth*
  il pleuvra *it will rain*

---

other ways of talking about the future

As in English, there are two other ways of talking about the future without using the future tense:

- You can use the present tense in sentences like these:
  Je rentre à Londres demain. *I'm returning to London tomorrow.*
  Il part à onze heures. *He's leaving at 11 o'clock.*

- You can use **aller** *to go* to translate *going to do something*. The following verb is in the infinitive:
  Je vais visiter mes parents. *I'm going to visit my parents.*
  Il va venir plus tard. *He's going to come later.*
  Qu'est-ce que tu vas faire? *What are you going to do?*
  Si tu n'étudies pas, tu vas rater les examens. *If you don't study you're going to fail the exams.*

  But don't use it if you want to talk about a state of mind. Just use the future tense instead:
  Je serai très content de vous voir. *I'm going to be/I will be very happy to see you.*

---

conditional

The conditional has the same stem as the future tense (i.e. the infinitive) but a different set of endings.

	travailler *to work*	**finir** *to finish*	**vendre** *to sell*
je	travailler**ais**	finir**ais**	vendr**ais**
tu	travailler**ais**	finir**ais**	vendr**ais**
il/elle	travailler**ait**	finir**ait**	vendr**ait**
nous	travailler**ions**	finir**ions**	vendr**ions**
vous	travailler**iez**	finir**iez**	vendr**iez**
ils/elles	travailler**aient**	finir**aient**	vendr**aient**

The conditional has a lot in common with the future tense:
- Both have the distinctive r before all the endings.
- The same verbs are irregular in the future and the conditional, and they're irregular in a similar way – the stem is the same for both, with only the endings differing:

	future	conditional
être *to be*	je serai	je serais
avoir *to have*	j'aurai	j'aurais
aller *to go*	j'irai	j'irais
faire *to do*	je ferai	je ferais
pouvoir *to be able*	je pourrai	je pourrais
vouloir *to want*	je voudrai	je voudrais
savoir *to know*	je saurai	je saurais
devoir *to have to*	je devrai	je devrais

- The conditional endings are exactly the same as the imperfect tense endings (page 148) – although they're on the same stem as the future tense.

word **power**

Although there are many irregular verbs in French, many follow similar patterns, so once you've learnt one verb you can apply the pattern to others. In particular, verbs derived from another verb (by adding a prefix) usually behave in the same way as the original verb:

- **revenir** *to come back*, **devenir** *to become*, **prévenir** *to warn*, **convenir** *to suit*, **se souvenir de** *to remember* behave like **venir** *to come*, as do **tenir** *to hold* and verbs derived from it e.g. **obtenir** *to obtain*:
  future: **je viendrai, je reviendrai, je deviendrai, je tiendrai** etc
  conditional: **je viendrais, je reviendrais, je tiendrais** etc

- **amener** *to bring*, **emmener** *to take (away)* behave like **mener** *to lead*:
  future: **je mènerai, j'amènerai, j'emmènerai**
  conditional: **je mènerais, j'amènerais, j'emmènerais**

- **accueillir** *to greet* and **recueillir** *to collect* are like **cueillir** *to pick*:
  future: **je cueillerai, j'accueillerai, je recueillerai**
  conditional: **je cueillerais, j'accueillerais, je recueillerais**

- **contredire** *to contradict*, **interdire** *to forbid*, **prédire** *to predict* behave like **dire** *to say*:
  future: **je dirai, je contredirai, j'interdirai, je prédirai**
  conditional: **je dirais, je contredirais, j'interdirais, je prédirais**

The following verbs ending in **-evoir** also follow the same pattern: **recevoir** *to receive*, **décevoir** *to disappoint*, **apercevoir** *to catch sight of* and **concevoir** *to conceive*:
future: **je recevrai, je décevrai, j'apercevrai, je concevrai**
conditional: **je recevrais, j'apercevrais, je concevrais**

Similarly, **acquérir** *to acquire*, **conquérir** *to conquer*, **s'enquérir de** *to ask about* behave in the same way:
future: **j'acquerrai, je conquerrai, je m'enquerrai de**
conditional: **j'acquerrais, je conquerrais, je m'enquerrais de**

when to use the conditional

- The conditional is used in French to say what *would* happen:
  Je préférerais rester ici. *I would/I'd prefer to stay here.*
  Que préféreriez-vous? *What would you prefer?*
  Ça me plairait beaucoup. *I would really like that.*
  lit. *That would really please me.*
  J'irais moi-même, mais je suis très occupé.
  I'd go myself but I'm very busy.
  Que feriez-vous? *What would you do?*
  J'aimerais bien … *I would like to …*
  Je savais qu'il viendrait. *I knew (that) he would come.*
  J'y irais si j'avais assez de temps. *I'd go there if I had enough time.*
  J'achèterais un yacht si je gagnais des millions. *I'd buy a yacht if I were a millionaire.* lit. *earned millions*

- You can use it to make a request sound polite:
  Je voudrais deux cafés. *I'd like two coffees.*
  Vous voudriez venir? *Would you like to come?*
  Pourriez-vous me dire? *Could you tell me?*
  Je pourrais vous poser une question? *Could I ask you a question?*
  Il me faudrait cinq citrons. *I'll need five lemons.*
  Je vous serais très reconnaissant. *I'd be very grateful to you.*

- The conditional of **devoir** *to have to* is used to translate *should* or *ought* when giving advice:
  Tu devrais lui dire merci. *You ought to say thank you to him/her.*
  Il devrait apprendre le français. *He should learn French.*

- The conditional is also used to show that there's uncertainty about the accuracy of what's being said. English uses speech marks or phrases like *it is alleged that, it was said that*.
  La victime serait déjà morte. *It is alleged that the victim is already dead.*
  Il y aurait cinq blessés dans l'accident. *There would appear to be five people injured in the accident.*

- As in English, the conditional is used in reported speech where the future tense was used in the actual words:

  Je lui ai dit qu'il vaudrait mieux répondre. *I told her it would be better to reply.*

  Il m'a dit qu'il irait bientôt à Lyon. *He told me he would soon be going to Lyon.*

  Elle m'a répondu qu'elle le verrait lundi prochain. *She replied to me that she would see him next Monday.*

- Just as French uses the future tense after **quand/lorsque** *when*, **pendant que/tant que** *while*, **aussitôt que/dès que** *as soon as* and **une fois que** *once* where English uses the present tense (page 141), so it uses the conditional after these words where English uses the past tense:

  Le chef a dit qu'une fois que mon collègue arriverait, je pourrais aller. *The boss said that as soon as my colleague arrived, I could go.*

  Il a promis que dès qu'il aurait assez d'argent, il le ferait. *He promised that as soon as he had enough money, he would do it.*

- The conditional phrase **on dirait que**, which literally means *one would say that*, is used to express possibility:

  On dirait qu'il va pleuvoir. *It looks as if it's going to rain.*

  On dirait qu'ils viennent de gagner. *You'd think they'd just won.*

  On dirait qu'elle a peur. *It's as if she's afraid.*

Would doesn't always indicate a conditional in English. It can also refer to something that used to happen regularly in the past, e.g. *When I was a child we would go to the beach every Sunday.* In sentences like these, you use the imperfect tense in French (page 148).

the imperfect

The imperfect is based on the **nous** form of the present tense: **nous travaillons, nous finissons, nous vendons, nous dormons, nous faisons, nous avons** etc. You simply take off the **-ons** ending and add the following instead:

	travailler *to work*	**finir** *to finish*	**vendre** *to sell*
je	travaill**ais**	finiss**ais**	vend**ais**
tu	travaill**ais**	finiss**ais**	vend**ais**
il/elle	travaill**ait**	finiss**ait**	vend**ait**
nous	travaill**ions**	finiss**ions**	vend**ions**
vous	travaill**iez**	finiss**iez**	vend**iez**
ils/elles	travaill**aient**	finiss**aient**	vend**aient**

Être *to be* is the only verb which doesn't conform to the above rule. It adds the imperfect endings to the irregular stem **ét-**:

j'étais	nous étions
tu étais	vous étiez
il/elle était	ils/elles étaient

All other verbs use the present tense **nous** form without **-ons**:
avoir *to have* j'avais, tu avais, il avait
faire *to do* je faisais, tu faisais, il faisait
aller *to go* j'allais, tu allais, il allait
dire *to say/tell* je disais, tu disais, il disait
partir *to leave* je partais, tu partais, il partait
manger *to eat* je mangeais, tu mangeais, il mangeait
commencer *to begin* je commençais, tu commençais, il commençait

Impersonal verbs (pages 188-189), which either don't have a **nous** form or rarely use it, have the following forms in the imperfect:
pleuvoir *to rain* il pleuvait
falloir *to be necessary* il fallait
plaire *to please* il plaisait
valoir *to be worth* il valait

... and when to use it

- The imperfect is used when talking about how things were, when describing people or things in the past, or when talking about events that happened regularly or carried on over a period. It translates *was* or *were doing* something, as well as *used to* or *would*.

  Quand j'étais petit, on allait tous les ans à Blackpool. *When I was little we used to/would go every year to Blackpool.*

  J'étais heureuse. *I was happy./I used to be happy.*

  Il portait un pantalon bleu. *He was wearing blue trousers.*

  Il préparait le repas quand nous sommes arrivés. *He was cooking the meal when we arrived.*

  Il y avait beaucoup de gens au concert. *There were a lot of people at the concert.*

  Au seizième siècle l'Angleterre avait une population de quatre millions d'habitants. *In the 16th century England had a population of four million.*

> Even when English uses the simple past to talk about things that happened over a period of time, or to describe a state of affairs in the past, in French you still need to use the imperfect tense: **Quand j'habitais en Ecosse je faisais souvent du ski.** *When I lived in Scotland I often went skiing.*

- The imperfect can be used after **si** *if* to make suggestions:

  Si on allait au cinéma? *Shall we go to the cinema?*

  Si on faisait un barbecue? *How about having a barbecue?*

- The imperfect of **être en train de** (page 103) can be used to emphasise the continuous nature of an activity:

  J'étais en train d'écrire quand l'ordinateur est tombé en panne. *I was in the middle of writing when the computer crashed.*

- The imperfect tense used after **depuis** *for, since* translates the English *had been doing* or *had done for/since*:

  Nous avions envie d'aller aux Antilles depuis longtemps. *We had wanted/been wanting to go to the West Indies for a long time.*

- The imperfect of **venir de** + infinitive means *had just done*:

  Il venait de partir quand elle a téléphoné. *He had just left when she phoned.*

past historic

For regular verbs the past historic is formed by removing **-er**, **-ir** or **-re** from the infinitive and adding these endings:

	travailler *to work*	**finir** *to finish*	**vendre** *to sell*
je	travaill**ai**	fin**is**	vend**is**
tu	travaill**as**	fin**is**	vend**is**
il/elle	travaill**a**	fin**it**	vend**it**
nous	travaill**âmes**	fin**îmes**	vend**îmes**
vous	travaill**âtes**	fin**îtes**	vend**îtes**
ils/elles	travaill**èrent**	fin**irent**	vend**irent**

Those **-er** verbs whose stems end in **c** or **g** (page 136) add a cedilla or insert **e** after the **g** to maintain the soft sound of the infinitive:
il commença *he began*; **vous mangeâtes** *you ate*

There are many verbs with an unpredictable past historic, although it's the stem that's irregular rather than the endings. Here are some of the more common:
faire *to do* je fis, tu fis, il fit, nous fîmes, vous fîtes, ils firent
venir *to come* je vins, tu vins, il vint, nous vînmes, vous vîntes, ils vinrent
voir *to see* je vis, tu vis, il vit, nous vîmes, vous vîtes, ils virent
naître *to be born* je naquis, tu naquis, il naquit, nous naquîmes, vous naquîtes, ils naquirent

Several have **u** in the endings:
vivre *to live* je vécus, tu vécus, il vécut, nous vécûmes, vous vécûtes, ils vécurent
pouvoir *to be able* je pus, tu pus, il put, nous pûmes, vous pûtes, ils purent
être *to be* je fus, tu fus, il fut, nous fûmes, vous fûtes, ils furent
avoir *to have* j'eus, tu eus, il eut, nous eûmes, vous eûtes, ils eurent

... and when to use it

- The past historic is used primarily in formal written French, for example, in works of literature, formal reports, essays and newspaper articles.

  In informal writing, such as letters and emails, and in spoken French, the perfect tense is used instead.

- The past historic describes a completed event in the past, where English usually uses the simple past:

  La guerre commença en 1939 et elle dura six ans. *The war began in 1939 and (it) lasted six years.*

  Les autres s'en allèrent immédiatement. *The others went away immediately.*

  Nous fîmes un grand voyage en Amérique du Sud. *We took a long trip to South America.*

  Le prince demanda à la princesse de l'épouser. Ils se marièrent et vécurent heureux à tout jamais. *The prince asked the princess to marry him. They got married and lived happily ever after.*

Be careful of the word *was* in English. It's not always used for the imperfect, i.e. to talk about how things used to be in the past or events that carried on over a period of time (page 149). You also find it in sentences like these where the action is completed:

Il fut ambassadeur de France pendant dix ans. *He <u>was</u> the French ambassador for ten years.*

Charles de Gaulle naquit le vingt-deux novembre 1890 et mourut le neuf novembre 1970. *Charles de Gaulle <u>was</u> born on 22 November 1890 and died on 9 November 1970.*

checkpoint 16

1   When you come across a new verb, you have to know its infinitive before you can look it up in a dictionary. Decide whether each of the following is in the present, future, conditional, imperfect or past historic, and what person it is, then work out what the infinitive is.

E.g. aimera: future, il/elle → aimer

voudrais	finissait	viendrons
eurent	vais	enverra
pourrais	étaient	regarda
préfériez	dites	recevront
faisions	mourra	fut
devrais	tiennent	serons
pars	saurez	plaisait

The meanings of the infinitives are given with the answers (page 263) for you to work out the translation of the above words.

2   Replace the ending of these infinitives with the person and tense in brackets.

arriver (je, future)   choisir (il/elle imperfect)
demander (tu, conditional)   payer (nous, present)
vouloir (ils, imperfect)   comprendre (tu, future)
sortir (il, present)   nettoyer (je, future)
penser (il/elle, imperfect)   écrire (vous, conditional)
offrir (tu, present)   attendre (ils/elles, present)
commencer (je, imperfect)   continuer (ils/elles, future)

3   Pair these phrases to make four grammatically correct sentences.

A	B
Quand j'avais cinq ans	mais je n'ai pas de temps
Moi, je le ferais avec plaisir	nous pourrons aller au cinéma
Je vous téléphonerai	nous habitions à Besançon
Si tu es libre demain	quand elle arrivera

Verbs: compound tenses

Compound tenses are those which are made up of two parts:

- an auxiliary, i.e. support verb. Like English, French uses **avoir** *have* for the majority of verbs.
- the past participle of the main verb. Regular English past participles end in *-ed*: *lived, worked, believed,* while many others are irregular: *eaten, thought, begun.*

In French the four main compound tenses are:

- **perfect**, which uses the present tense of **avoir**:
  j'ai travaillé *I have worked, I worked*
- **pluperfect**, which uses the imperfect tense of **avoir**:
  j'avais travaillé *I had worked*
- **future perfect**, which uses the future tense of **avoir**:
  j'aurai travaillé *I will have worked*
- **conditional perfect**, which uses the present conditional of **avoir**:
  j'aurais travaillé *I would have worked*

The majority of verbs use **avoir** as the auxiliary verb, and there's a list of verbs that use **être** on page 159. The main difference between the two groups is that with verbs using **être** the past participle changes to agree with the subject of the verb.

As in English, past participles, despite their name, are also used in constructions which don't relate to the past – in passive constructions, for instance: *prizes are awarded, these pictures will be taken down.*

the past participle

In English, the past participle is the form of a verb that comes after *has/have* in the perfect tense: *worked, played, taken, been*.

To form past participles in French, you change the infinitive like this:

	infinitive	past participle
-er → -é	**travailler** *to work*	**travaillé** *worked*
-ir → -i	**finir** *to finish*	**fini** *finished*
-re → -u	**vendre** *to sell*	**vendu** *sold*

Not all verbs follow these patterns. Many have irregular past participles, just as English does: *lived, played, wanted, finished, decided* are regular past participles while *given, thought, spent, eaten* are irregular and have to be learnt individually. The irregular ones don't necessarily coincide in the two languages.

- The past participle of every **-er** verb ends in **-é**, even that of **aller** *to go*, which is irregular in other tenses: **allé** *been, gone*.

- A few **-re** verbs have a past participle ending in **-i**: **suivre** *to follow* → **suivi** *followed*; **rire** *to laugh* → **ri** *laughed*; **suffire** *to be enough* → **suffi** *been enough*.

- **-aindre**, **-eindre** and **-oindre** verbs have a past participle ending in **-t**: **peindre** *to paint* → **peint** *painted*; **craindre** *to fear* → **craint** *feared*; **joindre** *to attach* → **joint** *attached*.

- Many **-ir** verbs which aren't regular in the present tense still have past participles ending in **-i**: **dormir** *to sleep* → **dormi** *slept*; **sortir** *to go out* → **sorti** *gone out*; **partir** *to leave* → **parti** *left*; **servir** *to serve* → **servi** *served*; **cueillir** *to pick* → **cueilli** *picked*.

- Verbs in the **ouvrir** *to open* group (page 134) have a past participle ending in **-ert**: **découvrir** *to discover* → **découvert** *discovered*; **offrir** *to offer* → **offert** *offered*.

- Some **-ir** verbs that are irregular in the present and future tenses have a past participle ending **-u**: **venir** *to come* → **venu** *come*; **tenir** *to hold* → **tenu** *held*; **courir** *to run* → **couru** *run*.

- Many other verbs have an irregular past participle ending in **-u**:

lire *to read*	→	**lu** *read*
voir *to see*	→	**vu** *seen*
boire *to drink*	→	**bu** *drunk*
savoir *to know*	→	**su** *known*
pouvoir *to be able*	→	**pu** *been able*
vouloir *to want*	→	**voulu** *wanted*
croire *to believe*	→	**cru** *believed*
plaire *to please*	→	**plu** *pleased*
pleuvoir *to rain*	→	**plu** *rained*
falloir *to be necessary*	→	**fallu** *been necessary*
valoir *to be worth*	→	**valu** *been worth*
résoudre *to resolve*	→	**résolu** *resolved*
recevoir *to receive*	→	**reçu** *received*
décevoir *to disappoint*	→	**déçu** *disappointed*
vivre *to live*	→	**vécu** *lived*
connaître *to know*	→	**connu** *known*
paraître *to appear*	→	**paru** *appeared*

- The irregular past participles of some verbs are still recognisable because they're similar to the infinitive or present tense forms:

dire *to say*	→	**dit** *said*
faire *to do*	→	**fait** *made*
prendre *to take*	→	**pris** *taken*
conduire *to drive*	→	**conduit** *driven*
écrire *to write*	→	**écrit** *written*
cuire *to cook*	→	**cuit** *cooked*

- Others aren't as easily recognisable:

être *to be*	→	**été** *been*
avoir *to have*	→	**eu** *had*
devoir *to have to*	→	**dû** *had to*
mettre *to put*	→	**mis** *put*
mourir *to die*	→	**mort** *died*
naître *to be born*	→	**né** *been born*
(s')asseoir *to sit down*	→	**assis** *sat down*

use of the past participle

- The main use of the past participle is after **avoir** and **être** in compound tenses: perfect, pluperfect, future perfect, conditional perfect.
  Je vous ai téléphoné hier. *I called you yesterday.*
  J'avais déjà vendu la voiture. *I'd already sold the car.*
  Le train sera parti. *The train will have left.*
  J'aurais préféré l'autre. *I would have preferred the other one.*

- As in English, many past participles are used as adjectives, which means they must agree with their accompanying noun:
  un steak bien cuit *a well-cooked steak*
  fromage râpé *grated cheese*
  Quels sont vos passe-temps préférés? *What are your favourite (preferred) hobbies?*
  Les fenêtres sont fermées. *The windows are closed.*

- You can use a past participle after the infinitives **avoir** and **être** to mean *to have done something* (past or perfect infinitive):
  Enchanté(e) d'avoir fait votre connaissance. *I'm delighted to have met you.*

  You must use this form after **après** *after*:
  Après avoir préparé le repas, il s'est lavé les mains. *After having cooked (after cooking) the meal, he washed his hands.*
  Après s'être assise, elle a allumé son ordinateur. *After having sat down (after sitting down), she switched on her computer.*

- Past participles are also used with **être** to form the passive (see opposite).

 In both English and French there are past participles which have become nouns in their own right: **un fiancé**, **une mariée** *a bride*, **un mort** *a dead man*, **une plongée** *a dive*.

the passive

In both French and English, a past participle can be used with any tense of **être** *to be* to form the passive. This is when something is done ***to*** the subject, rather than ***by*** it: e.g. *the room was booked by Annie* rather than *Annie booked the room.*

- In French the past participle agrees with the subject:
  Le vin blanc est servi frais. *White wine is served chilled.*
  Cette fenêtre sera fermée. *This window will be closed.*
  Les prix ont été réduits de 10%. *The prices have been reduced by 10%.*
  Les fenêtres ont été fermées. *The windows have been closed.*

- The passive often includes **par** *by*:
  La chambre a été réservée par Annie. *The room was booked by Annie.*
  Le gâteau était fait par ma grand-mère. *The cake was made by my grandmother.*
  Le traité sera signé par le président demain. *The treaty will be signed by the president tomorrow.*

- The passive is used far less often in French than in English because French has other ways of expressing the English passive. The most common is to use **on** *one*, *they*, *we* (page 78):
  On m'a invité à la cérémonie. *I was invited to the ceremony.*
  lit. *They invited me to the ceremony.*
  On a réduit les prix de 10%. *The prices have been reduced by 10%.*
  lit. *They have reduced the prices by 10%.*
  On avait organisé un séminaire. *A seminar had been organised.*

- Some verbs can be made reflexive to translate English passive sentences:
  Le vin blanc se boit frais. *White wine is drunk chilled.*
  Comment ça s'écrit? *How is it spelt?* lit. *How does it write itself?*

the perfect tense: i) with avoir

The perfect tense of the majority of verbs is made up of the present tense of **avoir** *to have* plus the past participle of the main verb (pages 154-155).

travailler *to work*	j'	ai travaillé
	tu	as travaillé
	il/elle	a travaillé
	nous	avons travaillé
	vous	avez travaillé
	ils/elles	ont travaillé

finir *to finish*	j'	ai fini
	tu	as fini
	il/elle	a fini
	nous	avons fini
	vous	avez fini
	ils/elles	ont fini

vendre *to sell*	j'	ai vendu
	tu	as vendu
	il/elle	a vendu
	nous	avons vendu
	vous	avez vendu
	ils/elles	ont vendu

Most negative pairs, e.g. **ne … pas**, **ne … jamais**, **ne … rien**, usually go around the **avoir** part of the tense, together with any object pronouns:
Il n'a pas travaillé hier. *He didn't work yesterday.*
Le roman 'David Copperfield'? Je ne l'ai pas lu. *The novel 'David Copperfield'? I haven't read it.*

But **personne** *no-one* and **nulle part** *nowhere* go after the past participle:
Je n'ai vu personne. *I didn't see anyone./I haven't seen anyone.*
Nous ne l'avons trouvé nulle part. *We didn't find him anywhere.*

> Usually the past participle doesn't change its ending when used after **avoir**. For the only exception, see page 161.

ii) with être

A small group of verbs use **être** *to be* instead of **avoir** for the perfect tense. Most of them describe movement or a change of state:

aller *to go*	**entrer** *to enter*	**retourner** *to return*
venir *to come*	**sortir** *to go out*	**rentrer** *to return*
arriver *to arrive*	**monter** *to go up*	**tomber** *to fall*
partir *to leave*	**descendre** *to go down*	**rester** *to stay*
naître *to be born*	**mourir** *to die*	

- Verbs derived from the above verbs also take **être**: **devenir** *to become*, **revenir** *to come back*, **ressortir** *to go out again*.

- All reflexive verbs (page 116) take **être**, e.g. **se lever** *to get up*, **s'amuser** *to have a good time, enjoy oneself*.

- Their past participle is formed in exactly the same way as verbs that use **avoir**, but it has to agree with the subject:

	m	f
je	suis allé	suis allée
tu	es allé	es allée
il/elle	est allé	est allée
nous	sommes allés	sommes allées
vous	êtes allé(s)	êtes allée(s)
ils/elles	sont allés	sont allées

- In a mixed group, the past participle is masculine plural:
Luc et Madeleine sont arrivés.

- The use of **on** *we* is unusual in the perfect tense with **être** as it takes **est** but the past participle is in the plural: **on est arrivés.**

- The past participle of reflexive verbs also agrees with the subject in most circumstances (see page 161 for exceptions)

	m	f
je	me suis levé	me suis levée
tu	t'es levé	t'es levée
il/elle	s'est levé	s'est levée
nous	nous sommes levés	nous sommes levées
vous	vous êtes levé(s)	vous êtes levée(s)
ils/elles	se sont levés	se sont levées

when to use the perfect tense

- You use the French perfect tense for both the English simple past *I worked, I ate, I went* and the perfect *I have worked, I have eaten, I have gone*:
  J'ai acheté deux billets. *I (have) bought two tickets.*
  Il est allé en France. *He went to France./He's gone to France.*
  Nous nous sommes bien amusés. *We (have) had a good time.*

- You use the perfect tense in questions starting with *did* as well as *has/have*:
  Tu as acheté une nouvelle voiture? *Did you buy a new car?/Have you bought a new car?*
  Il est allé à Londres? *Did he go to London?/Has he gone to London?*

  It's also used when *did* is used in a negative:
  Elle n'est pas arrivée. *She didn't arrive./She hasn't arrived.*
  On n'est pas bien amusés. *We didn't have a good time./We haven't had a good time.*

- The perfect tense is used to describe completed actions or events which occurred once or several times in the past. If they happened regularly, or over a period of time, you use the imperfect (page 148).
  Compare: **J'ai rendu visite à ma mère deux fois l'année dernière.**
  I visited my mother twice last year.
  with: **Je rendais visite à ma mère tous les jours l'année dernière.**
  I visited my mother every day last year.

- You use the perfect tense in *negative* sentences containing **depuis** *for, since*:
  Je ne l'ai pas vu depuis longtemps. *I haven't seen him for a long time.*

  This is different from *positive* sentences with **depuis**, where you use the present tense (page 139):
  J'habite ici depuis longtemps. *I've been living here for a long time.*

object pronouns and the perfect tense

- Object pronouns go before **avoir** in the compound tenses.
  When **avoir** verbs are preceded by a direct object pronoun (**me**, **te**, **le**, **la**, **nous**, **vous**, **les**), the past participle agrees with the pronoun:
  Jacques, je t'ai vu hier. *Jacques, I saw you yesterday.*
  Madeleine? Je l'ai vue en ville. *Madeleine? I saw her in town.*
  Mes amis? Oui, je les ai vus. *My friends? Yes, I saw them.*
  Mes chaussures? Oui, je les ai trouvées. *My shoes? Yes, I've found them.*

- When the direct object is a noun, it usually comes after the verb, so there's no agreement. Occasionally a direct object noun comes before the verb and in that case the rule about preceding direct objects and past participle agreement applies:
  J'ai acheté les chaussures. *I bought the shoes.* (Shoes are the object and come after the verb, so there's no agreement.)
  Quelles chaussures avez-vous achetées? *Which shoes did you buy?* (Shoes are the object and they precede the verb, so there's agreement.)
  Voici les chaussures que j'ai achetées. *Here are the shoes I bought.*

- Occasionally an **être** verb takes a direct object. In these instances it forms the perfect tense with **avoir** and obeys all the rules of **avoir** verbs:
  Il a sorti la voiture du garage. Il l'a sortie du garage. *He took the car out of the garage. He took it out of the garage.*
  Il a monté les marches. Ils les a montées. *He went up the steps. He went up them.*

- When a reflexive verb has a direct object ***noun***, the past participle no longer changes to agree:
  Elle s'est lavée. *She got washed.*
  Elle s'est lavé les mains. *She washed her hands.*

But, if you want to say *she washed <u>them</u>* the past participle agrees with the direct object pronoun: **elle se les est lavées**, because the direct object pronoun precedes the verb.

checkpoint 17

1   What are the past participles of these verbs? 11 of them are regular and 13 irregular.

choisir; envoyer; faire; venir; regarder; être; connaître; entendre; entrer; partir; payer; avoir; attendre; naître; mettre; dire; penser; boire; mourir; descendre; pouvoir; pleuvoir; ouvrir; réussir

2   Fill the gaps to create the perfect tense.

a elle _____ dormi   b j' _____ fini

c nous _____ sortis   d tu t' _____ amusé

e on _____ téléphoné   f vous _____ arrivés

g ils _____ acheté   h elles _____ allées

3   Add an extra letter to the past participle if required.

a Je n'ai pas parlé_ avec Marie-France.

b Marie-France? Non, je ne l'ai pas vu_.

c Les enfants sont allé_ à l'école.

d Tu t'es bien amusé_, Céline?

e Ils se sont rencontré_ dans un café.

4   Choose the correct tense from the brackets.

a Je _____ de commencer quand elle est arrivée. (suis venu/venais)

b Vous _____ vos amis hier? (avez vu/voyiez)

c Et si on _____ un pique-nique? (a fait/faisait)

d L'année dernière on _____ à Biarritz. (est allés/allait)

e Elle _____ les yeux bleus. (a eu/avait)

f Il y _____ depuis deux ans quand il a rencontré sa femme. (a habité/habitait)

g La guerre _____ en 1914. (a commencé/commençait)

h Il _____ un journal quand elle est entrée. (a lu/lisait)

the pluperfect

The only difference between the formation of the pluperfect and the
tense is that the pluperfect uses the imperfect of **avoir** or **être** instead
present. The same verbs use **avoir** or **être**; the rules for agreement are th
same; pronouns and negative words go in the same place.

travailler	j'	avais travaillé	
to work	tu	avais travaillé	
	il/elle	avait travaillé	
	nous	avions travaillé	
	vous	aviez travaillé	
	ils/elles	avaient travaillé	

		m	f
aller	j'	étais allé	étais allée
to go	tu	étais allé	étais allée
	il/elle	était allé	était allée
	nous	étions allés	étions allées
	vous	étiez allé(s)	étiez allée(s)
	ils/elles	étaient allés	étaient allées

se lever	je	m'étais levé	m'étais levée
to get up	tu	t'étais levé	t'étais levée
	il/elle	s'était levé	s'était levée
	nous	nous étions levés	nous étions levées
	vous	vous étiez levé(s)	vous étiez levée(s)
	ils/elles	s'étaient levés	s'étaient levées

You use the pluperfect when in English you'd say *had done something*:
J'avais fini. *I had finished.*
Je lui ai téléphoné mais elle était déjà partie. *I phoned her but she had
already left.*
Margaux a dit qu'elle avait fini son travail. *Margaux said that she had
finished her work.*
Mes parents m'ont écrit qu'ils étaient allés au Louvre. *My parents wrote
to me that they had been to the Louvre.*

the future perfect

The future tense of **avoir** or **être** and a past participle give you the future perfect. The same rules for agreement and position of pronouns apply as for the other compound tenses.

travailler	j'	aurai travaillé	
to work	tu	auras travaillé	
	il/elle	aura travaillé	
	nous	aurons travaillé	
	vous	aurez travaillé	
	ils/elles	auront travaillé	

		m	f
aller	je	serai allé	serai allée
to go	tu	seras allé	seras allée
	il/elle	sera allé	sera allée
	nous	serons allés	serons allées
	vous	serez allé(s)	serez allée(s)
	ils/elles	seront allés	seront allées

se lever	je	me serai levé	me serai levée
to get up	tu	te seras levé	te seras levée
	il/elle	se sera levé	se sera levée
	nous	nous serons levés	nous serons levées
	vous	vous serez levé(s)	vous serez levée(s)
	ils/elles	se seront levés	se seront levées

You use the future perfect when in English you'd say *will have done something*:
J'aurai fini mon travail avant cinq heures. *I will have finished my work by five o'clock.*
Demain à cette heure il sera arrivé en Australie. *By this time tomorrow he will have arrived in Australia.*

You also use it after **quand**, **lorsque** *when*, **aussitôt que**, **dès que** *as soon as*, **pendant que**, **tant que** *while* and **une fois que** *once*, where the main verb is in the future tense in French, and where English would use the perfect tense:
Tu pourras regarder la télé quand tu auras fait la vaisselle. *You can (will be able to) watch TV when you've washed the dishes.*
Aussitôt que j'aurai écrit mon mémoire, j'irai en vacances. *As soon as I've written my dissertation I'll go on holiday.*

the conditional perfect

The conditional tense of **avoir** or **être** and a past participle give you the conditional perfect. The same rules for agreement and position of pronouns apply as for the other compound tenses.

travailler	j'	aurais travaillé	
to work	tu	aurais travaillé	
	il/elle	aurait travaillé	
	nous	aurions travaillé	
	vous	auriez travaillé	
	ils/elles	auraient travaillé	

		m	f
aller	je	serais allé	serais allée
to go	tu	serais allé	serais allée
	il/elle	serait allé	serait allée
	nous	serions allés	serions allées
	vous	seriez allé(s)	seriez allée(s)
	ils/elles	seraient allés	seraient allées

		m	f
se lever	je	me serais levé	me serais levée
to get up	tu	te serais levé	te serais levée
	il/elle	se serait levé	se serait levée
	nous	nous serions levés	nous serions levées
	vous	vous seriez levé(s)	vous seriez levée(s)
	ils/elles	se seraient levés	se seraient levées

You use the conditional perfect when in English you'd say *would*, *should* or *could have done something*:

J'aurais payé. *I would have paid.*
J'aurais dû leur dire. *I should have told them.*
J'aurais bien aimé faire ça. *I would have liked to do that.*
Vous auriez pu me conduire. *You could have given me a lift.*
Je serais allé si je ne m'étais pas levé tard. *I would have gone if I hadn't got up late.*
Si j'avais su que tu venais, j'aurais invité Charles. *If I had known that you were coming I would have invited Charles.*

checkpoint 18

1   Change these sentences from the present to the tense
    indicated.

    a **Il comprend.** .... pluperfect

    b **Je finis mon travail.** .... future perfect

    c **Nous y allons.** .... conditional perfect

    d **Qu'est-ce qu'elle fait?** .... pluperfect

    e **Ils se promènent dans le parc.** .... conditional perfect

    f **Tu commences avant cinq heures?** .... future perfect

    g **Je dois parler avec lui.** .... conditional perfect

    h **Si vous savez.** .... pluperfect

2   Choose a noun from list A and match it with a phrase from
    list B to form a passive sentence.

    A   B

    La maison   avait été emmené chez le vétérinaire

    Les vedettes   sera vendue

    Le chien   ont été renovés

    Mes cousins   ont été invités

    Les bâtiments anciens   étaient habillées par Jean Paul
       Gaultier

3   Which of these verbs has a past participle that does not end
    in -u? boire, plaire, croire, recevoir, cuire, tenir, entendre

4   Rewrite these sentences beginning après followed by a past or
    perfect infinitive.
    Example: Il a servi le client, puis il a fermé la bouteille →
    Après avoir servi le client, il a fermé la bouteille.

    a **Elle est sortie de la voiture, puis elle a vu son amie.**

    b **Elle a vu son amie, puis elle a traversé la rue.**

    c **Il s'est levé, puis il a bu une tasse de café.**

    d **Il a bu son café, puis il est sorti.**

    e **Ils sont arrivés à l'aéroport, puis ils ont changé de l'argent.**

Present participle, imperative, subjunctive

French verb endings not only provide information about tense, i.e. whether things are happening in the past, present or future, they indicate other functions of the verb too.

These functions include:

- **participles**: the past participle, which is used in compound tenses (pages 154-156), and the present participle, ending in **-ant**, which is the equivalent of the -ing ending in English – although in French it's used much less and not always in the same way.

- the **imperative**, which is used to tell somebody what to do. In English there's only one version but there are two in French because of the two different words for you: **tu** and **vous**.

  There's also a **nous** imperative, used to say Let's … This is usually identical to the present tense.

- the **subjunctive**, which is no longer used much in English but is used regularly in certain circumstances in French. A verb in the subjunctive doesn't convey hard fact but is usually the second verb of a sentence, following another verb expressing someone's attitude or opinion, doubt or uncertainty.

  The sort of phrase that triggers a subjunctive includes words like wish, doubt, fear, suggest, permit, forbid, deny, possible and probable, followed by **que** that. And some prepositions are always followed by the subjunctive.

the present participle

The present participle ends in *-ing* in English and **-ant** in French. It is formed by taking the **nous** form of the present tense, e.g. **nous travaillons, nous finissons, nous faisons**, and replacing **-ons** with **-ant**: **travaillant, finissant, faisant**.

There are only three exceptions:
être → **étant** *being*　　　**savoir** → **sachant** *knowing*
avoir → **ayant** *having*

- Many present participles have become adjectives, in which case they agree with the subject:
  une ville charmante *a charming town*
  une question étonnante *an astonishing question*
  des tables pliantes *folding tables*

- Some present participles have become nouns:
  un représentant *representative* lit. *one representing*
  un participant lit. *one participating*

- The present participle can also be used as a verb, describing something the subject of the main verb is doing. When used in this way it never changes – it doesn't agree with the subject:
  Tous les trains venant de Lille ont quelques minutes de retard.
  All trains coming from Lille are running a few minutes late.

- The name 'present participle' is something of a misnomer, as the present participle doesn't only appear in present tense sentences:
  Ayant soif, elle a acheté une bouteille d'eau. *Being thirsty, she bought a bottle of water.*
  Ayant faim, je vais acheter un sandwich. *As I'm* (lit. *being*) *hungry, I'm going to buy a sandwich.*
  Relisant ton mémoire tu trouveras sans doute des fautes de frappe.
  When you re-read (lit. *re-reading*) *your dissertation you'll no doubt find typos.*

- Ne ... pas etc. go round it, and object pronouns come before it:
  Ne le voyant pas, je n'ai pas dit 'Bonjour'. *As I didn't see him* (lit. *not seeing him*), *I didn't say 'Hello'.*

Very often the present participle is used after **en**, when it becomes known as the **gerund**: **en travaillant, en finissant, en vendant**.

- The gerund is used to talk about two actions happening at the same time, when both verbs have the same subject. The English translation often includes *while/when* or *on ... -ing*:
  En faisant la vaisselle, elle a perdu sa bague. *She lost her ring while doing the washing-up.*
  En sortant de la maison, j'ai vu Claudine. *On coming out of the house I saw Claudine.*

- It's also used to describe the manner in which something is done or how something happened:
  Il est sorti de la maison en courant. *He came running out of the house.*
  J'ai perdu cinq kilos en faisant beaucoup d'exercice. *I lost five kilos by doing lots of exercise.*
  Elle s'est cassé la jambe en tombant d'un cheval. *She broke her leg falling off a horse.*

The suffix *-ing* is very common in English, but it's usually ***not*** the equivalent of the French present participle or gerund.

- It's often part of a continuous tense: *I am working, she was doing*, which are translated in French by the present or imperfect tenses: **je travaille, elle faisait**.

- It comes after another verb: *We like dancing, I prefer swimming*. French uses the infinitive here: **On aime danser, Je préfère nager**.

- It comes after prepositions: *before leaving, without paying, instead of going home*. French uses the infinitive here too: **avant de partir, sans payer, au lieu de rentrer**.

- English words ending in *-ing* are often nouns: *Smoking and drinking are bad for your health*. French prefers to use a different kind of noun: **Le tabac et l'alcool sont mauvais pour la santé** or an infinitive: **Fumer et boire, c'est mauvais pour la santé**.

the imperative

The imperative is used to give instructions: *turn left, come in, don't worry*, and make suggestions: *let's go, let's not worry*. There are three forms: **tu**, **vous** and **nous**.

	travailler *to work*	finir *to finish*	vendre *to sell*
tu	travaille	finis	vends
vous	travaillez	finissez	vendez
nous	travaillons	finissons	vendons

- Regular imperatives are identical to the present tense, except for the **tu** form of -er verbs, which drops the **-s**:
  tu travailles *you work, you're working*; **Travaille!** *Work!*
  tu manges *you eat, you're eating*; **Mange!** *Eat!*
  The **-s** returns when the verb is followed by **y** or **en**:
  Manges-en! *Eat some!*

- Verbs like **ouvrir** *to open*, which use regular -er endings in the present tense (page 134), behave in the same way:
  tu ouvres *you open*; **Ouvre la porte!** *Open the door!*

- **Aller** *to go* is irregular only in the **tu** form, and it loses and regains the -s in the same way as other verbs:
  Va chez le dentiste! *Go to the dentist!*
  Vas-y! *Go (on)!*

- **Être**, **avoir** and **savoir** have the following irregular imperatives (**tu, vous, nous**):
  être *to be*: **sois, soyez, soyons**
  avoir *to have*: **aie, ayez, ayons**
  savoir *to know*: **sache, sachez, sachons**
  Soyez sages, mes enfants! *Be good, children!*
  Ayez la bonté d'attendre. *Be so kind as to wait.* lit. *Have the goodness to wait.*
  Sache que je t'aime. *Know that I love you.*

... and how to use it

You use the imperative to tell someone what to do, to give advice and to make suggestions:

Tournez à gauche. *Turn left.*
Entre. *Come in.*
Allons-y. *Let's go.*

To make imperatives negative, you put **ne ... pas** or **ne** and another negative round the verb:

Ne parlez pas! *Don't speak!*
Ne dites rien! *Don't say anything!*
N'aie jamais peur! *Never be afraid!*

Object pronouns come after the imperative in positive sentences and follow the usual order (page 84). **Me** changes to **moi** when it's the only pronoun or when it appears with **le, la, les** or **y**. In these instances **moi** comes at the end of the sequence:

Aide-moi! *Help me!*
Donne-moi les chocolats! Donne-les-moi! *Give me the chocolates! Give them to me!*
Emmènes-y-moi! *Take me there!*

Reflexive pronouns also come after the imperative and are joined to it by a hyphen. **Te** changes to **toi:**

Assieds-toi! *Sit down!*
Levez-vous! *Stand up!*
S'en aller is an exception:
Va-t-en!/Allez-vous-en! *Go away!*

Object and reflexive pronouns come before the verb in negative imperatives. They follow the usual order (page 84):

Ne m'en donnez pas! *Don't give me any!*
Ne le lui envoie pas! *Don't send it to him!*
Ne vous inquiétez pas! *Don't worry!*
Ne t'assieds jamais! *Never sit down!*

Although there's a spelling difference in the **tu** imperative, it makes no difference when you're talking – all regular imperatives sound exactly the same as the present tense.

alternatives to the imperative

- To tone down a command, you can use **pouvoir** *to be able to* in the present tense or the conditional:
  Tu peux me dire ...? *Can you tell me ...?*
  Pourriez-vous me traduire cette phrase? *Could you translate this sentence for me?*

- You can also use **il faut** *it is necessary* or **devoir** *to have to*:
  Il faut partir maintenant. *You must leave now.*
  Vous devez vous reposer. *You have to rest.*
  Tu devrais lui téléphoner. *You ought to phone him/her.*
  Vous devriez répondre avant vendredi. *You should reply by Friday.*

- The infinitive is often used in written instructions, such as signs or recipes:
  Mettre votre ceinture de sécurité. *Wear your seatbelt.*
  Ne pas stationner. *No parking.*
  Ajouter la farine et mélanger. *Add the flour and mix in.*

- In formal French **veuillez** is used. It's a very polite way of asking someone to do something, and it's followed by another verb in the infinitive. It's the only imperative form of **vouloir** and is regularly used in both spoken and written French:
  Veuillez patienter. *Please wait.*
  Veuillez nous excuser. *Do please excuse us.*
  Veuillez répondre aussitôt que possible. *Please reply as soon as possible.*
  Veuillez agréer, Monsieur/Madame, l'expression de mes sentiments distingués. This is the standard ending for a formal letter, the equivalent of *Yours faithfully.*

- The **nous** form of the imperative is not that common, except in the phrase **Allons-y** *Let's go*. Other ways of saying *let's* are **si on** + imperfect and **pourquoi ne pas** + infinitive:
  Si on faisait un pique-nique? *Let's have a picnic./What about having a picnic?*
  Pourquoi ne pas faire un pique-nique? *Let's have a picnic./Why not have a picnic?*

checkpoint 19

1   Identify the imperatives in this set of directions:

"Alors, ne prenez pas la première rue à gauche, mais continuez tout droit jusqu'aux feux. Tournez à gauche, traversez la place, puis prenez la deuxième rue à droite. Ne vous inquiétez pas – ce n'est pas loin".

2   If you followed the directions on this map, would you end up at A, B, C or D?

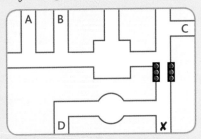

3   Is the person giving the directions using **tu** or **vous**? How would he/she give them using the other one?

4   Make grammatically correct sentences out of the jumbled-up words, adding hyphens if needed:
   a   en pas ne donne lui
   b   lève ne pas te
   c   envoyez leur les

5   Replace the underlined phrases with a present participle:
   a   Les étudiants <u>qui viennent</u> des Etats-Unis doivent remplir ce formulaire.
   b   <u>Puisqu'elle avait</u> faim, elle a mangé tous les sandwichs.
   c   Une fille, <u>qui lisait</u> un livre, était assise dans le coin.
   Replace the underlined words with a gerund (en + present participle):
   d   <u>Quand on a vu</u> la neige, on a décidé de jouer dans le jardin.
   e   <u>Quand je suis sorti</u> du bâtiment, j'ai vu les policiers.
   f   Elle lisait, <u>pendant qu'elle mangeait</u>.

the subjunctive: present tense

There are four tenses of the subjunctive: present, imperfect, perfect and pluperfect. In practice, only the present and perfect subjunctive are used in modern-day French. The others are very rarely found outside literature from previous centuries.

To form the **present subjunctive** of regular -er, -ir and -re verbs, take the ils/elles form of the present indicative (page 134) – **travaillent, finissent, vendent** – remove the -ent and add these endings:

	travailler *to work*	**finir** *to finish*	**vendre** *to sell*
je	travaille	finisse	vende
tu	travailles	finisses	vendes
il/elle	travaille	finisse	vende
nous	travaillions	finissions	vendions
vous	travailliez	finissiez	vendiez
ils/elles	travaillent	finissent	vendent

- The endings are the same for all three groups.
- The subjunctive of regular -er verbs in the je, tu, il/elle and ils/elles forms is the same as the indicative.
- The subjunctive of the ils/elles forms of -ir and -re verbs is the same as the indicative.
- The subjunctive of all nous and vous forms is the same as the imperfect indicative.

Many verbs have some irregularities in the present subjunctive (pages 176–177). Être *to be* and avoir *to have* are completely irregular.

	être	**avoir**
je	sois	aie
tu	sois	aies
il/elle	soit	ait
nous	soyons	ayons
vous	soyez	ayez
ils/elles	soient	aient

... and past tenses

The **perfect subjunctive** is the present subjunctive of **avoir** (page 174) or **être** (page 174) followed by the past participle.

	travailler *to work*	aller *to go*
je/j'	aie travaillé	sois allé(e)
tu	aies travaillé	sois allé(e)
il/elle	ait travaillé	soit allé(e)
nous	ayons travaillé	soyons allé(e)s
vous	ayez travaillé	soyez allé(e)(s)
ils/elles	aient travaillé	soient allé(e)s

To form the **imperfect subjunctive**, take the stem of the past historic (page 150) and add these endings:

	travailler *to work*	finir *to finish*	vendre *to sell*
je	travaill**asse**	fin**isse**	vend**isse**
tu	travaill**asses**	fin**isses**	vend**isses**
il/elle	travaill**ât**	fin**ît**	vend**ît**
nous	travaill**assions**	fin**issions**	vend**issions**
vous	travaill**assiez**	fin**issiez**	vend**issiez**
ils/elles	travaill**assent**	fin**issent**	vend**issent**

If there's a **u** in the past historic endings, that **u** remains in the imperfect subjunctive: être: **je fusse**; avoir: **j'eusse**; devoir: **je dusse**.

The **pluperfect subjunctive** is the imperfect subjunctive of **avoir** or **être** followed by the past participle:

je/j'	eusse travaillé	fusse allé(e)
tu	eusses travaillé	fusses allé(e)
il/elle	eût travaillé	fût allé(e)
nous	eussions travaillé	fussions allé(e)s
vous	eussiez travaillé	fussiez allé(e)(s)
ils/elles	eussent travaillé	fussent allé(e)s

irregular subjunctives

Many verbs that are irregular in some other tenses form their present subjunctive in the same way as regular verbs, i.e. their stem is based on the **ils/elles** form of the present indicative:

conduire	*to drive*	je conduise, tu conduises, il/elle conduise, nous conduisions, vous conduisiez, ils/elles conduisent
connaître	*to know*	je connaisse, tu connaisses, il/elle connaisse, nous connaissions, vous connaissiez, ils/elles connaissent
dire	*to say*	je dise, tu dises, il/elle dise, nous disions, vous disiez, ils/elles disent
écrire	*to write*	j'écrive, tu écrives, il/elle écrive, nous écrivions, vous écriviez, ils/elles écrivent
mettre	*to put*	je mette, tu mettes, il/elle mette, nous mettions, vous mettiez, ils/elles mettent
ouvrir	*to open*	j'ouvre, tu ouvres, il ouvre, nous ouvrions, vous ouvriez, ils/elles ouvrent
partir	*to leave*	je parte, tu partes, il/elle parte, nous partions, vous partiez, ils/elles partent

The verbs listed on page 137, which double up the final consonant of the stem or add a grave accent to the **e** in the je, tu, il/elle and ils/elles forms of the present indicative, or change **y** to **i**, do so in the present subjunctive too:

acheter	*to buy*	j'achète, tu achètes, il/elle achète, nous achetions, vous achetiez, ils/elles achètent
appeler	*to call*	j'appelle, tu appelles, il/elle appelle, nous appelions, vous appeliez, ils/elles appellent
employer	*to use*	j'emploie, tu emploies, il/elle emploie, nous employions, vous employiez, ils/elles emploient

Many other irregular verbs form their present subjunctive in the regular way for the **je**, **tu**, **il/elle** and **ils/elles** forms, but their **nous** and **vous** forms have a different stem, which is identical to their present indicative stem:

boire	*to drink*	**je boive, tu boives, il/elle boive, nous buvions, vous buviez, ils/elles boivent**
croire	*to believe*	**je croie, tu croies, il/elle croie, nous croyions, vous croyiez, ils/elles croient**
devoir	*to have to*	**je doive, tu doives, il/elle doive, nous devions, vous deviez, ils/elles doivent**
prendre	*to take*	**je prenne, tu prennes, il/elle prenne, nous prenions, vous preniez, ils/elles prennent**
recevoir	*to receive*	**je reçoive, tu reçoives, il/elle reçoive, nous recevions, vous receviez, ils/elles reçoivent**
venir	*to come*	**je vienne, tu viennes, il/elle vienne, nous venions, vous veniez, ils/elles viennent**
voir	*to see*	**je voie, tu voies, il/elle voie, nous voyions, vous voyiez, ils/elles voient**

Similarly, some irregular verbs have different stems in the **nous** and **vous** forms:

aller	*to go*	**j'aille, tu ailles, il/elle aille, nous allions, vous alliez, ils/elles aillent**
vouloir	*to want*	**je veuille, tu veuilles, il/elle veuille, nous voulions, vous vouliez, ils/elles veuillent**

Other verbs which have an irregular subjunctive keep the same stem throughout:

faire	*to do*	**je fasse, tu fasses, il/elle fasse, nous fassions, vous fassiez, ils/elles fassent**
pouvoir	*to be able*	**je puisse, tu puisses, il/elle puisse, nous puissions, vous puissiez, ils/elles puissent**
savoir	*to know*	**je sache, tu saches, il/elle sache, nous sachions, vous sachiez, ils/elles sachent**

when to use the subjunctive: 1

In English, the subjunctive is no longer widely used, and appears most often in expressions like these: *if only it were true; be that as it may; until death do us part; perish the thought.*

In French, it's needed whenever opinions and attitudes are involved, when you're talking about things that aren't actually fact.

The subjunctive is generally the second verb in a sentence, introduced by **que**, and it's only needed when the subjects of the two verbs are different – if they're the same, the second verb is in the infinitive (page 114).

The types of verbs that are followed by **que** and the subjunctive are verbs which express:

- wanting and liking:
  Je voudrais qu'il vienne. *I'd like him to come.*
  Je préfère que tu y ailles seul. *I'd prefer you to go (there) alone.*
  Tu souhaites que je sois différent? *Do you wish I were different?*

- suggesting, requiring and expecting:
  Je propose que nous fassions un barbecue chez moi. *I suggest that we have a barbecue at my place.*
  Je demande que tu reviennes de bonne heure. *I'm asking you to come back early.*
  J'attends qu'il vienne. *I expect him to come./I expect he'll come.*
  But **espérer** *to hope* is **not** followed by the subjunctive:
  J'espère qu'il viendra. *I hope he will come.*

- ordering, permission and forbidding:
  Il a ordonné que vous fassiez attention. *He's ordered you to pay attention.*
  La loi interdit qu'on boive de l'alcool dans le métro. *The law forbids you to drink alcohol on the Underground.*
  Il permet qu'elle y aille. *He allows her to go there.*

- emotions, e.g. joy, anger, sadness, sorrow, disappointment:
  Je suis désolé que tu ne puisses pas venir. *I'm sorry that you can't come.*
  Je suis content que tu sois content. *I'm happy that you're happy.*

- doubt, denial and possibility:
  Je doute qu'elle soit coupable. *I doubt that she's guilty.*
  Le chef nie qu'il y ait un problème. *The boss denies there's a problem.*
  Il est possible qu'il l'ait fait. *It's possible that he did it.*

- fear: **ne** is sometimes added before the second verb, even if the meaning is not negative:
  J'ai peur qu'il (ne) soit arrêté. *I'm afraid he'll be arrested.*
  Je crains que le chien (ne) me morde. *I'm afraid the dog will bite me.*
  If **pas** were added to the above sentences they would mean *I'm afraid he <u>won't</u> be arrested* and *that the dog <u>won't</u> bite*.

- mental reaction or value judgement:
  Quel scandale qu'on ait gaspillé l'argent. *What a scandal that the money has been squandered.*
  Il est incroyable qu'elle ait raté l'examen. *It's unbelievable that she failed the exam.*

- thinking or believing in the negative only:
  Je ne pense pas que vous arriviez à l'heure. *I don't think you'll arrive on time.*
  But **Je pense que vous arriverez à l'heure** *I think you will arrive on time.*
  Je ne crois pas que les Anglais soient polis. *I don't believe that the English are polite.*
  But **Je crois que les Anglais sont polis.** *I believe the English are polite.*

- impersonal expressions such as **il est** or **il semble/paraît + nécessaire, essentiel, important, normal, possible, dommage** *a pity*, **urgent, utile** *useful*, and **il est temps** *it's time* and **il vaut mieux** *it's better*:
  Il est urgent que nous sachions tous les détails. *It's urgent that we know all the details.*
  Il est temps qu'il me dise la verité. *It's time he told me the truth.*

  Il faut *it's necessary* can be followed by an infinitive or a subjunctive:
  il (me) faut partir or **il faut que je parte** *I must leave.*

when to use the subjunctive: 2

- Several conjunctions have to be followed by the subjunctive. The most widely used are **bien que, quoique** *although*, **jusqu'à ce que** *until*, **en attendant que** *while*, **afin que, pour que** *so that*, **à condition que** *provided that*, **sans que** *without*:

  Téléphone-moi afin que je sache où tu es. *Phone me so that I know where you are.*

  C'est un bon film bien qu'il soit très long. *It's a good film although it's very long.*

  Vous ne pouvez pas sortir jusqu'à ce que vous finissiez votre travail. *You can't go until you finish your work.*

  Je veux sortir sans que le chef me voie. *I want to leave without the boss seeing me.*

- A few conjunctions can also take an (optional) **ne** which doesn't have a negative meaning: **avant que** *before*, **à moins que** *unless*, **de peur que, de crainte que** *for fear that*:

  avant qu'il (ne) soit trop tard *before it's too late*

  Je ne viendrai pas à moins qu'il (ne) m'invite. *I won't come unless he invites me.*

  J'ai peur qu'ils (ne) me voient ici. *I'm afraid they'll see me here.*

The subjunctive is also used:

- in clauses beginning with **qui** or **que** after a superlative or **premier** *first*, **dernier** *last*, **seul** *only*:

  C'est la seule chose qu'il comprenne. *It's the only thing he understands.*

  C'est l'homme le plus intéressant que je connaisse. *He's the most interesting man I know.*

  C'est la plus belle ville que j'aie jamais vue. *It's the most beautiful town I've ever seen.*

- after **ne ... personne** *nobody*, as well as **rien qui** *nothing who/which* and **quelqu'un qui** *someone who* in questions only:

  Je ne connais personne qui puisse le faire. *I don't know anyone who can do it.*

  Y a-t-il quelqu'un qui sache la réponse? *Is there anyone who knows the answer?*

- after the indefinite expressions **quoi que, quel que** *whatever*, **qui que** *whoever*, **où que** *wherever*:
  quoi que vous veuillez savoir *whatever you want to know*
  qui que vous soyez *whoever you may be*
  quelles que soient les difficultés *whatever the difficulties may be*
  où que vous alliez *wherever you go*

  But not with **chaque fois que** *whenever*:
  chaque fois que je vais en ville *whenever I go to town*

- in a few familiar phrases:
  Vive la France! *Long live France!*
  Que Dieu te bénisse! *(May) God bless you!*
  Qu'ils mangent de la brioche! *Let them eat cake!*
  advienne que pourra *come what may*
  ainsi soit-il *so be it*

---

present or perfect subjunctive?

The present subjunctive is used for actions that take place at the same time as, or later than, the action of the verb in the first part of the sentence:
Je veux que tu partes maintenant/à deux heures. *I want you to leave now/at two o'clock.*
Je ne pense pas qu'il vienne. *I don't think he's coming/he will come.*
Je ne pensais pas qu'il vienne. *I didn't think he would come.*

The perfect subjunctive is used for actions that have taken place earlier than the action of the verb in the first part of the sentence:
Je ne pense pas qu'il soit arrivé. *I don't think he's arrived.*
Je suis content que vous soyez venu. *I'm pleased (that) you came.*
J'étais content que vous soyez venu. *I was pleased you came.*

checkpoint 20

1   Write the present subjunctive of the following:

    a il .... (partir)   b nous .... (être)

    c je .... (choisir)   d vous .... (venir)

    e elles .... (boire)   f tu .... (dire)

    g nous .... (prendre)   h on .... (vouloir)

    i j' .... (aller)   j vous .... (pouvoir)

    k elle .... (amener)   l il .... (avoir)

2   Which of these is **not** followed by the subjunctive?

    a avant que, après que, afin que, à moins que

    b proposer que, permettre que, espérer que, préférer que, souhaiter que

3   Write the correct verb in the gaps, choosing the correct form of one of être, faire, venir, vouloir or avoir.

    a Je voudrais que tu .... me voir.

    b Je suis désolé que tu n' .... pas trouvé ta montre.

    c Je ne pense pas qu'il .... coupable.

    d Je ne connais personne qui .... le faire.

    e C'est essentiel qu'elle .... ses devoirs.

4   Make the first verb in these sentences negative, which means that the following verb must be in the subjunctive.
    Example: Je pense qu'elle est arrivée → Je ne pense pas qu'elle soit arrivée.

    a Je pense qu'il a fini.

    b Je crois qu'elle sait la réponse.

    c Je pense que tu es trop timide.

5   Convert these commands into a sentence beginning Je veux que ...
    Example: Viens ici ! → Je veux que tu viennes ici.

    a Finis maintenant!

    b Faites attention!

    c Allons-y!

    d Ecoutez-moi!

    e Dis la vérité!

Key verbs

In French, as in most languages, some verbs are used more frequently than others. These include verbs like **aimer** *to like*, **aller** *to go*, **donner** *to give*, **dire** *to say*, **manger** *to eat* and **penser** *to think*, which relate to basic human activity.

Some verbs are used very frequently because their grammatical uses extend beyond their fundamental meaning:

- **Devoir** *to have to*, **pouvoir** *to be able to* and **vouloir** *to want to,* known as modal verbs, are used with the infinitive of a second verb.
- **Être** *to be* and **avoir** *to have* are used with a past participle to form past tenses (pages 158–159).
- **Avoir** also features in many expressions that don't use the word *have* in English.
- **Faire** *to do/make* is used in a whole range of situations when it's not translated as *do* or *make*.

These are all irregular and written out in full in the verb tables.

Some common French verbs don't have a direct equivalent in English. Both **savoir** and **connaître** translate *to know*, but they're not at all interchangeable. **Savoir** means to know information and facts, and to know how to do something, whereas you use **connaître** when you're talking about knowing or being acquainted with a person or a place.

modal verbs

Devoir *to have to*, **pouvoir** *to be able to* and **vouloir** *to want to,* are known as modal verbs. They don't impart much information on their own, so they're always followed by another verb (or sometimes a noun). All three verbs are irregular (pages 217, 238, 253) and they all behave in a similar way when followed by another verb.

- Verbs which follow a modal verb are always in the infinitive:
  Tu dois changer à Lille. *You have to change at Lille.*
  Vous pouvez choisir. *You can choose.*
  Je veux aller au théâtre. *I want to go to the theatre.*
  Je peux sortir? Puis-je sortir? *Can I go out?*
  Elle n'a pas pu venir. *She couldn't come.*

- Reflexive verbs change their reflexive pronoun to agree:
  Je voudrais me reposer. *I'd like to rest.*
  Tu dois te lever tôt demain. *You must get up early tomorrow.*
  Nous devons nous dépêcher. *We have to hurry.*

- When there are object pronouns, they go in front of the infinitive:
  Je veux y aller. *I want to go there.*
  Vous pouvez m'aider? *Can you help me?*
  Je voudrais lui en donner. *I'd like to give him some.*

- The modal verbs form their perfect tense and other compound tenses with **avoir**:
  Je n'ai pas pu résister. *I couldn't resist.*
  Je n'ai pas voulu assister au séminaire. *I didn't want to attend the seminar.*
  Tu aurais dû me le dire. *You should have told me.*

devoir

Devoir has a non-modal meaning; it can mean *to owe*:
Je vous dois combien? *How much do I owe you?*
Vous me devez cinquante euros. *You owe me 50 euros.*
This meaning is entirely separate from its use as a modal verb, when it has the following range of English translations:

- *have to, must, should, am/is/are supposed to* – present tense:
  Je dois rentrer. *I have to go back home.*
  Elle doit être chez son copain. *She must be at her friend's house.*
  Elle doit arriver ce soir. *She's supposed to be arriving this evening./She should arrive this evening.*
  Tu dois partir à quelle heure? *What time do you have to leave?*

- *had to, was/were supposed to* – perfect and imperfect; *must have* – perfect:
  J'ai dû louper l'émission. *I had to miss the programme.*
  Il a dû partir très tôt. *He had to leave very early.*
  J'ai dû le voir. *I must have seen him.*
  Je devais y aller avec eux. *I was supposed to go there with them.*
  Je devais rester à la maison toute la semaine. *I had to stay at home all week.*
  Si on devait choisir un mot ... *If you had to choose one word...*

- *ought to, should* – conditional:
  Vous devriez partir maintenant. *You should leave now.*
  Tu devrais lui téléphoner. *You ought to phone her.*
  Elle ne devrait pas avoir peur. *She shouldn't be afraid.*

- *should have, ought to have* – conditional perfect:
  J'aurais dû vous prévenir. *I ought to have warned you.*
  Vous n'auriez pas dû le faire. *You shouldn't have done it.*

Devoir and **il faut** both mean *to have to*. **Devoir** implies a sense of obligation, while **falloir** is stronger and implies necessity:
Il faut y aller./Il faut que tu y ailles. *You must go there./You need to go there.*
Il ne faut pas en parler. *You/We mustn't speak about it.*
Il a fallu partir de bonne heure. *We had to leave early.*

pouvoir

Pouvoir *to be able to* is a modal verb with a range of English translations:

- *can, may, might* – present tense:
  Tu peux m'aider? *Can you help me?*
  On ne peut pas venir aujourd'hui. *We can't come today.*
  Il peut être absent. *He may/might be absent.*
  Je peux payer par carte de crédit? *Can I pay by credit card?*
  Je peux sortir? *May I go out?*

- *could* – imperfect, perfect, conditional and subjunctive:
  Je pouvais les aider. *I could help them (was able to help).*
  J'ai pu parler avec lui. *I could speak/managed to speak to him.*
  Je pourrais venir demain. *I could come tomorrow.*
  Je pourrais t'aider si tu veux. *I could help you if you wish.*
  Vous pourriez me dire ...? *Could you tell me ...?*

- *could have, might have* – conditional perfect:
  J'aurais pu t'aider. *I could have helped you.*
  Nous aurions pu venir hier. *We could have come yesterday.*
  Tu aurais pu te faire mal. *You might have hurt yourself.*

- **Il se peut** means *it is possible*. It's followed by the subjunctive:
  Il se peut qu'elle vienne. *(It's possible) she might come.*

- If *can/could* has the meaning of knowing how to do something, you use **savoir** *to know (how to)* in French:
  Il s'est cassé la jambe et ne peut pas jouer au foot. *He's broken his leg and can't play football.*
  Je sais jouer du piano. *I can play the piano.*

- Verbs of seeing, hearing etc don't need to be preceded by **pouvoir**, where English has *can*:
  Vous voyez ce bâtiment-là? *Can you see that building?*
  Je ne vous entends pas très bien. *I can't hear you very well.*

- Sometimes **peut-être** *perhaps, maybe* is used with another verb to translate *may* or *might*:
  Je vais peut-être le voir demain. *I might go to see him tomorrow.*

---

vouloir

Vouloir *to want* can be followed by a noun.
Je veux/voudrais un café. *I want/I'd like a coffee.*
Nous voudrions une chambre à deux lits. *We'd like a double room.*
Je voulais une plus grande chambre. *I wanted a bigger room.*

It can also be followed by another verb. Used in this way, it's a modal verb and it has a range of English translations:

- *want*, *will* – present:
  Je ne veux pas rester ici. *I don't want to stay here.*
  Nous voulons visiter le musée. *We want to visit the museum.*
  Qu'est-ce que tu veux faire? *What do you want to do?*
  Voulez-vous signer ici? *Will you/Would you like to sign here?*

- *wanted* – imperfect and perfect, with different meanings; *refused to* in the negative perfect:
  Je voulais sortir. *I wanted to go out* (and this might or might not have happened).
  J'ai voulu sortir. *I wanted to go out* (and this is what happened).
  Je n'ai pas voulu sortir. *I refused to go out.*

- *would like*, *would have liked* – conditional and conditional perfect:
  Je voudrais voir le nouveau film. *I'd like to see the new film.*
  J'aurais voulu vivre dans les années vingt. *I would like to have lived in the twenties.*

- *please* – imperative, very formal:
  Veuillez attendre. *Please wait.*
  Veuillez m'excuser. *Please excuse me.*

Vouloir bien means *to be glad/willing to*:
Je veux bien le faire. *I'll be glad to do it.*
Il veut bien la voir, mais elle ne veut pas le voir. *He's happy to see her, but she doesn't want to see him.*

Vouloir dire means *to mean*:
Qu'est-ce que ça veut dire? *What does that mean?*
Que veut dire 'gaspiller'? *What does 'gaspiller' mean?*

impersonal verbs

Impersonal verbs are so called because they only have an *it* (**il**) form in the various tenses.

They include:

- **il y a** *there is, there are*:
  Il y a un bon restaurant au centre ville. *There's a good restaurant in the town centre.*
  Il y a beaucoup de monde ici. *There are a lot of people here.*
  Il y a quelqu'un? *Is anybody there?*
  Non, il n'y avait personne. *No, there was nobody there.*
  Il doit y avoir une alternative. *There must be an alternative.*

- weather verbs and expressions:
  il pleut *it's raining*; **il neige** *it's snowing*; **il gèle** *it's freezing*
  il fait beau/mauvais/du vent *it's fine/bad weather/windy*
  Il a plu hier. *It rained yesterday.*
  J'éspère qu'il ne va pas pleuvoir. *I hope it's not going to rain.*
  Il a fait si beau! *It was such beautiful weather!*

- **Il faut** from **falloir** *to have to, to be necessary*. It's used when it's clear who the subject is.
  Il faut partir avant dix-huit heures. *I/you/we have to leave before six pm.*
  Il a fallu partir tôt. *I/You/We had to leave early.*
  Il faudrait payer à l'avance. *You would have to pay in advance.*

  Il faut can also be used with a personal pronoun or it can be followed by a clause in the subjunctive (page 179):
  Il me/te/nous faut partir tôt. *I/You/We have to leave early.*
  Il faut que nous partions tôt. *We have to leave early.*
  Il faudra que nous partions tôt. *We will have to leave early.*

  Il ne faut pas doesn't mean *it isn't necessary*. It means *one must not*, or *you may not*:
  Il ne faut pas entrer. *You mustn't go in.*

  For *it isn't necessary*, you use **il n'est pas nécessaire de** or **il n'y a pas besoin de**.

- **Il vaut mieux** (from **valoir**) *it's/it would be better/best*:
  Il vaut mieux partir. *It would be better to leave.*
  Il vaut mieux que tu partes. *It would be better if you left.*
  Il vaudrait mieux ne rien dire. *It would be better to say nothing.*

- **il paraît que** *it appears (that)*, **il (me) semble que** *it seems (to me) (that)*,
  on dirait que *it looks as if* lit. *one would say that*:
  Il paraît qu'elle est arrivée hier. *It appears she arrived yesterday.*
  Il me semble qu'il a peu d'amis. *It seems to me that he has few friends.*
  On dirait qu'il va neiger. *It looks as if it's going to snow.*

- **il reste** *there is/are … left*:
  Il reste encore du pain. *There's still some bread left.*
  Il ne restait que deux tranches de jambon. *There were only two slices of ham left.*

- **il manque** *there is/are not enough* lit. *is/are lacking*:
  Il manque du lait. *There's not enough milk.*
  Il ne me manque pas d'idées. *I'm not short of ideas.*

- **il suffit de** *you just need to* lit. *it's enough to*:
  Il suffit de suivre la consigne. *You just need to follow the instructions.*
  Il suffit d'expliquer. *You just need to explain.*

- Reflexive impersonal verbs include: **il s'agit de** *it's about/a question of*,
  il se trouve que *it just so happens that*, **il se peut que** *it's possible that*:
  De quoi s'agit il? *What's it about?*
  Il ne s'agissait plus de son honnêteté. *It was no longer a question of his honesty.*
  Il se trouve que je ne l'ai pas vue. *As it happens, I didn't see her.*
  Il se peut qu'il le fasse. *It's possible that he'll do it.*
  Il se peut que je sois enceinte. *It's possible that I'm pregnant./I might be pregnant.*

- Many impersonal expressions use **être** and start with **il est** (page 190).

être

Être *to be* is the most used and the most irregular verb in French, as in English.

- As well as its basic use, **être** is used with a past participle to form the past tenses of certain verbs (page 159):
Il est arrivé en retard. *He (has) arrived late.*
Elle est morte. *She (has) died.*
Nous étions partis avant neuf heures. *We had left before nine o'clock.*
Il sera parti en vacances. *He will have gone on holiday.*
Ils seraient rentrés. *They would have come back.*

- It's also used to form the passive:
Son visage était couvert. *His face was covered.*
La maison a été rénovée. *The house has been renovated.*

- **Il est** with an adjective creates an impersonal expression:
Il est nécessaire/essentiel. *It's necessary/essential.*
Il est recommandé. *It's recommended/advisable.*
Il est facile/difficile. *It's easy/difficult.*
Il est possible/impossible. *It's possible/impossible.*
Il est probable. *It's probable.*
Il est utile/inutile. *It's useful/pointless.*

These impersonal expressions can be followed by **de** plus an infinitive:
Il est essentiel de savoir. *It's essential to know.*
Il est inutile de s'inquiéter. *It's pointless worrying.*
But if the following verb has its own subject, they're followed by **que** even when English doesn't use *that*. Some expressions need the subjunctive (page 179):
Il est possible que ce soit vrai. *It's possible that it is true.*
Il est probable que vous recevrez la lettre demain. *It's likely that you'll receive the letter tomorrow.*
Il est essentiel qu'elle sache la vérité. *It's essential that she knows the truth.*

In impersonal phrases, the **il** doesn't refer to anything in particular. For guidelines on when to use **c'est** and when to use **il est**, see page 73.

avoir

Avoir translates *to have* or *have got*.

Nous avons trois enfants. *We've got three children.*
Je n'ai pas beaucoup de temps. *I don't have much time.*
Elle a mal à la tête. *She has a headache.*
Il a du flair pour les affaires. *He has a flair for business.*
Il a le béguin pour elle. *He's got a crush on her.*
Qu'est-ce que tu as? *What's the matter?/What's your problem/complaint?*

It's used with a past participle to form past tenses (page 158):
J'ai compris. *I have understood.*
Vous avez mangé? *Have you eaten?*
Elles avaient fini? *Had they finished?*

Avoir also features in many expressions that don't use the word *have* in English. For example, **avoir lieu** means *to take place*, while **avoir besoin de** means *to need.* The following are some of the ways **avoir** is used:

- talking about age:
  L'enfant a quel age? *How old is the child?*
  Il a huit ans. *He's eight years old.*

- saying what you feel like physically:
  avoir sommeil *to feel sleepy*
  avoir faim/soif *to be hungry/thirsty*; **avoir chaud/froid** *to be hot/cold*
  avoir mal au cœur, avoir des nausées *to feel sick*
  avoir le mal de mer/le mal de l'air *to be seasick/airsick*
  avoir le vertige *to feel dizzy*

- saying what you feel like mentally:
  avoir peur *to be afraid*; **avoir honte** *to be ashamed*
  avoir envie de *to feel like*
  avoir raison/tort *to be right/wrong*
  avoir de la compassion pour *to sympathise with, to feel for*
  avoir du respect pour *to respect*

- everyday phrases:
  avoir de la chance *to be lucky*
  avoir de bonnes intentions *to mean well*
  avoir de la patience avec *to bear with*
  avoir confiance en *to put one's trust in, to rely on*

faire

The basic translations of **faire** are *to do* and *to make*:

Il n'y a rien à faire. *There's nothing to do.*
Qu'est-ce que tu fais? *What are you doing?*
Ils ont fait l'amour. *They made love.*
On a fait une erreur/une faute. *We made a mistake.*
faire la cuisine *to do the cooking*
faire la lessive *to do the washing*
faire de la recherche *to do research*

It's also used in many other ways that don't have *do* or *make* in the English translation.

- It's used to talk about the weather:
  Il fait beau/mauvais temps. *It's fine/awful weather.*
  Il fait du vent/du brouillard. *It's windy/foggy.*
  Il fait chaud/froid. *It's hot/cold.*
  Il fait trente degrés à l'ombre. *It's 30 degrees in the shade.*

- It can translate *take* or *have*:
  faire une pause *to take a break*
  faire une excursion *to take a trip*
  faire une sieste *to have a nap*
  faire la grasse matinée *to have a lie-in*

- It's used for many sports and activities:
  faire du sport *to do/play sport*
  faire une promenade *to go for a walk*
  faire de l'escalade *to go climbing*
  faire une randonnée *to go hiking*
  faire de l'équitation *to go horseriding*
  faire de la montgolfière *to go hot air ballooning*
  faire du ski *to go skiing*
  faire du ski nautique *to go water-skiing*
  faire du jogging *to jog*
  faire de la voile *to sail*
  faire de la planche à voile *to windsurf*
  faire de la planche à roulettes *to skateboard*
  faire de la planche à neige/faire du snowboard *to snowboard*

faire du canoë *to go canoeing*
faire du deltaplane *to go hang-gliding*
faire du saut à l'élastique *to bungee jump*

- It's used before another verb in the infinitive to mean *have something done*:
  J'ai fait nettoyer la voiture. *I've had the car cleaned.*
  Tu as fait réparer le pneu? *Have you had the tyre repaired?*
  Il a fait bâtir un garage. *He's had a garage built.*
  Nous avons fait agrandir la maison. *We've had the house extended.*

- It has many other varied translations:
  faire attention (à) *to pay attention (to)*
  faire l'imbécile *to play the fool*
  faire le malade *to pretend to be ill*
  faire des bêtises *to get into mischief*
  faire la connaissance de *to meet (for the first time)*
  faire du stop *to hitch-hike*
  faire la fête *to party*
  faire jour/nuit *to be daylight/night-time*
  faire la queue *to queue*
  faire le pont *to make a long weekend of it*
  faire les bagages *to pack*
  faire les courses/du shopping *to go shopping*
  faire la grève *to go on strike*
  faire un numéro de téléphone *to dial a number*
  faire des éxperiences *to experiment*
  faire justice soi-même *to take the law into one's own hands*

- It also features in many phrases:
  Ça ne fait rien. *It doesn't matter.*
  Ça fait combien? *How much is that?*
  Fais/faites voir. *Show me.*
  Pour ce que ça fait! *For all the good it does!*
  Ça me fait rire. *That makes me laugh.*
  Elle sait y faire. *She's got the knack.*
  Ça ne se fait pas. *That's not the done thing.*
  J'ai mieux à faire. *I've got better things to do.*
  Faites commes chez vous. *Make yourself at home.*
  faire d'une pierre deux coups *to kill two birds with one stone*

checkpoint 21

1   Fill each gap with one of the following words: **avez, a, ai, fera, sont, ont, fait, faites, fais, être**

   a Le weekend je .... de la planche à voile.

   b Qu'est-ce que vous .... ? Vous lisez?

   c Vous .... besoin de quelque chose?

   d Elles .... arrivées hier.

   e J'espère qu'il va .... là demain.

   f Mon fils .... six ans.

   g J' .... mal aux dents.

   h J'espère qu'il .... beau demain.

   i Il .... du vent.

   j Ils nous .... téléphoné hier soir.

2   Rephrase these sentences using **Il faut que**:
   Example: Il me faut aller. → Il faut que j'aille.

   a Il te faut partir.   b Il nous faut lui téléphoner.

   c Il me faut faire les devoirs.   d Il vous faut vous lever tôt.

3   What word(s) are missing?

   a .... aller au cinéma. *I'd like to go to the cinema.*

   b .... attendre. *You (vous) ought to wait.*

   c .... commencer? *Do they (f) want to start?*

   d .... téléphoné. *I should have phoned.*

   e Est-ce qu' .... nager ici? *Can one swim here?*

   f .... voir. *I want to see.*

   g .... jouer du violon? *Can you (tu) play the violin?*

   h .... payer. *We could have paid.*

   i .... m'aider? *Can you (tu) help me?*

   j .... partir maintenant. *She must leave now.*

4   When you're tired, which of these are you most likely to feel like doing: **faire du stop, faire les courses, faire la grasse matinée, faire de l'escalade**?

Verbs followed by prepositions

French verbs are linked to other words in a sentence in various ways. They can be:

- followed directly by another verb. This second verb is always in the infinitive in French, even though in English it can be an infinitive, e.g. *to think*, *to work*, or a gerund, e.g. *thinking*, *working*:
  Je veux voyager. *I want to travel.*
  J'aime voyager. *I like travelling.*

- followed by **à** or **de** before the second verb. More often than not, the preposition has no equivalent in English:
  continuer à voyager *to continue travelling*
  décider de voyager *to decide to travel*

- followed by **à** + person + **de** + verb:
  dire à quelqu'un d'entrer *to tell (to) somebody to come in*

- followed directly by a noun:
  inviter quelqu'un *to invite somebody*
  manger quelque chose *to eat something*

- followed by **à** or **de** before the noun. There are also a few verbs that are followed by other prepositions:
  parler à quelqu'un *to talk to somebody*
  parler de quelqu'un *to talk of/about somebody*
  entrer dans une maison *to enter (into) a house*

  It's not always this straightforward because the preposition often has no equivalent in English or has an unexpected translation:
  jouer au foot *to play football*
  remplir d'eau *to fill with water*

verbs followed by à

Some French verbs are always linked to the rest of the sentence by à.
The most common are listed opposite.

- When these verbs are followed by another verb, this is always in the infinitive in French, whatever the English translation may be. Although there's no English equivalent for à with most verbs, it has a translation with a few:

  Il voudrait renoncer à fumer. *He'd like to give up smoking.*
  Je n'arrive pas à fermer ma valise. *I can't manage to close my suitcase.*
  Je t'encourage à lire ce livre. *I encourage you to read this book.*
  Ce produit sert à enlever des taches. *This product is used for getting rid of stains.*
  Ils se sont amusés à participer au concours. *They enjoyed taking part in the competition.*

  You can use y, meaning *it* in this instance (page 81), to replace the phrase introduced by à:

  Il voudrait y renoncer. *He'd like to give it up.*
  Je n'y arrive pas. *I can't manage to do it.*
  Je t'y encourage. *I encourage you to do it.*
  Ce produit y sert. *This product is used for it.*

- When these verbs are followed by a noun, à often has no equivalent in English or has an unexpected translation. Le or les after à combine with it to become au or aux (page 48):

  Tu veux jouer au tennis? *Do you want to play tennis?*
  Il ressemble beaucoup à son grand-père. *He looks a lot like his grandfath*
  Je me suis habitué aux lentilles de contact. *I've got used to contact lense*

- When the object of these verbs is a pronoun rather than a noun, it's an indirect object pronoun (page 79) if it refers to a person and y when it refe to anything else:

  J'ai téléphoné à Dominic. *I've phoned Dominic.*
  Je lui ai téléphoné. *I've phoned him.*
  Elle obéit à ses parents. *She obeys her parents.*
  Elle leur obéit. *She obeys them.*
  Je pense beaucoup à l'avenir. *I think a lot about the future.*
  J'y pense beaucoup. *I think about it a lot.*

acheter à *to buy from*
aider à *to help to*
s'amuser à *to enjoy oneself doing*
apprendre à *to learn how to*
arriver à *to manage to, succeed in doing*
assister à *to attend*
s'attendre à *to expect to*
avoir à *to have to, be obliged to*
chercher à *to attempt to*
commencer à *to begin to*
consentir à *to consent to*
consister à *to consist in*
continuer à *to continue to*
convenir à *to suit, be suitable for*
emprunter à *to borrow from*
encourager à *to encourage s.o. to*
enseigner à *to teach s.o. to*
s'habituer à *to get used to*
hésiter à *to hesitate to*
s'intéresser à *to be interested in*
inviter à *to invite s.o. to*
jouer à *to play (a game or a sport)*
se mettre à *to start to, set about*
obéir à *to obey*
obliger à *to force, oblige s.o. to*
parler à *to talk to*
penser à *to think of/about*
permettre à *to permit*
persister à *to persist in*
plaire à *to please*
se préparer à *to prepare oneself to*
promettre à *to promise*
réfléchir à *to consider*

renoncer à *to give up*
répondre à *to answer*
résister à *to resist*
ressembler à *to resemble*
réussir à *to succeed in*
servir à *to be used for*
tarder à *to delay, be late in*
téléphoner à *to phone*
tenir à *to be keen to*

verbs followed by de

Some French verbs are always linked to the rest of the sentence by **de**. The most common are listed opposite.

- When these verbs are followed by another verb, this is always in the infinitive in French, whatever the English translation may be. Although there's no English equivalent for **de** with most verbs, it has a translation with a few:

  J'ai oublié de fermer la porte à clé. *I've forgotten to lock the door.*
  Je n'ai pas envie d'y aller. *I don't feel like going (there).*
  Elle a décidé d'y retourner. *She's decided to go back (there).*
  Je rêve d'habiter dans le sud de la France. *I dream of living in the South of France.*
  Elle refuse de travailler. *She refuses to work.*

- When these verbs are followed by a noun, **de** is translated in a variety of ways or sometimes not translated at all. **Le** or **les** after **de** combine with it to become **du** or **des** (page 48):

  Elle ne parle jamais de sa famille. *She never talks about her family.*
  Tu as besoin du CD? *Do you need the CD?*
  Il s'est aperçu des erreurs. *He noticed the mistakes.*
  Je l'ai rempli d'eau. *I filled it with water.*

- To translate *it/them,* when referring to things rather than people, you replace **de** + noun with **en** (page 82):

  Elle n'en parle jamais. *She never talks about it/them.*
  Tu en as besoin? *Do you need it/them?*
  Il s'en est aperçu. *He noticed it/them.*

accepter de *to agree to, to accept*
accuser de *to accuse s.o. of*
s'agir de *to be a question of*
s'apercevoir de *to notice*
s'approcher de *to approach*
s'arrêter de *to stop*
avoir besoin de *to need*
avoir envie de *to feel like*
avoir honte de *to be ashamed of*
avoir l'intention de *to intend*
avoir peur de *to be afraid of*
avoir raison de *to be right to*
avoir tort de *to be wrong in*
cesser de *to stop*
changer de *to change*
choisir de *to choose to*
conseiller de *to advise s.o. to*
convenir de *to admit to, acknowledge*
craindre de *to fear*
décider de *to decide to*
se dépêcher de *to hurry to*
dépendre de *to depend on*
empêcher de *to prevent sth/s.o. from*
en avoir marre de *to be fed up with*
essayer de *to try to*
s'étonner de *to be surprised to/at*
être sur le point de *to be about to*
s'excuser de *to apologise for*
se fatiguer de *to get tired of*
féliciter de *to congratulate s.o. on*
finir de *to finish*
se garder de *to be careful not to*

jouer de *to play (an instrument)*
jouir de *to enjoy*
manquer de *to lack*
se méfier de *to distrust, be careful about*
menacer de *to threaten to*
mériter de *to deserve to*
se moquer de *to make fun of*
s'occuper de *to be busy with*
offrir de *to offer to*
oublier de *to forget to*
parler de *to talk about*
penser de *to think of, have an opinion about*
persuader de *to persuade s.o. to*
se plaindre de *to complain about*
prier de *to beg, request s.o. to*
profiter de *to make the most of*
promettre de *to promise to*
proposer de *to suggest*
rappeler de *to remind s.o. to*
se rappeler de *to remember to*
refuser de *to refuse to*
regretter de *to regret*
remercier de *to thank s.o. for*
se rendre compte de *to realise, be aware of*
rêver de *to dream of*
rire de *to laugh at*
risquer de *to risk*
se servir de *to make use of*
se souvenir de *to remember*
terminer de *to finish*
se vanter de *to boast about*
venir de (faire) *to have just (done)*

verb + à + person + de + infinitive

Whereas in English you ask or tell someone to do something without a preposition, in French you ask or tell **to** them to do something:

J'ai demandé à mon mari de m'aider. *I asked my husband to help me.*
Demande à ta mère de me téléphoner. *Ask your mother to phone me.*
Il a dit à Luc de s'en aller. *He told Luc to go away.*

There are several verbs which behave in the same way:

apprendre à qn* de *to teach s.o. to*
commander à qn de *to order s.o. to*
conseiller à qn de *to advise s.o. to*
défendre à qn de *to ban s.o. from*
demander à qn de *to ask s.o. to*
dire à qn de *to tell s.o. to*
interdire à qn de *to forbid s.o. to, ban s.o. from*
ordonner à qn de *to order s.o. to*
permettre à qn de *to allow s.o. to*
promettre à qn de *to promise s.o. to*
proposer à qn de *to propose to s.o. that*
recommander à qn de *to recommend to s.o. that*
suggérer à qn de *to suggest to s.o. that*

***qn = quelqu'un** *someone*

Je recommande à tout le monde d'étudier le français. *I recommend that everyone study French.*
Je conseillerais aux étudiants de répondre. *I'd advise the students to reply.*
J'ai promis à ta sœur de venir demain. *I promised your sister I'd come tomorrow.*

To replace à + person with a pronoun, you use an indirect object pronoun (page 79):
Tu peux lui demander d'attendre? *Can you ask her to wait?*
Je leur conseillerais de répondre. *I'd advise them to reply.*
Dis-lui de venir demain. *Tell her to come tomorrow.*

verb + dans, par, pour, en

A few verbs are followed by **dans**, **par**, **pour** or **en** + a noun or another verb:

- **commencer** *to start* and **finir/terminer** *to finish* can be followed by **par** *by* + an infinitive:
  J'ai commencé par lire de courts romans. *I started by reading short novels.*
  (compare this with **J'ai commencé à lire** *I started to read*)
  Elle a fini par remercier le public. *She finished by thanking the public.*
  (compare this with **Elle a fini de remercier le public** *She finished thanking the public*)

- **entrer dans** *to enter*
  Nous sommes entrés dans la cathédrale. *We entered the cathedral.*
  La Turquie veut entrer dans l'Union européenne. *Turkey wants to join (lit. enter) the European Union.*

- **avoir confiance en** *to trust*
  Je n'ai plus confiance en lui. *I don't trust him any more.*
  Tu as confiance en son jugement? *Do you trust his judgement?*

- **Pour** followed by a verb in the infinitive has the sense of *for, in order to*:
  Nous travaillons pour vivre. *We work in order to live.*
  Il faut donner pour recevoir. *You must give in order to receive.*
  Je l'ai fait pour t'aider. *I did it to help you.*
  Cliquer ici pour imprimer la page. *Click here to print the page.*

verbs with no preposition in French

Although these verbs have a preposition before a noun in English, they don't need one in French – they have a direct object:

attendre *to wait **for***
chercher *to look **for***
demander *to ask **for***
écouter *to listen **to***
payer *to pay **for*** (can also be followed by **pour**)
regarder *to look **at***

J'attends un de mes amis. *I'm waiting for one of my friends.*
Je cherche mon passeport. *I'm looking for my passport.*
J'ai demandé une bière. *I've asked for a beer.*
Moi, je paie les repas des autres. *I'll pay for the others' meals.*
Tu voudrais regarder les photos? *Would you like to look at the photos?*

checkpoint 22

1　Does à, de or d' belong in the gap?

　a J'ai promis　venir. *I've promised to come.*

　b Tu peux aider Robert　porter les valises? *Can you help
　Robert to carry the suitcases?*

　c Elle a essayé　apprendre. *She's tried to learn.*

　d Elle a honte　être pauvre. *She's ashamed of being poor.*

　e Je voudrais apprendre　faire du ski. *I'd like to learn to ski.*

　f Il s'est fatigué　attendre. *He got tired of waiting.*

　g Tu as peur　sortir? *Are you afraid of going out?*

　h Tu as raison　ne pas sortir. *You're right not to go out.*

2　To fill these gaps, you need the combination of preposition + *the*.
　Check with page 48 if you need to.

　a Je voudrais parler　directeur. *I'd like to talk to the manager.*

　b Ça dépend　temps. *It depends on the weather.*

　c Vous devriez répondre　lettre. *You ought to reply to
　the letter.*

　d J'en ai marre　service ici. *I'm fed up with the service here.*

　e Que penses-tu　film? *What do you think of the film?*

　f Je m'intéresse　art moderne. *I'm interested in modern art.*

　g Vous avez besoin　ciseaux? *Do you need the scissors?*

　h Je me suis habitué　chaleur. *I've got used to the heat.*

3　Translate these into French.

　a *They're* (m) *waiting for the train.*

　b *I like playing tennis.*

　c *She forgot to pay.*

　d *We're about to leave.*

　e *She's looking for her bag.*

　f *Do you* (tu) *need any money?*

　g *I've asked for a hundred euros.*

　h *We hope to come back next year.*

Verb tables

The following pages present 50 key verbs, which are listed on page 254 for easy reference. They include:

- **travailler** *to work*, **finir** *to finish* and **vendre** *to sell*, which provide the regular patterns for **-er** verbs, **-ir** verbs and **-re** verbs.

- the reflexive verb **se laver** *to get washed*, which is regular.

- **commencer** *to begin* and **manger** *to eat*, which illustrate the spelling changes that verbs with **c** or **g** before **-er** undergo in some tenses.

- **acheter** *to buy* and **appeler** *to call*, which illustrate the spelling changes that verbs with **e** or **é** as the vowel in the syllable before **-er** undergo in some tenses, and **employer** *to use*, which illustrates the spelling changes that verbs with **y** before the **-er** undergo in some tenses.

- key irregular verbs such as **être** *to be*, **avoir** *to have*, **aller** *to go* and the modal verbs **devoir** *to have to*, **pouvoir** *to be able to* and **vouloir** *to want to*.

- other irregular verbs such as **dire** *to say* and **prendre** *to take*, which provide the pattern for verbs that behave in the same way. These are listed underneath.

All 50 verbs are written out in all persons in the present, future, conditional, imperfect, past historic, perfect and present subjunctive.
The perfect tense shows you whether the verb takes **avoir** or **être** in the compound tenses. All you need then do to form the pluperfect (page 163), future perfect (page 164) and conditional perfect (page 165) is to change the tense of **avoir/être**.

1   acheter *to buy*

	present	future	conditional
j'	achète	achèterai	achèterais
tu	achètes	achèteras	achèterais
il/elle	achète	achètera	achèterait
nous	achetons	achèterons	achèterions
vous	achetez	achèterez	achèteriez
ils/elles	achètent	achèteront	achèteraient

	imperfect	past historic	perfect
j'	achetais	achetai	ai acheté
tu	achetais	achetas	as acheté
il/elle	achetait	acheta	a acheté
nous	achetions	achetâmes	avons acheté
vous	achetiez	achetâtes	avez acheté
ils/elles	achetaient	achetèrent	ont acheté

	present subjunctive
j'	achète
tu	achètes
il/elle	achète
nous	achetions
vous	achetiez
ils/elles	achètent

present participle **achetant**

past participle **acheté**

imperative **achète, achetons, achetez**

Verbs where **e** or **é** change to **è** include **amener** *to bring*, **emmener** *to take*, **espérer** *to hope*, **geler** *to freeze*, **se lever** *to get up*, **préférer** *to prefer*.

2 aller *to go*

	present	future	conditional
je/j'	vais	irai	irais
tu	vas	iras	irais
il/elle	va	ira	irait
nous	allons	irons	irions
vous	allez	irez	iriez
ils/elles	vont	iront	iraient

	imperfect	past historic	perfect
je/j'	allais	allai	suis allé(e)
tu	allais	allas	es allé(e)
il/elle	allait	alla	est allé(e)
nous	allions	allâmes	sommes allé(e)s
vous	alliez	allâtes	êtes allé(e)(s)
ils/elles	allaient	allèrent	sont allé(e)s

	present subjunctive
j'	aille
tu	ailles
il/elle	aille
nous	allions
vous	alliez
ils/elles	aillent

present participle **allant**

past participle **allé**

imperative **va** (**vas** before **y**), **allons**, **allez**

3   appeler *to call*

	present	future	conditional
j'	appelle	appellerai	appellerais
tu	appelles	appelleras	appellerais
il/elle	appelle	appellera	appellerait
nous	appelons	appellerons	appellerions
vous	appelez	appellerez	appelleriez
ils/elles	appellent	appelleront	appelleraient

	imperfect	past historic	perfect
j'	appelais	appelai	ai appelé
tu	appelais	appelas	as appelé
il/elle	appelait	appela	a appelé
nous	appelions	appelâmes	avons appelé
vous	appeliez	appelâtes	avez appelé
ils/elles	appelaient	appelèrent	ont appelé

	present subjunctive
j'	appelle
tu	appelles
il/elle	appelle
nous	appelions
vous	appeliez
ils/elles	appellent

present participle **appelant**

past participle **appelé**

imperative **appelle, appelons, appelez**

Épeler *to spell*, **jeter** *to throw*, **rappeler** *to remind*, **s'appeler** *to be called* also double the consonant before -er in some persons and tenses

4 s'asseoir *to sit down*

There are two ways of conjugating this verb in the present tense.
The first of the two forms is the most common.

	present	future
je	m'assieds/assois	m'assiérai
tu	t'assieds/assois	t'assiéras
il/elle	s'assied/assoit	s'assiéra
nous	nous asseyons/assoyons	nous assiérons
vous	vous asseyez/assoyez	vous assiérez
ils/elles	s'asseyent/assoient	s'assiéront

	conditional	imperfect	past historic
je	m'assiérais	m'asseyais	m'assis
tu	t'assiérais	t'asseyais	t'assis
il/elle	s'assiérait	s'asseyait	s'assit
nous	nous assiérions	nous asseyions	nous assîmes
vous	vous assiériez	vous asseyiez	vous assîtes
ils/elles	s'assiéraient	s'asseyaient	s'assirent

	perfect	present subjunctive
je	me suis assis(e)	m'asseye
tu	t'es assis(e)	t'asseyes
il/elle	s'est assis(e)	s'asseye
nous	nous sommes assis(es)	nous asseyions
vous	vous êtes assis(e)(s)	vous asseyiez
ils/elles	se sont assis(es)	s'asseyent

present participle **s'asseyant**

past participle **assis**

imperative **assieds-toi, asseyons-nous, asseyez-vous**

5   avoir *to have*

	present	future	conditional
j'	ai	aurai	aurais
tu	as	auras	aurais
il/elle	a	aura	aurait
nous	avons	aurons	aurions
vous	avez	aurez	auriez
ils/elles	ont	auront	auraient

	imperfect	past historic	perfect
j'	avais	eus	ai eu
tu	avais	eus	as eu
il/elle	avait	eut	a eu
nous	avions	eûmes	avons eu
vous	aviez	eûtes	avez eu
ils/elles	avaient	eurent	ont eu

	present subjunctive
j'	aie
tu	aies
il/elle	ait
nous	ayons
vous	ayez
ils/elles	aient

present participle **ayant**

past participle **eu**

imperative **aie, ayons, ayez**

6 **battre** *to beat*

	present	future	conditional
je	**bats**	**battrai**	**battrais**
tu	**bats**	**battras**	**battrais**
il/elle	**bat**	**battra**	**battrait**
nous	**battons**	**battrons**	**battrions**
vous	**battez**	**battrez**	**battriez**
ils/elles	**battent**	**battront**	**battraient**

	imperfect	past historic	perfect
je/j'	**battais**	**battis**	**ai battu**
tu	**battais**	**battis**	**as battu**
il/elle	**battait**	**battit**	**a battu**
nous	**battions**	**battîmes**	**avons battu**
vous	**battiez**	**battîtes**	**avez battu**
ils/elles	**battaient**	**battirent**	**ont battu**

	present subjunctive
je	**batte**
tu	**battes**
il/elle	**batte**
nous	**battions**
vous	**battiez**
ils/elles	**battent**

present participle **battant**

past participle **battu**

imperative **bats, battons, battez**

7 boire *to drink*

	present	future	conditional
je	bois	boirai	boirais
tu	bois	boiras	boirais
il/elle	boit	boira	boirait
nous	buvons	boirons	boirions
vous	buvez	boirez	boiriez
ils/elles	boivent	boiront	boiraient

	imperfect	past historic	perfect
je/j'	buvais	bus	ai bu
tu	buvais	bus	as bu
il/elle	buvait	but	a bu
nous	buvions	bûmes	avons bu
vous	buviez	bûtes	avez bu
ils/elles	buvaient	burent	ont bu

	present subjunctive
je	boive
tu	boives
il/elle	boive
nous	buvions
vous	buviez
ils/elles	boivent

present participle **buvant**

past participle **bu**

imperative **bois, buvons, buvez**

8 **commencer** *to begin*

	present	future	conditional
je	**commence**	**commencerai**	**commencerais**
tu	**commences**	**commenceras**	**commencerais**
il/elle	**commence**	**commencera**	**commencerait**
nous	**commençons**	**commencerons**	**commencerions**
vous	**commencez**	**commencerez**	**commenceriez**
ils/elles	**commencent**	**commenceront**	**commenceraient**

	imperfect	past historic	perfect
je/j'	**commençais**	**commençai**	**ai commencé**
tu	**commençais**	**commenças**	**as commencé**
il/elle	**commençait**	**commença**	**a commencé**
nous	**commencions**	**commençâmes**	**avons commencé**
vous	**commenciez**	**commençâtes**	**avez commencé**
ils/elles	**commençaient**	**commencèrent**	**ont commencé**

	present subjunctive
je	**commence**
tu	**commences**
il/elle	**commence**
nous	**commencions**
vous	**commenciez**
ils/elles	**commencent**

present participle **commençant**

past participle **commencé**

imperative **commence, commençons, commencez**

Verbs where **c** changes to **ç** include **annoncer** *to announce*,
avancer *to advance*, **lancer** *to throw*, **menacer** *to threaten*,
pincer *to pinch,* **rincer** *to rinse.*

9   conduire *to drive*

	present	future	conditional
je	conduis	conduirai	conduirais
tu	conduis	conduiras	conduirais
il/elle	conduit	conduira	conduirait
nous	conduisons	conduirons	conduirions
vous	conduisez	conduirez	conduiriez
ils/elles	conduisent	conduiront	conduiraient

	imperfect	past historic	perfect
je/j'	conduisais	conduisis	ai conduit
tu	conduisais	conduisis	as conduit
il/elle	conduisait	conduisit	a conduit
nous	conduisions	conduisîmes	avons conduit
vous	conduisiez	conduisîtes	avez conduit
ils/elles	conduisaient	conduisirent	ont conduit

	present subjunctive
je	conduise
tu	conduises
il/elle	conduise
nous	conduisions
vous	conduisiez
ils/elles	conduisent

present participle **conduisant**

past participle **conduit**

imperative **conduis, conduisons, conduisez**

Verbs which follow the same pattern include **construire** *to build*, **cuire** *to cook*, **détruire** *to destroy*, **réduire** *to reduce* and **traduire** *to translate*.

10 connaître *to know*

	present	future	conditional
je	connais	connaîtrai	connaîtrais
tu	connais	connaîtras	connaîtrais
il/elle	connaît	connaîtra	connaîtrait
nous	connaissons	connaîtrons	connaîtrions
vous	connaissez	connaîtrez	connaîtriez
ils/elles	connaissent	connaîtront	connaîtraient

	imperfect	past historic	perfect
je/j'	connaissais	connus	ai connu
tu	connaissais	connus	as connu
il/elle	connaissait	connut	a connu
nous	connaissions	connûmes	avons connu
vous	connaissiez	connûtes	avez connu
ils/elles	connaissaient	connurent	ont connu

	present subjunctive
je	connaisse
tu	connaisses
il/elle	connaisse
nous	connaissions
vous	connaissiez
ils/elles	connaissent

present participle **connaissant**

past participle **connu**

imperative **connais, connaissons, connaissez**

Verbs which follow the same pattern as **connaître** include **apparaître** *to appear*, **disparaître** *to disappear* and **paraître** *to seem*.

11 courir *to run*

	present	future	conditional
je	cours	courrai	courrais
tu	cours	courras	courrais
il/elle	court	courra	courrait
nous	courons	courrons	courrions
vous	courez	courrez	courriez
ils/elles	courent	courront	courraient

	imperfect	past historic	perfect
je/j'	courais	courus	ai couru
tu	courais	courus	as couru
il/elle	courait	courut	a couru
nous	courions	courûmes	avons couru
vous	couriez	courûtes	avez couru
ils/elles	couraient	coururent	ont couru

	present subjunctive
je	coure
tu	coures
il/elle	coure
nous	courions
vous	couriez
ils/elles	courent

present participle **courant**

past participle **couru**

imperative **cours, courons, courez**

12 craindre *to fear*

	present	future	conditional
je	crains	craindrai	craindrais
tu	crains	craindras	craindrais
il/elle	craint	craindra	craindrait
nous	craignons	craindrons	craindrions
vous	craignez	craindrez	craindriez
ils/elles	craignent	craindront	craindraient

	imperfect	past historic	perfect
je/j'	craignais	craignis	ai craint
tu	craignais	craignis	as craint
il/elle	craignait	craignit	a craint
nous	craignions	craignîmes	avons craint
vous	craigniez	craignîtes	avez craint
ils/elles	craignaient	craignirent	ont craint

	present subjunctive
je	craigne
tu	craignes
il/elle	craigne
nous	craignions
vous	craigniez
ils/elles	craignent

present participle **craignant**

past participle **craint**

imperative **crains, craignons, craignez**

Verbs that follow the pattern of **craindre** include **se plaindre** *to complain*.

13 croire *to believe*

	present	future	conditional
je	crois	croirai	croirais
tu	crois	croiras	croirais
il/elle	croit	croira	croirait
nous	croyons	croirons	croirions
vous	croyez	croirez	croiriez
ils/elles	croient	croiront	croiraient

	imperfect	past historic	perfect
je/j'	croyais	crus	ai cru
tu	croyais	crus	as cru
il/elle	croyait	crut	a cru
nous	croyions	crûmes	avons cru
vous	croyiez	crûtes	avez cru
ils/elles	croyaient	crurent	ont cru

	present subjunctive
je	croie
tu	croies
il/elle	croie
nous	croyions
vous	croyiez
ils/elles	croient

present participle **croyant**

past participle **cru**

imperative **crois, croyons, croyez**

14 devoir *to have to*

	present	future	conditional
je	dois	devrai	devrais
tu	dois	devras	devrais
il/elle	doit	devra	devrait
nous	devons	devrons	devrions
vous	devez	devrez	devriez
ils/elles	doivent	devront	devraient

	imperfect	past historic	perfect
je/j'	devais	dus	ai dû
tu	devais	dus	as dû
il/elle	devait	dut	a dû
nous	devions	dûmes	avons dû
vous	deviez	dûtes	avez dû
ils/elles	devaient	durent	ont dû

	present subjunctive
je	doive
tu	doives
il/elle	doive
nous	devions
vous	deviez
ils/elles	doivent

present participle devant

past participle dû

imperative dois, devons, devez

15 dire *to say*

	present	future	conditional
je	dis	dirai	dirais
tu	dis	diras	dirais
il/elle	dit	dira	dirait
nous	disons	dirons	dirions
vous	dites	direz	diriez
ils/elles	disent	diront	diraient

	imperfect	past historic	perfect
je/j'	disais	dis	ai dit
tu	disais	dis	as dit
il/elle	disait	dit	a dit
nous	disions	dîmes	avons dit
vous	disiez	dîtes	avez dit
ils/elles	disaient	dirent	ont dit

	present subjunctive
je	dise
tu	dises
il/elle	dise
nous	disions
vous	disiez
ils/elles	disent

present participle **disant**

past participle **dit**

imperative **dis, disons, dites**

Verbs which follow the same pattern as **dire** include **contredire** *to contradict*, **interdire** *to forbid* and **prédire** *to predict*.

16 dormir *to sleep*

	present	future	conditional
je	dors	dormirai	dormirais
tu	dors	dormiras	dormirais
il/elle	dort	dormira	dormirait
nous	dormons	dormirons	dormirions
vous	dormez	dormirez	dormiriez
ils/elles	dorment	dormiront	dormiraient

	imperfect	past historic	perfect
je/j'	dormais	dormis	ai dormi
tu	dormais	dormis	as dormi
il/elle	dormait	dormit	a dormi
nous	dormions	dormîmes	avons dormi
vous	dormiez	dormîtes	avez dormi
ils/elles	dormaient	dormirent	ont dormi

	present subjunctive
je	dorme
tu	dormes
il/elle	dorme
nous	dormions
vous	dormiez
ils/elles	dorment

present participle **dormant**

past participle **dormi**

imperative **dors, dormons, dormez**

	present	future	conditional
j'	écris	écrirai	écrirais
tu	écris	écriras	écrirais
il/elle	écrit	écrira	écrirait
nous	écrivons	écrirons	écririons
vous	écrivez	écrirez	écririez
ils/elles	écrivent	écriront	écriraient

	imperfect	past historic	perfect
j'	écrivais	écrivis	ai écrit
tu	écrivais	écrivis	as écrit
il/elle	écrivait	écrivit	a écrit
nous	écrivions	écrivîmes	avons écrit
vous	écriviez	écrivîtes	avez écrit
ils/elles	écrivaient	écrivirent	ont écrit

	present subjunctive
j'	écrive
tu	écrives
il/elle	écrive
nous	écrivions
vous	écriviez
ils/elles	écrivent

present participle **écrivant**

past participle **écrit**

imperative **écris, écrivons, écrivez**

Verbs which follow the same pattern as **écrire** include **décrire** *to describe*.

18 employer *to use*

	present	future	conditional
j'	emploie	emploierai	emploierais
tu	emploies	emploieras	emploierais
il/elle	emploie	emploiera	emploierait
nous	employons	emploierons	emploierions
vous	employez	emploierez	emploieriez
ils/elles	emploient	emploieront	emploieraient

	imperfect	past historic	perfect
j'	employais	employai	ai employé
tu	employais	employas	as employé
il/elle	employait	employa	a employé
nous	employions	employâmes	avons employé
vous	employiez	employâtes	avez employé
ils/elles	employaient	employèrent	ont employé

	present subjunctive
j'	emploie
tu	emploies
il/elle	emploie
nous	employions
vous	employiez
ils/elles	emploient

present participle **employant**

past participle **employé**

imperative **emploie, employons, employez**

Verbs which follow the same pattern include **appuyer** *to press*, **s'ennuyer** *to be bored*, **essuyer** *to wipe*, **nettoyer** *to clean* and **(se) noyer** *to drown*.

19 envoyer *to send*

	present	future	conditional
j'	envoie	enverrai	enverrais
tu	envoies	enverras	enverrais
il/elle	envoie	enverra	enverrait
nous	envoyons	enverrons	enverrions
vous	envoyez	enverrez	enverriez
ils/elles	envoient	enverront	enverraient

	imperfect	past historic	perfect
j'	envoyais	envoyai	ai envoyé
tu	envoyais	envoyas	as envoyé
il/elle	envoyait	envoya	a envoyé
nous	envoyions	envoyâmes	avons envoyé
vous	envoyiez	envoyâtes	avez envoyé
ils/elles	envoyaient	envoyèrent	ont envoyé

	present subjunctive
j'	envoie
tu	envoies
il/elle	envoie
nous	envoyions
vous	envoyiez
ils/elles	envoient

present participle **envoyant**

past participle **envoyé**

imperative **envoie, envoyons, envoyez**

20 être *to be*

	present	future	conditional
je	suis	serai	serais
tu	es	seras	serais
il/elle	est	sera	serait
nous	sommes	serons	serions
vous	êtes	serez	seriez
ils/elles	sont	seront	seraient

	imperfect	past historic	perfect
je/j'	étais	fus	ai été
tu	étais	fus	as été
il/elle	était	fut	a été
nous	étions	fûmes	avons été
vous	étiez	fûtes	avez été
ils/elles	étaient	furent	ont été

	present subjunctive
je	sois
tu	sois
il/elle	soit
nous	soyons
vous	soyez
ils/elles	soient

present participle étant

past participle été

imperative sois, soyons, soyez

21 faire *to do, make*

	present	future	conditional
je	fais	ferai	ferais
tu	fais	feras	ferais
il/elle	fait	fera	ferait
nous	faisons	ferons	ferions
vous	faites	ferez	feriez
ils/elles	font	feront	feraient

	imperfect	past historic	perfect
je/j'	faisais	fis	ai fait
tu	faisais	fis	as fait
il/elle	faisait	fit	a fait
nous	faisions	fîmes	avons fait
vous	faisiez	fîtes	avez fait
ils/elles	faisaient	firent	ont fait

	present subjunctive
je	fasse
tu	fasses
il/elle	fasse
nous	fassions
vous	fassiez
ils/elles	fassent

present participle **faisant**

past participle **fait**

imperative **fais, faisons, faites**

22 falloir *to be necessary*

	present	future	conditional
il	**faut**	**faudra**	**faudrait**

	imperfect	past historic	perfect
il	**fallait**	**fallut**	**a fallu**

	present subjunctive
il	**faille**

23 finir *to finish*

	present	future	conditional
je	finis	finirai	finirais
tu	finis	finiras	finirais
il/elle	finit	finira	finirait
nous	finissons	finirons	finirions
vous	finissez	finirez	finiriez
ils/elles	finissent	finiront	finiraient

	imperfect	past historic	perfect
je/j'	finissais	finis	ai fini
tu	finissais	finis	as fini
il/elle	finissait	finit	a fini
nous	finissions	finîmes	avons fini
vous	finissiez	finîtes	avez fini
ils/elles	finissaient	finirent	ont fini

	present subjunctive
je	finisse
tu	finisses
il/elle	finisse
nous	finissions
vous	finissiez
ils/elles	finissent

present participle **finissant**

past participle **fini**

imperative **finis, finissons, finissez**

24 se laver *to get washed*

	present	future	conditional
je	me lave	me laverai	me laverais
tu	te laves	te laveras	te laverais
il/elle	se lave	se lavera	se laverait
nous	nous lavons	nous laverons	nous laverions
vous	vous lavez	vous laverez	vous laveriez
ils/elles	se lavent	se laveront	se laveraient

	imperfect	past historic	perfect
je	me lavais	me lavai	me suis lavé(e)
tu	te lavais	te lavas	t'es lavé(e)
il/elle	se lavait	se lava	s'est lavé(e)
nous	nous lavions	nous lavâmes	nous sommes lavé(e)s
vous	vous laviez	vous lavâtes	vous êtes lavé(e)(s)
ils/elles	se lavaient	se lavèrent	se sont lavé(e)s

	present subjunctive
je	me lave
tu	te laves
il/elle	se lave
nous	nous lavions
vous	vous laviez
ils/elles	se lavent

present participle **(se) lavant**

past participle **lavé**

imperative **lave-toi, lavons-nous, lavez-vous**

25 lire *to read*

	present	future	conditional
je	lis	lirai	lirais
tu	lis	liras	lirais
il/elle	lit	lira	lirait
nous	lisons	lirons	lirions
vous	lisez	lirez	liriez
ils/elles	lisent	liront	liraient

	imperfect	past historic	perfect
je/j'	lisais	lus	ai lu
tu	lisais	lus	as lu
il/elle	lisait	lut	a lu
nous	lisions	lûmes	avons lu
vous	lisiez	lûtes	avez lu
ils/elles	lisaient	lurent	ont lu

	present subjunctive
je	lise
tu	lises
il/elle	lise
nous	lisions
vous	lisiez
ils/elles	lisent

present participle **lisant**

past participle **lu**

imperative **lis, lisons, lisez**

Verbs which follow the same pattern as **lire** include **élire** *to elect*.

26 manger *to eat*

	present	future	conditional
je	mange	mangerai	mangerais
tu	manges	mangeras	mangerais
il/elle	mange	mangera	mangerait
nous	mangeons	mangerons	mangerions
vous	mangez	mangerez	mangeriez
ils/elles	mangent	mangeront	mangeraient

	imperfect	past historic	perfect
je/j'	mangeais	mangeai	ai mangé
tu	mangeais	mangeas	as mangé
il/elle	mangeait	mangea	a mangé
nous	mangions	mangeâmes	avons mangé
vous	mangiez	mangeâtes	avez mangé
ils/elles	mangeaient	mangèrent	ont mangé

	present subjunctive
je	mange
tu	manges
il/elle	mange
nous	mangions
vous	mangiez
ils/elles	mangent

present participle **mangeant**

past participle **mangé**

imperative **mange, mangeons, mangez**

Verbs which add **e** after **g** as **manger** include **arranger** *to arrange*, **bouger** *to move*, **partager** *to share*, **protéger** *to protect* and **soulager** *to relieve*.

27 mettre *to put*

	present	future	conditional
je	mets	mettrai	mettrais
tu	mets	mettras	mettrais
il/elle	met	mettra	mettrait
nous	mettons	mettrons	mettrions
vous	mettez	mettrez	mettriez
ils/elles	mettent	mettront	mettraient

	imperfect	past historic	perfect
je/j'	mettais	mis	ai mis
tu	mettais	mis	as mis
il/elle	mettait	mit	a mis
nous	mettions	mîmes	avons mis
vous	mettiez	mîtes	avez mis
ils/elles	mettaient	mirent	ont mis

	present subjunctive
je	mette
tu	mettes
il/elle	mette
nous	mettions
vous	mettiez
ils/elles	mettent

present participle **mettant**

past participle **mis**

imperative **mets, mettons, mettez**

Verbs which follow the pattern of **mettre** include **admettre** *to admit*, **permettre** *to permit*, **promettre** *to promise* and **transmettre** *to transmit*.

28 mourir *to die*

	present	future	conditional
je	meurs	mourrai	mourrais
tu	meurs	mourras	mourrais
il/elle	meurt	mourra	mourrait
nous	mourons	mourrons	mourrions
vous	mourez	mourrez	mourriez
ils/elles	meurent	mourront	mourraient

	imperfect	past historic	perfect
je	mourais	mourus	suis mort(e)
tu	mourais	mourus	es mort(e)
il/elle	mourait	mourut	est mort(e)
nous	mourions	mourûmes	sommes mort(e)s
vous	mouriez	mourûtes	êtes mort(e)(s)
ils/elles	mouraient	moururent	sont mort(e)s

	present subjunctive
je	meure
tu	meures
il/elle	meure
nous	mourions
vous	mouriez
ils/elles	meurent

present participle **mourant**

past participle **mort**

imperative **meurs, mourons, mourez**

29 naître *to be born*

	present	future	conditional
je	nais	naîtrai	naîtrais
tu	nais	naîtras	naîtrais
il/elle	naît	naîtra	naîtrait
nous	naissons	naîtrons	naîtrions
vous	naissez	naîtrez	naîtriez
ils/elles	naissent	naîtront	naîtraient

	imperfect	past historic	perfect
je	naissais	naquis	suis né(e)
tu	naissais	naquis	es né(e)
il/elle	naissait	naquit	est né(e)
nous	naissions	naquîmes	sommes né(e)s
vous	naissiez	naquîtes	êtes né(e)(s)
ils/elles	naissaient	naquirent	sont né(e)s

	present subjunctive
je	naisse
tu	naisses
il/elle	naisse
nous	naissions
vous	naissiez
ils/elles	naissent

present participle **naissant**

past participle **né**

imperative **nais, naissons, naissez**

30 ouvrir *to open*

	present	future	conditional
j'	ouvre	ouvrirai	ouvrirais
tu	ouvres	ouvriras	ouvrirais
il/elle	ouvre	ouvrira	ouvrirait
nous	ouvrons	ouvrirons	ouvririons
vous	ouvrez	ouvrirez	ouvririez
ils/elles	ouvrent	ouvriront	ouvriraient

	imperfect	past historic	perfect
j'	ouvrais	ouvris	ai ouvert
tu	ouvrais	ouvris	as ouvert
il/elle	ouvrait	ouvrit	a ouvert
nous	ouvrions	ouvrîmes	avons ouvert
vous	ouvriez	ouvrîtes	avez ouvert
ils/elles	ouvraient	ouvrirent	ont ouvert

	present subjunctive
j'	ouvre
tu	ouvres
il/elle	ouvre
nous	ouvrions
vous	ouvriez
ils/elles	ouvrent

present participle **ouvrant**

past participle **ouvert**

imperative **ouvre, ouvrons, ouvrez**

Verbs which follow the same pattern as **ouvrir** include **couvrir** *to cover*, **découvrir** *to discover*, **offrir** *to offer* and **souffrir** *to suffer*.

31 partir *to leave*

	present	future	conditional
je	pars	partirai	partirais
tu	pars	partiras	partirais
il/elle	part	partira	partirait
nous	partons	partirons	partirions
vous	partez	partirez	partiriez
ils/elles	partent	partiront	partiraient

	imperfect	past historic	perfect
je	partais	partis	suis parti(e)
tu	partais	partis	es parti(e)
il/elle	partait	partit	est parti(e)
nous	partions	partîmes	sommes parti(e)s
vous	partiez	partîtes	êtes parti(e)(s)
ils/elles	partaient	partirent	sont parti(e)s

	present subjunctive
je	parte
tu	partes
il/elle	parte
nous	partions
vous	partiez
ils/elles	partent

present participle **partant**

past participle **parti**

imperative **pars, partons, partez**

Verbs which follow the same pattern include **sortir** *to go out*. **Mentir** *to lie* and **sentir** *to feel* have the same endings but take **avoir** not **être**.

32 peindre *to paint*

	present	future	conditional
je	peins	peindrai	peindrais
tu	peins	peindras	peindrais
il/elle	peint	peindra	peindrait
nous	peignons	peindrons	peindrions
vous	peignez	peindrez	peindriez
ils/elles	peignent	peindront	peindraient

	imperfect	past historic	perfect
je/j'	peignais	peignis	ai peint
tu	peignais	peignis	as peint
il/elle	peignait	peignit	a peint
nous	peignions	peignîmes	avons peint
vous	peigniez	peignîtes	avez peint
ils/elles	peignaient	peignirent	ont peint

	present subjunctive
je	peigne
tu	peignes
il/elle	peigne
nous	peignions
vous	peigniez
ils/elles	peignent

present participle **peignant**

past participle **peint**

imperative **peins, peignons, peignez**

Verbs which follow the same pattern as **peindre** include **atteindre** *to achieve, to reach* and **éteindre** *to extinguish/to switch off.*

33 plaire *to please*

	present	future	conditional
je	plais	plairai	plairais
tu	plais	plairas	plairais
il/elle	plaît	plaira	plairait
nous	plaisons	plairons	plairions
vous	plaisez	plairez	plairiez
ils/elles	plaisent	plairont	plairaient

	imperfect	past historic	perfect
je/j'	plaisais	plus	ai plu
tu	plaisais	plus	as plu
il/elle	plaisait	plut	a plu
nous	plaisions	plûmes	avons plu
vous	plaisiez	plûtes	avez plu
ils/elles	plaisaient	plurent	ont plu

	present subjunctive
je	plaise
tu	plaises
il/elle	plaise
nous	plaisions
vous	plaisiez
ils/elles	plaisent

present participle **plaisant**

past participle **plu**

imperative **plais, plaisons, plaisez**

Verbs which follow the same pattern as **plaire** include **se taire** *to keep quiet*.

34 pleuvoir *to rain*

	present	future	conditional
il	**pleut**	**pleuvra**	**pleuvrait**

	imperfect	past historic	perfect
il	**pleuvait**	**plut**	**a plu**

	present subjunctive
il	**pleuve**

present participle **pleuvant**

past participle **plu**

35 pouvoir *to be able*

	present	future	conditional
je	peux	pourrai	pourrais
tu	peux	pourras	pourrais
il/elle	peut	pourra	pourrait
nous	pouvons	pourrons	pourrions
vous	pouvez	pourrez	pourriez
ils/elles	peuvent	pourront	pourraient

	imperfect	past historic	perfect
je/j'	pouvais	pus	ai pu
tu	pouvais	pus	as pu
il/elle	pouvait	put	a pu
nous	pouvions	pûmes	avons pu
vous	pouviez	pûtes	avez pu
ils/elles	pouvaient	purent	ont pu

	present subjunctive
je	puisse
tu	puisses
il/elle	puisse
nous	puissions
vous	puissiez
ils/elles	puissent

present participle **pouvant**

past participle **pu**

36 prendre *to take*

	present	future	conditional
je	prends	prendrai	prendrais
tu	prends	prendras	prendrais
il/elle	prend	prendra	prendrait
nous	prenons	prendrons	prendrions
vous	prenez	prendrez	prendriez
ils/elles	prennent	prendront	prendraient

	imperfect	past historic	perfect
je/j'	prenais	pris	ai pris
tu	prenais	pris	as pris
il/elle	prenait	prit	a pris
nous	prenions	prîmes	avons pris
vous	preniez	prîtes	avez pris
ils/elles	prenaient	prirent	ont pris

	present subjunctive
je	prenne
tu	prennes
il/elle	prenne
nous	prenions
vous	preniez
ils/elles	prennent

present participle **prenant**

past participle **pris**

imperative **prends, prenons, prenez**

Verbs which follow the pattern of **prendre** include **apprendre** *to learn* and **comprendre** *to understand*.

37 recevoir *to receive*

	present	future	conditional
je	reçois	recevrai	recevrais
tu	reçois	recevras	recevrais
il/elle	reçoit	recevra	recevra
nous	recevons	recevrons	recevrions
vous	recevez	recevrez	recevriez
ils/elles	reçoivent	recevront	recevraient

	imperfect	past historic	perfect
je/j'	recevais	reçus	ai reçu
tu	recevais	reçus	as reçu
il/elle	recevait	reçut	a reçu
nous	recevions	reçûmes	avons reçu
vous	receviez	reçûtes	avez reçu
ils/elles	recevaient	reçurent	ont reçu

	present subjunctive
je	reçoive
tu	reçoives
il/elle	reçoive
nous	recevions
vous	receviez
ils/elles	reçoivent

present participle **recevant**

past participle **reçu**

imperative **reçois, recevons, recevez**

Verbs which follow the same pattern as **recevoir** include **apercevoir** *to catch sight of* and **décevoir** *to disappoint*.

38 résoudre *to solve*

	present	future	conditional
je	résous	résoudrai	résoudrais
tu	résous	résoudras	résoudrais
il/elle	résout	résoudra	résoudrait
nous	résolvons	résoudrons	résoudrions
vous	résolvez	résoudrez	résoudriez
ils/elles	résolvent	résoudront	résoudraient

	imperfect	past historic	perfect
je/j'	résolvais	résolus	ai résolu
tu	résolvais	résolus	as résolu
il/elle	résolvait	résolut	a résolu
nous	résolvions	résolûmes	avons résolu
vous	résolviez	résolûtes	avez résolu
ils/elles	résolvaient	résolurent	ont résolu

	present subjunctive
je	résolve
tu	résolves
il/elle	résolve
nous	résolvions
vous	résolviez
ils/elles	résolvent

present participle résolvant

past participle résolu

imperative résous, résolvons, résolvez

Verbs which follow the same pattern as résoudre include dissoudre *to dissolve*.

39 rire *to laugh*

	present	future	conditional
je	ris	rirai	rirais
tu	ris	riras	rirais
il/elle	rit	rira	rirait
nous	rions	rirons	ririons
vous	riez	rirez	ririez
ils/elles	rient	riront	riraient

	imperfect	past historic	perfect
je/j'	riais	ris	ai ri
tu	riais	ris	as ri
il/elle	riait	rit	a ri
nous	riions	rîmes	avons ri
vous	riiez	rîtes	avez ri
ils/elles	riaient	rirent	ont ri

	present subjunctive
je	rie
tu	ries
il/elle	rie
nous	riions
vous	riiez
ils/elles	rient

present participle **riant**

past participle **ri**

imperative **ris, rions, riez**

Verbs which follow the same pattern as **rire** include **sourire** *to smile*.

40 savoir *to know*

	present	future	conditional
je	sais	saurai	saurais
tu	sais	sauras	saurais
il/elle	sait	saura	saurait
nous	savons	saurons	saurions
vous	savez	saurez	sauriez
ils/elles	savent	sauront	sauraient

	imperfect	past historic	perfect
je/j'	savais	sus	ai su
tu	savais	sus	as su
il/elle	savait	sut	a su
nous	savions	sûmes	avons su
vous	saviez	sûtes	avez su
ils/elles	savaient	surent	ont su

	present subjunctive
je	sache
tu	saches
il/elle	sache
nous	sachions
vous	sachiez
ils/elles	sachent

present participle **sachant**

past participle **su**

imperative **sache, sachons, sachez**

41 servir *to serve*

	present	future	conditional
je	sers	servirai	servirais
tu	sers	serviras	servirais
il/elle	sert	servira	servirait
nous	servons	servirons	servirions
vous	servez	servirez	serviriez
ils/elles	servent	serviront	serviraient

	imperfect	past historic	perfect
je/j'	servais	servis	ai servi
tu	servais	servis	as servi
il/elle	servait	servit	a servi
nous	servions	servîmes	avons servi
vous	serviez	servîtes	avez servi
ils/elles	servaient	servirent	ont servi

	present subjunctive
je	serve
tu	serves
il/elle	serve
nous	servions
vous	serviez
ils/elles	servent

present participle **servant**

past participle **servi**

imperative **sers, servons, servez**

	present	future	conditional
je	suis	suivrai	suivrais
tu	suis	suivras	suivrais
il/elle	suit	suivra	suivrait
nous	suivons	suivrons	suivrions
vous	suivez	suivrez	suivriez
ils/elles	suivent	suivront	suivraient

	imperfect	past historic	perfect
je/j'	suivais	suivis	ai suivi
tu	suivais	suivis	as suivi
il/elle	suivait	suivit	a suivi
nous	suivions	suivîmes	avons suivi
vous	suiviez	suivîtes	avez suivi
ils/elles	suivaient	suivirent	ont suivi

	present subjunctive
je	suive
tu	suives
il/elle	suive
nous	suivions
vous	suiviez
ils/elles	suivent

present participle **suivant**

past participle **suivi**

imperative **suis, suivons, suivez**

Verbs which follow the same pattern as **suivre** include **poursuivre** *to chase*.

43 tenir *to hold*

	present	future	conditional
je	tiens	tiendrai	tiendrais
tu	tiens	tiendras	tiendrais
il/elle	tient	tiendra	tiendrait
nous	tenons	tiendrons	tiendrions
vous	tenez	tiendrez	tiendriez
ils/elles	tiennent	tiendront	tiendraient

	imperfect	past historic	perfect
je/j'	tenais	tins	ai tenu
tu	tenais	tins	as tenu
il/elle	tenait	tint	a tenu
nous	tenions	tînmes	avons tenu
vous	teniez	tîntes	avez tenu
ils/elles	tenaient	tinrent	ont tenu

	present subjunctive
je	tienne
tu	tiennes
il/elle	tienne
nous	tenions
vous	teniez
ils/elles	tiennent

present participle **tenant**

past participle **tenu**

imperative **tiens, tenons, tenez**

Verbs which follow the same pattern include **appartenir** *to belong*, **contenir** *to contain*, **entretenir** *to maintain*, **maintenir** *to keep* and **obtenir** *to obtain*.

	present	future	conditional
je	travaille	travaillerai	travaillerais
tu	travailles	travailleras	travaillerais
il/elle	travaille	travaillera	travaillerait
nous	travaillons	travaillerons	travaillerions
vous	travaillez	travaillerez	travailleriez
ils/elles	travaillent	travailleront	travailleraient

	imperfect	past historic	perfect
je/j'	travaillais	travaillai	ai travaillé
tu	travaillais	travaillas	as travaillé
il/elle	travaillait	travailla	a travaillé
nous	travaillions	travaillâmes	avons travaillé
vous	travailliez	travaillâtes	avez travaillé
ils/elles	travaillaient	travaillèrent	ont travaillé

	present subjunctive
je	travaille
tu	travailles
il/elle	travaille
nous	travaillions
vous	travailliez
ils/elles	travaillent

present participle **travaillant**

past participle **travaillé**

imperative **travaille, travaillons, travaillez**

45 valoir *to be worth*

	present	future	conditional
je	vaux	vaudrai	vaudrais
tu	vaux	vaudras	vaudrais
il/elle	vaut	vaudra	vaudrait
nous	valons	vaudrons	vaudrions
vous	valez	vaudrez	vaudriez
ils/elles	valent	vaudront	vaudraient

	imperfect	past historic	perfect
je/j'	valais	valus	ai valu
tu	valais	valus	as valu
il/elle	valait	valut	a valu
nous	valions	valûmes	avons valu
vous	valiez	valûtes	avez valu
ils/elles	valaient	valurent	ont valu

	present subjunctive
je	vaille
tu	vailles
il/elle	vaille
nous	valions
vous	valiez
ils/elles	vaillent

present participle **valant**

past participle **valu**

imperative **vaux, valons, valez**

	present	future	conditional
je	vends	vendrai	vendrais
tu	vends	vendras	vendrais
il/elle	vend	vendra	vendrait
nous	vendons	vendrons	vendrions
vous	vendez	vendrez	vendriez
ils/elles	vendent	vendront	vendraient

	imperfect	past historic	perfect
je/j'	vendais	vendis	ai vendu
tu	vendais	vendis	as vendu
il/elle	vendait	vendit	a vendu
nous	vendions	vendîmes	avons vendu
vous	vendiez	vendîtes	avez vendu
ils/elles	vendaient	vendirent	ont vendu

	present subjunctive
je	vende
tu	vendes
il/elle	vende
nous	vendions
vous	vendiez
ils/elles	vendent

present participle **vendant**

past participle **vendu**

imperative **vends, vendons, vendez**

	present	future	conditional
je	**viens**	**viendrai**	**viendrais**
tu	**viens**	**viendras**	**viendrais**
il/elle	**vient**	**viendra**	**viendrait**
nous	**venons**	**viendrons**	**viendrions**
vous	**venez**	**viendrez**	**viendriez**
ils/elles	**viennent**	**viendront**	**viendraient**

	imperfect	past historic	perfect
je	**venais**	**vins**	**suis venu(e)**
tu	**venais**	**vins**	**es venu(e)**
il/elle	**venait**	**vint**	**est venu(e)**
nous	**venions**	**vînmes**	**sommes venu(e)s**
vous	**veniez**	**vîntes**	**êtes venu(e)(s)**
ils/elles	**venaient**	**vinrent**	**sont venu(e)s**

	present subjunctive
je	**vienne**
tu	**viennes**
il/elle	**vienne**
nous	**venions**
vous	**veniez**
ils/elles	**viennent**

present participle **venant**

past participle **venu**

imperative **viens, venons, venez**

Verbs which follow the same pattern as **venir** include **convenir** *to suit*, **devenir** *to become* and **se souvenir (de)** *to remember*.

48 vivre *to live*

	present	future	conditional
je	vis	vivrai	vivrais
tu	vis	vivras	vivrais
il/elle	vit	vivra	vivrait
nous	vivons	vivrons	vivrions
vous	vivez	vivrez	vivriez
ils/elles	vivent	vivront	vivraient

	imperfect	past historic	perfect
je/j'	vivais	vécus	ai vécu
tu	vivais	vécus	as vécu
il/elle	vivait	vécut	a vécu
nous	vivions	vécûmes	avons vécu
vous	viviez	vécûtes	avez vécu
ils/elles	vivaient	vécurent	ont vécu

	present subjunctive
je	vive
tu	vives
il/elle	vive
nous	vivions
vous	viviez
ils/elles	vivent

present participle **vivant**

past participle **vécu**

imperative **vis, vivons, vivez**

Verbs which follow the same pattern as **vivre** include **survivre** *to survive*.

49 voir *to see*

	present	future	conditional
je	vois	verrai	verrais
tu	vois	verras	verrais
il/elle	voit	verra	verrait
nous	voyons	verrons	verrions
vous	voyez	verrez	verriez
ils/elles	voient	verront	verraient

	imperfect	past historic	perfect
je/j'	voyais	vis	ai vu
tu	voyais	vis	as vu
il/elle	voyait	vit	a vu
nous	voyions	vîmes	avons vu
vous	voyiez	vîtes	avez vu
ils/elles	voyaient	virent	ont vu

	present subjunctive
je	voie
tu	voies
il/elle	voie
nous	voyions
vous	voyiez
ils/elles	voient

present participle **voyant**

past participle **vu**

imperative **vois, voyons, voyez**

Verbs which follow the same pattern as **voir** include **prévoir** *to predict*.

50 vouloir *to want*

	present	future	conditional
je	veux	voudrai	voudrais
tu	veux	voudras	voudrais
il/elle	veut	voudra	voudrait
nous	voulons	voudrons	voudrions
vous	voulez	voudrez	voudriez
ils/elles	veulent	voudront	voudraient

	imperfect	past historic	perfect
je/j'	voulais	voulus	ai voulu
tu	voulais	voulus	as voulu
il/elle	voulait	voulut	a voulu
nous	voulions	voulûmes	avons voulu
vous	vouliez	voulûtes	avez voulu
ils/elles	voulaient	voulurent	ont voulu

	present subjunctive
je	veuille
tu	veuilles
il/elle	veuille
nous	voulions
vous	vouliez
ils/elles	veuillent

present participle voulant

past participle voulu

imperative veuillez

Verb index

Pages 203-253

1	acheter *to buy*	26	manger *to eat*
2	aller *to go*	27	mettre *to put*
3	appeler *to call*	28	mourir *to die*
4	s'asseoir *to sit down*	29	naître *to be born*
5	avoir *to have*	30	ouvrir *to open*
6	battre *to beat*	31	partir *to leave*
7	boire *to drink*	32	peindre *to paint*
8	commencer *to begin*	33	plaire *to please*
9	conduire *to drive*	34	pleuvoir *to rain*
10	connaître *to know*	35	pouvoir *to be able*
11	courir *to run*	36	prendre *to take*
12	craindre *to fear*	37	recevoir *to receive*
13	croire *to believe*	38	résoudre *to solve*
14	devoir *to have to*	39	rire *to laugh*
15	dire *to say*	40	savoir *to know*
16	dormir *to sleep*	41	servir *to serve*
17	écrire *to write*	42	suivre *to follow*
18	employer *to use*	43	tenir *to hold*
19	envoyer *to send*	44	travailler *to work*
20	être *to be*	45	valoir *to be worth*
21	faire *to do, make*	46	vendre *to sell*
22	falloir *to be necessary*	47	venir *to come*
23	finir *to finish*	48	vivre *to live*
24	se laver *to get washed*	49	voir *to see*
25	lire *to read*	50	vouloir *to want*

Irregular verbs are also highlighted on the following pages:

Present	134-135	Past participle	154-155
Future/Conditional	142, 144	Present participle	168
Imperfect	148	Imperative	170
Past historic	150	Subjunctive	174, 176-177

Grammar terms

Abstract nouns are the words for intangible things like *liberty*, *silence*, *poverty*, *fear*, *happiness*. They're the opposite of concrete nouns such as *table*, *dog*, *water*.

Adjectives are words that describe or add information to nouns and pronouns: ***small*** *car*, *It was **superb***, ***French*** *wine*, ***first*** *class*, ***my*** *name*, ***Which*** *hotel?*, ***those*** *people*.

Adverbs add information to adjectives, verbs and other adverbs: ***very*** *small car*, *She speaks **clearly***, *She speaks **really** clearly*.

Agreement Unlike English, adjectives and articles in French change according to the noun/pronoun they relate to, needing to agree, i.e. match, in terms of gender (masculine/feminine) and number (singular/plural).

Articles are *the* (definite article), *a/an* (indefinite article) and *some* (partitive article). French has more than English.

An **aspirated h** is silent but behaves like a consonant. That means that **le** and **la** don't shorten to **l'** and **liaisons** don't occur before a word beginning with an aspirated h.

Auxiliary verbs are verbs that support the main verb: *We **have** eaten*, ***Has** she gone?* In English, but not French, *do/does* is used as an auxiliary verb in questions like *Do you understand?*

Cardinal numbers are *one*, *two*, *three*, *four*, etc.

Comparatives are used when making comparisons. English has two ways of comparing with adjectives: adding *-er* as in *bigger*, *cheaper*, and using the word *more* as in *more expensive*. Apart from a small number of irregular comparatives, French uses the second alternative, with **plus** *more* or **moins** *less*.

Compound tenses are two-word tenses. Most English tenses are compound e.g. the perfect *I have waited,* the pluperfect *I had waited*, the future *I will wait* and the conditional *I would wait*. Just under half of French tenses are compound tenses.

The **conditional** is a verb form used to say what would or could happen: *I would like to go, Would/Could you help me?* The **conditional perfect** translates *would have*: *I would have liked to go*.

Conjunctions are linking words like *and*, *but*, *while*, *because*.

Consonants and **vowels** make up the alphabet. The French vowels are **a**, **e**, **i**, **o**, **u**, **y**; the rest: **b**, **c**, **d**, **f**, etc. are the consonants.

Continuous tenses are used to say *I am/was doing* something in English. French doesn't have specific continuous tenses; the same verb form in French can mean *I do/did* and *I am/was doing*.

The **definite article** is the word *the*, which has several French translations.

Demonstrative words are used to point things out. *This, these, that, those* are demonstrative adjectives; *this one, that one, these (ones), those (ones)* are demonstrative pronouns.

A **direct object** is directly at the receiving end of a verb. In the sentence *We saw John*, *we* is the subject, *saw* is the verb and *John* is the direct object. Compare with **indirect object**.

Direct object pronouns are *me, us, you, him, her, it, them*.

Feminine See **gender**.

Formal is used to describe **vous**, the word for *you* when talking to someone you don't know well. The informal word for *you* is **tu**.

The **future perfect** translates *will have*: *She will have gone to work*.

The **future tense** of a verb translates the English *will*: *We will be there, I'll go later, She'll be at work*.

Gender Every French noun is either masculine or feminine, as are any articles and adjectives that relate to that noun.

A **gerund** in English is a noun ending in *-ing* that has been formed from a verb: *reading, driving, knowing*.

Imperative is the verb form used to give instructions or commands: ***Wait*** *for me*, ***Don't do*** *that*, ***Turn*** *the top clockwise*.

The **imperfect tense** of a verb is used to describe how things were and to talk about things that happened over a period of time or repeatedly: *She **was** furious, We **were watching** the match, We **used to go** there often*.

An **impersonal verb** is a verb form that doesn't relate to people or things and generally starts with *it*: *It's raining, It's possible*.

The **indefinite article** is *a/an* in English; **un** or **une** in French.

The **indicative mood** is used for factual statements: *He **goes** to school*. See also **mood**.

An **indirect object** is usually separated from its verb by *to* or *for*. In the sentence *We talked to John*, *we* is the subject, *talked* is the verb and *John* is the indirect object. Compare with **direct object**.

Indirect object pronouns usually have *to* or *for* in front of **direct object pronouns**, e.g. *to/for me, to/for them*. In French they're a single word.

Infinitive French verbs are listed in a dictionary in the infinitive form, ending in **-er**, **-ir**, or **-re**. The English equivalent uses *to*: **manger** *to eat,* **choisir** *to choose,* **comprendre** *to understand,* **avoir** *to have.*

Informal is used to describe **tu**, the word for *you* when talking to a good friend, a family member or a child. The formal word for *you* is **vous**.

Interrogative words are used in questions, e.g. *who, what, when, where, how, why, how much/many.*

Intransitive verbs need only a subject to make sense: *go, laugh;* unlike **transitive verbs** which need a subject and a direct object.

Invariable words don't change to agree with/match anything else.

Irregular nouns, verbs or adjectives don't behave in a predictable way like regular ones, and have to be learnt separately.

Liaison happens when a normally silent consonant at the end of a word is pronounced because it is followed by a word beginning with a vowel: **vous avez**.

Masculine See **gender**.

Modal verbs are verbs like *want, be able to, must,* which are followed by other verbs: *I **want** to stay here, I **can** swim, You **ought** to leave.*

The **mood** of a verb defines how it's used, e.g. the **indicative mood** is used for factual statements: *He **goes** to school;* while the **subjunctive mood** indicates that hard facts are not involved: *If he **were** to go to school …*

Negatives are words like *not, never, nothing, nobody;* and *not … ever, not … anybody, not … anything.*

Nouns are the words for living beings, things, places and concepts: *son, doctor, dog, table, house, Scotland, time, freedom.* See also **proper nouns**.

Number refers to the difference between singular (one) and plural (more than one).

Numbers See **cardinal numbers** and **ordinal numbers**.

The **object** of a sentence is at the receiving end of the verb. It can be direct: *They have **two children**;* or indirect: *Anna talks **to the children**.*

Object pronoun. See **direct object pronouns, indirect object pronouns**.

Ordinal numbers are *first, second, third, fourth,* etc.

Parts of speech are the grammatical building blocks of a sentence: *adjective, article, noun, pronoun, verb,* etc.

The **passive** describes something done **to** the subject rather than **by** it: *The meat is cooked in the oven, The room was booked by my friend.*

The **past historic tense** is only in formal writing. It translates the English simple past tense: *I went, I did* etc. Spoken French uses the perfect tense.

The **past participle** of a verb is used with *have* when talking about the past: *I have **finished**, He has **eaten**, They had **gone***. Some past participles can also be used as adjectives: *the **finished** product*.

The **perfect tense** of a verb is used in French to talk about the past; equivalent to the English *I worked* and *I have worked*.

The **person** of a verb indicates who or what is doing something:
first person   =   the speaker: *I* (singular), *we* (plural)
second person =   the person(s) being addressed: *you*
third person   =   who/what is being talked about: *he/she/it/they*

Personal pronouns are words like *I*, *you*, *we*, *she*, *her*, *them*.

The **pluperfect tense** translates *had* done something: *She had worked hard all day*.

Plural means more than one.

Possessive relates to ownership: **possessive adjectives** are *my, our, your, his/her/its, their*; **possessive pronouns** are *mine, ours, yours, his/hers, theirs*.

Prepositions are words like *by, in, on, with, for, through, next to*. They relate a noun/pronoun to another part of the sentence by e.g. place, time, purpose: *It's **on** the back seat, We're here **until** Friday, I've got a letter **for** Tom*.

Present participles end in *-ing* in English. In French they end in **-ant**. They are used as adjectives or verbs.

The **present tense** of a verb is used to talk about things being done now: *I work, I'm working*.

Pronouns replace nouns to avoid the need to repeat them. They can be personal: *we, she, us*; demonstrative: *this one, those*; possessive: *mine, theirs*. They can also involve *one/ones*: *the big one, the red ones*.

Proper nouns are the names of specific people, places or organisations. They're written with a capital letter: *Sally, Cambridge, European Union*.

Reflexive pronouns are me, te, se, nous, vous, used as an integral part of **reflexive verbs** in French.

Reflexive verbs are made up of two words, the first of which is *se* in the infinitive form. There's no consistent English equivalent, although many reflexive verbs include *get* or *oneself* in the translation: **se marier** *to get married*, **s'amuser** *to enjoy oneself*.

Regular nouns, adjectives, verbs etc. behave in a predictable way, conforming to the pattern for that particular part of speech.

Relative pronouns are words like *which*, *who*, *that*, used to join together parts of a sentence without repeating the noun.

The **simple past tense** in English is, for example, *I worked*, *We ate*, *They spoke*. There's also a simple past tense in French, called the **past historic**, but it's never used when speaking – the **perfect tense** is used instead.

Simple tenses are one-word tenses like *I play*, *I played*. French has slightly more simple tenses than English.

Singular means one.

The **stem** of a French verb is what's left when you remove the **-er**, **-ir**, or **-re** ending of the infinitive. You can then add other endings to this stem.

Stressed pronouns are the pronouns used in French after prepositions: **moi, toi, lui, elle, nous, vous, eux, elles**.

The **subject** of a sentence is whoever or whatever is carrying out the verb: ***They*** *have two children*, ***Anna*** *reads the paper*, ***This house*** *cost a lot of money*, ***Peace*** *is possible*.

Subject pronouns are *I, we, you, he, she, it, they*.

Subjunctive is a form of a verb that's more widely used in French than English. It equates to the English *may* or *were*: ***May*** *all your dreams come true*, *if I **were** rich*, but it's also used in a range of well-defined grammatical circumstances. See also **mood**.

Superlative is the *most/least* … when comparing several things. In English you can add *-est* to many adjectives: *biggest*, *cheapest*, or you can use *most*: *most expensive*. There's no French equivalent of *-est*; it uses **le/la/les plus**.

A **syllable** is a unit that contains a vowel and consists of a single sound: *can* has one syllable, *can-ter* has two, while *Can-ter-bu-ry* has four.

The **tense** of a verb indicates when something is done:

in the past	perfect tense: *I (have) worked*
	imperfect tense: *I was working*, *I used to work*
now	present tense: *I work*, *I'm working*
in the future	future tense: *I will work*

Transitive verbs need both a **subject** and a **direct object**: *use, give, throw*, unlike **intransitive verbs** which need only a subject: *sleep, sit, sneeze*. Some verbs can be used both transitively and intransitively: *The pilot flew the plane* (transitive), *I flew at eight o'clock this morning* (intransitive).

Verbs are words like *to go, to sleep, to eat, to like, to have, to be, to think*; they refer to doing and being.

Vowels and **consonants** make up the alphabet. In French, vowels are the sounds made by the letters **a**, **e**, **i**, **o**, **u**, **y**; the rest **b**, **c**, **d**, etc are consonants.

Answers

1 *a* Sofia N; glossy ADJ; magazine N; organises V; interviews N; hires V; professional ADJ; models N; photographers N; travels V; world N; boyfriend N; well-known ADJ; actor N; *b* my ADJ; father N; comes V; Toulouse N; lives V; Paris N; works V; central ADJ; office N; large ADJ; company N; *c* prepared V; fantastic ADJ; meal N; ate V; grilled ADJ; fish N; fresh ADJ; asparagus N; new ADJ; potatoes N; drank V; superb ADJ; French ADJ; white ADJ; wine N; dessert N; incredible ADJ

2 *a* very ADV; reasonable ADJ; rather ADV; dilapidated ADJ; really ADV; small ADJ; overgrown ADJ; *b* superbly ADV; terribly ADV; uneven ADJ; deliberately ADV; unfair ADJ

Checkpoint 1 Page 24
1 les oignons; les hindous; les Européens
2 comme
3 François; Louis; Nicolas; Thérèse
4 doo-bluh vay, doo-bluh vay, doo-bluh vay or trois doo-bluh vay
5 arobase
6 L'adresse de l'Académie française est 23, quai de Conti, 75006 Paris
7 It rises
8 y
9 ravi

Checkpoint 2 Page 32
1 *a* zéro; *b* virgule
2 smaller
3 huit; dix-huit; vingt-huit; soixante-dix-huit; quatre-vingt-huit

4 2.400.000 or 2 400 000
5 *a* It's five o'clock; *b* at seven o'clock in the evening; *c* after midnight; *d* yesterday evening at seven o'clock; *e* at half past eight; *f* 1st August; *g* about one o'clock; *h* next Friday; *i* at 11 o'clock on the dot; *j* until ten o'clock
6 *a* il est onze heures; *b* à neuf heures; *c* à midi; *d* après dix-huit heures; *e* à neuf heures pile; *f* demain à dix heures; *g* hier à dix heures; *h* dimanche à seize heures; *i* à sept heures tous les jours; *j* avant trois heures de l'après-midi
7 *a* en; *b* dans; *c* pendant
8 about two weeks/about a fortnight
9 le premier janvier; le vingt-cinq décembre; le trente et un décembre
10 16.44
11 soixante-dix
12 en mille/mil sept cent quatre-vingt-neuf; or en dix-sept cent quatre-vingt-neuf
13 printemps
14 75%

Checkpoint 3 Page 42
1 gâteau m; chou-fleur m; personne f; toilette f; médecin m; pare-brise m; collègue m/f; victime f; chaussure f; cousine f; silence m; enfant m/f
2 porcs; neveux; cadeaux; chats; souris; cafés; choux; monuments; personnes; yeux; lieux; fonctionnaires; prix; pneus; enfants; messieurs; chevaux; hôpitaux; grenouilles; pays

3 feminine
4 book and pound
5 several female musicians
6 personne; vedette; victime or idole
7 *a* biologie; *b* inflation; *c* probabilité; *d* criminologiste; *e* obstacle; *f* absence; *g* journalisme
8 mother-in-law and stepmother
9 Have a good day
10 storm (tempest)
11 traductrice

Checkpoint 4 Page 50

1 un chef; une infirmière; un/une secrétaire; une vedette; une université; une solution; une personne; un gâteau; une eau minérale; une vache; un musée; une ville; un village; un lycée; une serveuse

2 le chef; l'infirmière; le/la secrétaire; la vedette; l'université; la solution; la personne; le gâteau; l'eau minérale; la vache; le musée; la ville; le village; le lycée; la serveuse

3 *a* à la gare; *b* à l'hôtel de ville; *c* aux Halles; *d* au Louvre; *e* de l'eau minérale; *f* des pommes; *g* du Brie; *h* de la bière

4 *a* Vous êtes français?; *b* Vous êtes étudiant?; *c* Parlez-vous anglais? (or Vous parlez anglais?); *d* Vous aimez la cuisine chinoise?

Checkpoint 5 Page 60

1 *a* le premier ministre: prime minister; *b* la Maison Blanche: White House; *c* un centre sportif: sports centre; *d* la musique populaire: pop music; *e* une carte verte: green card; *f* les grandes villes françaises: big French towns; *g* Les Nations

Unies: United Nations; *h* une coïncidence heureuse: happy coincidence; *i* deuxième classe: second class; *j* les femmes fatales; *k* l'art moderne: modern art; *l* la communauté locale: local community

2 *a* simple; *b* long; *c* dernier; *d* haut; *e* faux; *f* important; *g* public; *h* clair

3 *a* accessible; *b* brutal; *c* ethnique; *d* stagnant; *e* biologique; *f* copieux; *g* radical; *h* portable; *i* susceptible; *j* prestigieux

4 *a* after; une attraction fatale; *b* before; un cher collègue or une chère collègue; *c* before; la seule personne; *d* after; les films français

5 *a* le blanc; les grandes; le vieux; la verte foncé; *b* quelque chose d'impossible; quelque chose de différent; rien de nouveau; rien de spécial

Checkpoint 6 Page 68

1 *a* absolu; *b* simple; *c* constant; *d* récent; *e* vrai; *f* précis; *g* lent; *h* courant; *i* complet; *j* effectif; *k* brillant; *l* doux

2 *a* autrement; *b* sérieusement; *c* scientifiquement; *d* généralement; *e* fréquemment; *f* malheureusement; *g* actuellement; *h* évidemment; *i* franchement; *j* agressivement; *k* poliment; *l* énormément

3 *a* exactement/précisément; *b* mieux; *c* vite; *d* mal; *e* souvent/fréquemment; *f* fort

4 *a* plus dur; *b* meilleures, moins chères; *c* le plus intéressant; *d* que; *e* le plus lent; *f* pire/plus

mauvais; *g* mieux; *h* le plus grand
… du monde; *i* aussi … que

Checkpoint 7 Page 73
1   *a* cette; *b* ces; *c* cet; *d* cette;
    e ce; *f* cet; *g* cette; *h* ces; *i* cet;
    j cette; *k* ces; *l* cet
2   *a* celle; *b* ceux; *c* celui; *d* celles;
    e celui; *f* celui; *g* celles

Checkpoint 8 Page 76
1   *a* son; *b* leur; *c* vos; *d* notre;
    e ton; *f* votre; *g* leurs; *h* mon;
    i nos; *j* mes
2   *a* le mien; *b* les siennes; *c* la
    sienne; *d* les nôtres; *e* les tiens;
    f le vôtre; *g* le sien; *h* le leur

Checkpoint 9 Page 83
1 y; 2 y; 3 en; 4 y; 5 en; 6 en; 7 en;
8 y; 9 y; 10 en

Checkpoint 10 Page 88
1   Bonjour, c'est moi.
2   *a* tu; *b* vous; *c* vous; *d* vous
3   *a* – vi; *b* – v; *c* – iv; *d* – ii; *e* – i
4   *a* le; *b* me; *c* leur; *d* l'; *e* nous;
    f lui; *g* les; *h* nous
5   Vous voulez l'écouter? Il faut les
    acheter.
6   *a* avec elles; *b* pour moi; *c* sans
    eux; *d* sauf toi; *e* après nous;
    f chez lui
7   They know each other. (speaking
    about women)
8   Moi, je l'ai fait./Je l'ai fait, moi.
9   *c*
10 Il nous l'a donné.

Checkpoint 11 Page 96
1   *a* dis donc!; *b* Qu'est-ce que vous
    en pensez?; *c* Bof!; *d* à mon avis;
    e Je suis d'accord; de toute façon
    – anyway – is left over
2   *a* lequel; *b* laquelle; *c* lequel;
    d lesquelles; *e* lesquels
3   où
4   *a* qui; *b* que; *c* qui; *d* dont;

e dont; *f* que
5   d'autre part
6   plutôt – the others give a reason
    for something

Checkpoint 12 Page 108
1   *a* en; *b* pour; *c* par; *d* aux;
    e depuis; *f* à, du; *g* dans; *h* avec
2   *a* a house near the sea;
    b my uncle's house; *c* a house
    with white walls; *d* a house in
    the shade; *e* a house costing two
    million euros; *f* a house designed
    by (or owned by) Sir Christopher
    Wren; *g* a wooden house;
    h a house without a garage;
    i a three-storey house;
    j a house under the bridge; *k* the
    house opposite; *l* the house at the
    end of the road
3   *a* la sœur de Michelle; *b* un
    numéro de téléphone; *c* le jus de
    tomate; *d* une bouteille de vin;
    e à mardi; *f* c'est à moi;
    g l'article de demain; *h* quelque
    chose de différent
4   un verre à champagne
5   sur la television means on top of
    the television and à la television
    means (showing) on television,
    i.e. broadcast.
6   en face du parking
7   un sandwich <u>au</u> fromage; un
    roman <u>d</u>'amour; <u>en</u> été; <u>en</u> nylon

Checkpoint 13 Page 120
1   arrival, deep
2   dream
3   -er, -ir, -re; the largest group is -er
4   tense
5   je/I; ils, elles/they
6   past historic
7   Il a décidé de ne pas rester ici.
8   pull
9   irregular verb; reflexive verb
10 to kiss

11 dominer; illustrer; isoler; simuler; commercialiser; maximiser

12 disinfect; irrigate; subjugate; disarm; disintegrate; relegate

Checkpoint 14 Page 132

1 *a* Il n'est pas étudiant; *b* Ce n'était pas bien; *c* Je ne le connais pas; *d* On n'y va pas souvent; *e* Nous ne nous sommes pas promenés sur la plage; *f* Je n'ai pas bu de vin.

2 *a* plus; *b* guère; *c* que; *d* aucune

3 Je ne joue ni au tennis ni au golf.

4 ne ... nulle part

5 *a* Personne ne m'a téléphoné; *b* Elle ne visite jamais personne; *c* Je n'ai vu aucun de mes amis.

6 est-ce que

7 qui

8 *a – ii; b – i; c – iii*

9 n'est-ce pas for both

10 *a* quelle; *b* quelles; *c* lequel; *d* laquelle

Checkpoint 15 Page 139

1 dites; arrivent; finissent; nageons; offre; espèrent; pars; menaçons; nettoie; craignez

2 *a* Nous allons/On va à Paris demain; *b* Il est en train de parler; *c* Elle vient d'être ici; *d* Je travaille ici depuis cinq ans.

3 offrir

Checkpoint 16 Page 152

1 from left to right: conditional, je or tu → vouloir, to want; imperfect, il/elle → finir, to finish; future, nous → venir, to come; past historic, ils/elles → avoir, to have; present, je → aller, to go; future, il/elle → envoyer, to send; conditional, je or tu → pouvoir, to be able; imperfect, ils/elles → être, to be; past historic, il/elle →

regarder, to look at; conditional, vous → préférer, to prefer; present, vous → dire, to say; future, ils/elles → recevoir, to receive; imperfect, nous → faire, to do; future, il/elle → mourir, to die; past historic, il/elle → être, to be; conditional, je or tu → devoir, to have to; present, ils/elles → tenir, to hold; future, nous → être, to be; present, je or tu → partir, to leave; future, vous → savoir, to know; imperfect, il/elle → plaire, to please

2 from left to right: j'arriverai; il/elle choisissait; tu demanderais; nous payons; ils/elles voulaient; tu comprendras; il/elle sort; je nettoierai; il/elle pensait; vous écririez; tu offres; ils/elles attendent; je commençais; ils/elles continueront

3 Quand j'avais cinq ans nous habitions à Besançon.
Moi, je le ferais avec plaisir mais je n'ai pas de temps.
Je vous téléphonerai quand elle arrivera.
Si tu es libre demain nous pourrons aller au cinéma.

Checkpoint 17 Page 162

1 choisi; envoyé; fait; venu; regardé; été; connu; entendu; entré; parti; payé; eu; attendu; né; mis; dit; pensé; bu; mort; descendu; pu; plu; ouvert; réussi

2 *a* a; *b* ai; *c* sommes; *d* es; *e* a; *f* êtes; *g* ont; *h* sont

3 *a* none required; *b* vue; *c* allés; *d* amusée; *e* rencontrés

4 *a* venais; *b* avez vu; *c* faisait; *d* est allés; *e* avait; *f* habitait; *g* a commencé; *h* lisait

Checkpoint 18 Page 166

1 *a* Il avait compris; *b* J'aurai fini mon travail; *c* Nous y serions allés; *d* Qu'est-ce qu'elle avait fait?; *e* Ils se seraient promenés dans le parc; *f* Tu auras commencé avant cinq heures?; *g* J'aurais dû parler avec lui; *h* Si vous aviez su.

2 La maison sera vendue.
Les vedettes étaient habillées par Jean Paul Gaultier.
Le chien avait été emmené chez le vétérinaire.
Mes cousins ont été invités.
Les bâtiments anciens ont été renovés.

3 cuire

4 *a* Après être sortie de la voiture, elle a vu son amie; *b* Après avoir vu son amie, elle a traversé la rue; *c* Après s'être levé, il a bu une tasse de café; *d* Après avoir bu son café, il est sorti; *e* Après être arrivés à l'aéroport, ils ont changé de l'argent.

Checkpoint 19 Page 173

1 "Alors, ne <u>prenez</u> pas la première rue à gauche, mais <u>continuez</u> tout droit jusqu'aux feux. <u>Tournez</u> à gauche, <u>traversez</u> la place, puis <u>prenez</u> la deuxième rue à droite. <u>Ne</u> <u>vous</u> <u>inquiétez</u> <u>pas</u> – ce n'est pas loin".

2 A

3 vous; ne prends pas; continue; tourne; traverse; prends; ne t'inquiète pas.

4 *a* ne lui en donne pas; *b* ne te lève pas; *c* envoyez-les-leur

5 *a* venant; *b* ayant; *c* lisant; *d* en voyant; *e* en sortant; *f* en mangeant

Checkpoint 20 Page 182

1 *a* parte; *b* soyons; *c* choisisse; *d* veniez; *e* boivent; *f* dises; *g* prenions; *h* veuille; *i* aille; *j* puissiez; *k* amène; *l* ait

2 *a* après que; *b* espérer que

3 *a* viennes; *b* aies; *c* soit; *d* veuille; *e* fasse

4 *a* Je ne pense pas qu'il ait fini; *b* Je ne crois pas qu'elle sache la réponse; *c* Je ne pense pas que tu sois trop timide.

5 *a* Je veux que tu finisses maintenant; *b* Je veux que vous fassiez attention; *c* Je veux que nous y allions; *d* Je veux que vous m'écoutiez; *e* Je veux que tu dises la vérité.

Checkpoint 21 Page 194

1 *a* fais; *b* faites; *c* avez; *d* sont; *e* être; *f* a; *g* ai; *h* fera; *i* fait; *j* ont

2 *a* Il faut que tu partes; *b* Il faut que nous lui téléphonions; *c* Il faut que je fasse les devoirs; *d* Il faut que vous vous leviez tôt.

3 *a* Je voudrais; *b* Vous devriez; *c* Elles veulent; *d* J'aurais dû; *e* on peut; *f* Je veux; *g* Tu sais; *h* Nous aurions pu; *i* Tu peux; *j* Elle doit

4 faire la grasse matinée

Checkpoint 22 Page 202

1 *a* de; *b* à; *c* d'; *d* d'; *e* à; *f* d'; *g* de; *h* de

2 *a* au; *b* du; *c* à la; *d* du; *e* du; *f* à l'; *g* des; *h* à la

3 *a* Ils attendent le train; *b* J'aime jouer au tennis; *c* Elle a oublié de payer; *d* Nous sommes sur le point de partir; *e* Elle cherche son sac; *f* Tu as besoin d'argent?; *g* J'ai demandé cent euros; *h* Nous espérons revenir l'année prochaine.

Index

à 98-99
    with definite article 48
    with object pronouns 84
    in prepositions 98
    after verbs 196-197, 200
a/an 44
a see avoir
accents 18
    on capital letters 22
adjectives 51
    endings/agreement 54-57
    position 58, 59
    irregular 57
    comparative/superlative 66-67
    demonstrative 70
    interrogative quel 125
    invariable 57
    possessive 74
    after rien, quelque chose 53
adverbs 61
    comparison 66-67
    formation 62
    phrases as adverbs 63
    of quantity 64
    position 64
    bien, mieux 67
    mal, pire 67
agreement
    of adjectives 54
    of articles 44, 46
    of past participles 159, 161
à la, à l', au, aux 48
aller 205
    perfect tense 159
    future meaning 143
alphabet 19
any
    du, de la, de l', des 49

en 83
anybody, not anybody 129, 158, 180
anything, not anything 129
articles 43
    definite 46
    indefinite 44
    partitive 49
as … as 67
at à 98
au, aux, à la, à l' 48
aucun (ne … aucun) 49, 130
aussi … que 67
auxiliary verbs 153
avoir 191, 208
    compound tenses 153
    to form perfect tense 158
be see être
better, best 67
bien 67
by
    de 100
    en 102-103
    par 105
ça 72
can pouvoir 184, 186
capital letters 21-22
cardinal numbers 26-27
ce 70, 72
    ce, cette, ces 70
    ce, c'est 72-73
ceci 72
cedilla 18
    in nous form of -er verbs 136
cela 72
celui, celle 71
cent 27
    omission of article 45

ce qui, ce que 92
c'est, ce sont 72, 73
ceux see celui
ci 72
-ci 70, 71
comma 20, 25
commands 170-171
    with object pronouns 85
comme
    exclamations 126
    like 20
comparatives 66-67
compound nouns 38
compound tenses 153
    perfect 158-161
    pluperfect 163
    future perfect 164
    conditional perfect 165
conjunctions
    followed by subjunctive 180
    conditional 144
    when to use 146-147
    conditional perfect 165
connaître 213
    cf savoir 183
consonants 17
could pouvoir 186
dans 104
    after verbs 201
date 30
days of the week 30
de 100-101
    with definite article 48
    after verbs 198-200
    after superlatives 66
    with object pronouns 84
    with lequel 93
decimal point 25
definite article 46
    with prepositions 48
demi 45
demonstrative

adjectives 70
    pronouns 71
depuis 106
    with imperfect 149
devoir 217
    modal verb 184-185
direct object pronouns 80
    position 84
do, make see faire
dont 94
du, de la, de l', des 48
each other 86
elle, elles
    subject pronouns 78
    emphatic pronouns 87
emphatic pronouns 87
en
    pronoun 82-83, 84, 198
    preposition 102-103
    after verbs 201
    in gerund 169
-er verbs
    regular model 247
    spelling variations 136-137
est see être
est-ce que 122
étais see être
été see être
être 190, 223
    compound tenses 153
    to form perfect tense 159
eu see avoir
eus see avoir
eux emphatic pronoun 87
exclamations 126
faire 192-193, 224
falloir 185, 188, 225
fasse see faire
il faut see falloir
feminine
    gender 33
    nouns 33

definite article 46
indefinite article 44
noun suffixes 37
finir model -**ir** verb 226
for
    depuis, pendant 106
    par, pour 105
    not translated 80, 201
from **de** 100-101
fus see **être**
future perfect tense 164
future tense 140-143
gender 33
gerund 169
grammar terms 254-259
ne ... guère 129
h pronunciation 17
half 45
    time: *half past* 29
hardly 129
have see **avoir**
he 78
her
    object pronoun 79
    possessive adjective 74
hers 75
herself 86
him 79
himself 86
his
    possessive adjective 74
    possessive pronoun 75
how exclamations 126
hundred 27
    omission of article 45
I subject pronoun 78
if **si**
    with future 141
il, ils
    subject pronoun 78
    il est 73
    il y a 188
imperative 170-171

with object pronouns 85
imperfect indicative 148-149
imperfect subjunctive 175
impersonal
    verbs 188-189
    expressions 190
    with subjunctive 179
in
    à 98
    dans 104
    de 101
    en 102
    sur 104
    after superlatives 66
indefinite article 44
indicative mood 110
indirect object pronouns 80
    position 84
infinitive 114-115
    after modal verbs 184
instructions 170-171, 114
interrogatives 122-125
intonation 18
invariable adjectives 57
-**ir** verbs
    regular model 226
it
    subject pronoun 78, 112
    object pronoun 79
its 74
ne ... jamais 129
je 78
la
    definite article 46
    direct object pronoun 79
-**là** 70, 71
laquelle see **lequel**
se laver modal reflexive verb 227
le
    definite article 46
    direct object pronoun 79
least 66-67
lequel, laquelle

relative pronoun 93
interrogative pronoun 125
les
definite article 46
direct object pronoun 79
less 65-66
let's see imperative
leur
possessive adjective 74
possessive pronoun 75
indirect object pronoun 79
liaison 17
lui
indirect object pronoun 79
emphatic pronoun 87
ma see **mon**
make see **faire**
mal 67
masculine
gender 33
nouns 33
definite article 46
indefinite article 44
noun suffixes 36
me
reflexive pronoun 86
object pronoun 79
me 79, 87
meilleur 67
-même *(self)* 86
mes see **mon**
midday, midnight 29
mien, mienne 75
mieux 67
might/might have **pouvoir** 186
mil 30
mille 27
omission of article 45
in years 30
milliard 27
million 27
mine 75

modal verbs 184
moi
emphatic pronoun 87
object pronoun after
imperative 171
moindre 67
moins 65-66
mon, ma, mes 74
months 30
mood of verb 110
more
comparative 65-66
encore de 64
most
superlative 66-67
la plupart 64
must
devoir 185
falloir 185, 188
my 74
myself 86
ne
in negatives 127-131
ne … ni … ni 129
ne … nulle part 129
ne … pas 127-128
after some verbs 179
after some conjunctions 180
negatives 127-131
list of negatives 128
negative commands 131
negative infinitive 115, 131
negative questions 131
neither … nor 129
n'est-ce pas 123
never 129
nobody 129, 180
not 127
nothing, not … anything 129
notre, nos 74
nôtre 75
nouns 33

gender 34-38
    plural endings 39
    compound nouns 38
    two nouns together 101
noun suffixes 36, 37
nous
    subject pronoun 78
    object pronoun 79
    emphatic pronoun 87
    reflexive pronoun 86
nowhere 129
numbers 25
    cardinal 26-27
    ordinal 28
object pronouns 79-80, 84-85
    with the perfect tense 85, 161
of **de** 100
of it, of them **en** 82-83
on
    personal pronoun 78-79
    nous as emphatic pronoun 87
on
    sur 104
    à 98
one
    cardinal number 26
    pronoun (*this/that one*) 71
    one another 86
only **ne ... que** 129
opinions 95
ordinal numbers 28
où
    question word 123
    in time expressions 94
ought **devoir** 185
our, ours 74-75
ourselves 86
par 105, 107
    after verbs 201
participle
    past 154-156
    present 168-169

partitive article 49
passive 157
past historic 150-151
past infinitive 115
past participle 154-156
pendant 106
perfect subjunctive 175
perfect tense 158
    with **avoir** 158
    with **être** 159
    with object pronouns 161
    modal verbs 184
    reflexive verbs 159
    when to use 160
person of verb 112
personal pronouns 77
(ne ...) personne 129, 158, 180
peu 67
pire 67
pluperfect indicative 163
pluperfect subjunctive 175
plural
    of nouns 39
    of **un, une** 44
    of definite article 46
    of adjectives 54-57
plus 65-66
    ne ... plus 129
possession 74-75
possessive
    adjectives 74
    pronouns 75
pour 105
    after verbs 201
pouvoir 238
    modal verb 184, 186
premier 28
prendre 239
prepositions 97, 107
    with definite article 48
    followed by emphatic

pronouns 87
    with verbs 195, 80
present indicative 134-139
present participle 168
present subjunctive 174
pronouns
    personal 77
    emphatic 87
    object 79-80, 84-85
    with modal verbs 183
    with compound tenses 161
    with perfect tense 85
    with reflexive verbs 161
    demonstrative 71
    interrogative 125
    possessive 75
    reflexive 86
    relative 92, 93
    subject 78, 87
pronunciation 16-17
punctuation 20
    with numbers 25
quand
    question word 123
    with future 141
    with future perfect 164
quantity expressions 64
que
    than 66
    relative pronoun 92
    introducing subjunctive
    178-179, 180
    in exclamations 126
    what 124
    that 92
    in **ne ... que** 129
    que de 126
quel, quelle
    question word 125
    used in exclamations 126
quelque chose 53
quelques 49

quelqu'un 180
qu'est-ce qui/que 124
questions 122
qui
    question word 124
    relative pronoun 92
qui est-ce qui/que 124
quoi 93, 124
-re verbs regular model 249
reflexive pronouns 86
    with reflexive verbs 117
    with the imperative 171
reflexive verbs 116-117
    regular **-er** model 227
    tenses 116-117
    imperative 171
    infinitive after modal verbs 184
    impersonal verbs 189
relative pronouns 92, 93, 94
rien
    ne ... rien 129
    + adjective 53
    with subjunctive 180
sa see **son**
sans 106
    with infinitive 130
savoir 243
    cf **pouvoir** 186
    cf **connaître** 183
se reflexive pronoun 86
seasons 30
se laver model reflexive verb 227
-self 86
s'en aller 83
ses see **son**
shall
    suggestions 149
    future 141
she 78
should **devoir** 185
si *if*
    with future 141

in suggestions 149
si yes 131
sien, sienne 75
simple tenses 133
    conditional 144
    future 140
    imperfect 148
    present 134
    past historic 150
since 106, 149
sois, soyons see être
some 49, 83
someone 180
something 53
sommes see être
son, sa, ses 74
sont see être
stem of verb 133
stress 18
stressed (emphatic) pronouns 87
subject pronouns 78-79
subjunctive 174
    selecting tense 181
    when to use 178-181
suffixes for nouns 36, 37
suggestions 149
suis see être
superlative 66-67
    with subjunctive 180
sur 104
ta see ton
te
    object pronoun 79
    reflexive pronoun 86
tenir 246
tense 110
    simple 133
    compound 153
    conditional 144
    future 140-143
    conditional perfect 165
    future perfect 164
    imperfect 148-149

    past historic 150-151
    perfect 158-161
    present 134-139
    pluperfect 163
tes see ton
than 65-66
that
    that, this 70
    relative pronoun 92
the 46
their, theirs 74, 75
them 79
themselves 86
there **y** 81
they 78
this, that 70
thousand 27
    omission of article 45
tien, tienne 75
time 29
time expressions 31
to
    infinitive 114
    à 98
    en 102
    pour 105
toi
    emphatic pronoun 87
    in imperative 171
ton, ta, tes 74
train, en train de 103
travailler model -er verb 247
tu 78
un, une
    indefinite article 44
    cardinal number 26
va, vais, vont see aller
valoir 248
vendre, model -re verb 249
venir 250
venir de
    with present tense 138
    with imperfect tense 149

verbs
    overview 109
    verb tables 203
    infinitive 114-115
    stem 133
    mood 110
    person 112
    tense 110
    simple tenses 133
    compound tenses 153
    reflexive 116-117
    auxiliary 153
    indicative 110
    imperative 170-171
    gerund 169
    modal 184
    passive 157
    past participle 154-156
    subjunctive 174
    with à 196, 200
    with de 198-200
    with dans, en, par, pour 201
    with object pronoun 84-85
votre, vos 74
vôtre 75
vouloir 253
    modal verb 184, 187
vous
    subject pronoun 78
    emphatic pronoun 87
    object pronoun 79
    reflexive pronoun 86
vowels 16
want, wish vouloir 187
was, imperfect 149, 151
we 78
were, imperfect 149
what
    question word 124
    qu'est-ce qui/que 124
    quoi 93
    quel? 125

ce qui, ce que 92
ce dont 94
in exclamations 126
when? see quand ·
    translated by où 94
where? 123
which (one)? 125
which, relative pronoun
    qui, que 92
    lequel 93
while
    with present participle 169
who? 124
who, whom relative pronoun 92
whose
    question word 124
    relative pronoun 94
why? 123
will
    future 140-143
    future perfect 164
    vouloir 141
with
    translated by à 99
without 106, 130
word order 90
worse, worst 67
would
    conditional 144
    imperfect 149
y 81, 196
    position 84
years 30
you
    subject pronoun 78
    object pronoun 79
your, yours 74-75
yourself 86